# The Fish and Game Cookbook

## Over 200 Time-Honored Recipes

### Sylvia Bashline

THE LYONS PRESS

To Jim, who says he taught me everything I know,
my mother and dad, who helped me to be a person,
and Tina and Zoa, who keep me honest.


Special thanks to Jack Samson, editor of *Field & Stream*, and
Bob Bell, editor of *Pennsylvania Game News*, for their permission
to use recipes previously published in those magazines.

Printed in Canada

10  9  8  7  6  5  4  3  2

Library of Congress Cataloging-in-Publication Data
Bashline, Sylvia G.
The fish and game cookbook: over 200 time-honored recipes /
Sylvia Bashline.
p. cm.
Includes index.
Originally published: The bounty of the earth cookbook.
New York : Lyons & Burford, 1994
ISBN 1-58574-011-X
1. Cookery (Game) 2. Cookery (Fish)
I. Bashline, Sylvia G. Bounty of the earth
cookbook. II. Title.

TX751 .B2683 2000
641.6'91—dc21                99-086263

# The
# Fish and Game
# Cookbook

# CONTENTS

# Foreword by
# Nick Sisley

No American male sportsman could help but be envious of Sylvia Bashline's husband. What a wife! She hunts, she shoots, she fishes and she prepares what she and her husband bring home in the most elegant manner anyone can imagine. Is there a hunter or fisherman in the country who doesn't wish that his wife had one or more of Sylvia's qualities, especially taking an intense interest in the outstanding preparation of our game and fish?

Notice that I said the Bashline meals were prepared, not merely cooked. Having been privileged to sit down at their dining room table many times, I know that their everyday lunches and suppers are events—happenings—occasions! Both Jim and Sylvia Bashline are food lovers who enjoy special game and fish concoctions fully as much as they savor well-prepared beef, pork, lamb or chicken. I owe any developed taste buds I have to the days I've sat at their table and enjoyed such dishes as broiled goose basted in mustard sauce, homemade bread filled with chopped hickory nuts and acorns, poached Atlantic salmon, smoked pheasant and a long list of other delectables. Almost every day the Bashlines eat as most of us dream of dining once or twice a year. (How they both stay so slim and trim is a wonder.)

Sylvia Bashline possesses boundless energy, great resourcefulness, a love for her work and the intensity to constantly seek perfection. This book is the extension of those remarkable qualities. You won't find one recipe she hasn't tested and probably retested! Even when she finds a delightful method for this game or that fish, she'll continue with her experimentation. Sure, she's encountered some duds over the years, but you won't find one of them in the ensuing pages.

As a writer, Sylvia Bashline has come on with a rush. While her popularity could have come on the coattails of her writer/husband, Jim Bashline, I know better. What Sylvia has done in recent years with the pen has drawn words of praise from those who don't know her husband, and in the knockdown, dog-eat-dog world of free-lance writing and book publishing, there's no room for second-raters. Readers are going to enjoy Sylvia's prose which introduces each chapter as much as they're going to enjoy the recipes they try.

Sometimes I wonder how many recipes in any given cookbook are tried by the readers. My guess is that the percentage is small. If you don't try most of the recipes in this book, you're missing out on some great dining. I know it's impossible to bag enough game and catch enough fish to try them all in one short year, but do make it a point to keep sampling. If there are a half dozen rabbits or squirrels or grouse or whatever in the freezer, take an inventory and map out a plan for testing as many recipes as possible.

The trouble with most game and fish cooking is that the cook is totally lacking in imagination—and that's just the way the meals turn out, dull. No wonder so much excellent wild meat goes to waste. It takes extra effort to cook with imagination and I think it's sad that so many of today's cooks don't have or take the time to prepare food with a flare. Most of today's kitchen scurriers look upon meal preparation as pure drudgery. How can their meals help but come out commonplace? Perhaps if they prepared their meals with more love, the family would be much more appreciative of their efforts. Mine is not meant to be a chauvinistic attitude, because many men, especially sportsmen, like to cook—and I'm one of them. Here's an idea! Can you and your family reserve one night a week for quality dining with both spouses donning an apron to prepare the evening meal? What better way to get started at whittling down the supply of game and fish in the freezer and to enjoy the eating so much more, too.

It's important to mention that Sylvia Bashline has made special notes in each chapter concerning wines and the ones that best suit each of the categories of game and fish. Few will disagree that a compatible wine adds immeasurably to the meal. The problem is that too few of us know enough about wine to choose a good one with any regularity. You can rely on Sylvia's suggestions in each chapter. You may want to experiment on your own after a first test, but lean on her wine judgment for the first time or two.

Whatever you do, don't put this cookbook on the shelf and forget it. Give it a special place in the kitchen, a nook where you'll see it often so you'll remember to use it regularly. That way you won't forget to try Sylvia's recommendations on the game and fish you acquire. Follow her directions and you won't be disappointed. Instead, you'll be eating like a king, and a lot more often!

NICK SISLEY

# Introduction
# to the
# 1994 Edition

This book is written for the millions of people who hunt and fish and need good, tested recipes to bring out the best from the bounty of the earth. Since it's my personal conviction that game and fish recipes should be easy to prepare, the ones in this book are, and the ingredients are readily available in most stores.

Most of the recipes were invented at least fifteen years ago (before the first edition was published); yet they are used daily in my home and in thousands of others across North America. Reports keep coming in from friends and strangers concerning their success (sometimes for the first time) in preparing a game or fish dish.

Before this new edition was published I carefully examined each recipe, looking for things that should be changed. I found few. To reflect changing life styles, some serving sizes were reduced, as was the amount of salt. However, I was proud of this book fifteen years ago and, like most "mothers," I'm still proud of it. I have a huge collection of fish and game cookbooks in my library but this is the one I turn to most often.

You won't find as many recipes for each species in this book as there are in others addressing the subject but each is well tested. In the chapter on doves, for instance, there are four recipes. Each is excellent and each is used in our home every fall; we don't need more.

Unfortunately, many game recipes appearing in print are not tested. In books, an easy way to tell is to look at the section on doves. Many of the untested recipes call for a serving of *one* dove. Have you ever tried to make do with one dove for dinner? I hope not.

This book will help you gain confidence in your ability to become an admired game and fish cook but you'll have to trust me in the beginning. If you have never tried rare goose before, do it now. Poaching trout may sound weird but try it. If you have only one pheasant to serve, it won't be wasted if you use a recipe from this book.

I use many natural ingredients. My recipes often call for butter, fresh mushrooms, long grain rice, or cream. If you are more comfortable working with margarine, canned mushrooms, minute rice, or evaporated milk, make the substitution. It won't affect the taste of the finished dish all that much. It's more important that you, as the cook, are at ease cooking the wild things.

Cooking evaporates the alcohol in wine, beer, and other beverages. However, if you wish to substitute bouillon, apple juice, or even water with a squirt of lemon juice, do so.

Some game and fish require using your fingers when eating. I serve game birds (whole or halves) on wooden platters with Rapala (trout-size) fillet knives. The knife is used on the breast meat and to remove the wings and legs from the carcass; then, these pieces are best handled with the fingers. With a bit of practice, it can be done gracefully. It's impossible to debone a shad without losing flesh even if you are an expert. We have learned to tackle shad using two hands; one works with a fork, the other removes bones. It works well.

Tongs are essential when cooking wild game. *Never* pierce meat with a fork. Succulent moisture is lost and so is flavor.

I am often "gifted" with game and fish since friends know how fond I am of it. All is accepted with gratitude but I often shake my head with dismay over freezing methods. I've received woodcock frozen in bread wrappers, venison in brown paper bags, and bluefish frozen with no protective covering. If it has been in the freezer only a few days, it might be okay. More often, it either has to be trimmed or even discarded. What a shame.

Freezing game and fish isn't hard. Small fish and game birds are best when covered with water and frozen in clean cardboard half-gallon milk cartons. Once frozen, cover the container with freezer paper and it will keep well for several months. With larger birds, fish, or mammals, I double-wrap before freezing. The first layer is an ample sheet of plastic wrap to exclude as much air as possible. The second layer is freezer paper. Always label packages with date and number of servings, as well as the cut of meat or species of fish. If you intend to keep game or fish longer than two months, try to store it in a freezer that doesn't have a frost-free feature. All food keeps longer when a fan isn't trying to draw the moisture from the packages.

Game and fish are what they eat. A hungry deer that has been filling its stomach with hemlock is not going to taste as good as one that has been feasting on apples and beechnuts. A carp that lives in warm, muddy water will have a different flavor from one from a cool, clean river.

I'm not sure what "gaminess" means. Sadly, I think most people are referring to the natural flavor of wild meat. It's more intense than domestic meat because the animal or bird has to work for a living. It tastes better to me and most of my friends. An off-flavor can occur if the meat is mishandled when being dressed but that's not gaminess—that's carelessness.

I'm often asked what woodcock tastes like, or dove, or squirrel. It tastes like what it is, just as pork or lamb or veal does. You have to eat it to know.

This book will make it easier for you to enjoy the wonderful, low-fat tastes of outdoor America fully—our bounty of the earth. *Relax* and go cook up a storm.

SYLVIA BASHLINE
March, 1994

# Ring-Necked
# Pheasant

Human beings have long been fascinated with the act of moving wild creatures from one part of the globe to another. In most cases, the introduction of an exotic species has caused more complications than benefits. The European carp and starling are good examples of unwanted guests in North America. The rabbit, when introduced into Australia, nearly ate up the country. And the gray squirrel found England so much to its liking that it has long been regarded there as a pest.

There are two outstanding success stories in North America, however. One is the brown trout, which came from Great Britain and Germany, and the other is the ring-necked pheasant. They have both created a biological niche for themselves. The brown trout filled in the gap that was widening as suitable native brook-trout water was being lost in the East. The ringneck set up housekeeping quite nicely in an expanding agricultural environment.

While the first stocking that really "took" occurred in Oregon in

1881, there were a few releases of pheasants from Europe before that time in the eastern United States. One of those was on the shore of the Delaware River in 1790 by Benjamin Franklin's son-in-law, Richard Bache. While there is no record of those birds surviving, there has been some speculation among Pennsylvania ringneck watchers that the tough, hardy flock that manage to flourish along the Schuylkill River (and Expressway) in the city limits of Philadelphia are descendants of those 18th-century birds.

One of the reasons that ringnecks were such a success in the United States is because they were an ideal addition to our native game birds. They live best in an area that is generally too far north for quail and too heavily cultivated for grouse. They are especially adaptable to the corn country of the nation. Many of the pheasants in the East make excellent use of the woodlots near farm fields for cover and protection. Undoubtedly those that run for the heavy brush and trees when crowded by predators—human or otherwise—survive to breed, thereby insuring good stock.

I came to pheasant hunting as a young adult. My black Labrador, Samantha, did too. In fact, Sam refused to pick up the first ringneck Jim downed in front of her. We were upset at the time, but now I suspect that she thought it was a chicken and not really worthy of her attention. A few strong admonitions, the bird forced into her mouth and an excellent pheasant dog came into being. She has since learned to love pheasant hunting and retrieving. Her specialty is chasing them down when they are wing-tipped and running to beat the band for the nearest multiflora rose hedgerow. I also have learned to respect this canny, tricky game bird after a background where the only bird to be hunted was the grouse.

In the game pocket, a big pheasant doesn't necessarily indicate an old pheasant, nor is a small bird always a young, tender individual. Separate the birds of the year from the old cocks by picking up the dead bird by its lower mandible. If the beak breaks, it's a youngster. The thumbnail will make an indentation in the spur of a young bird, whereas an older rooster spur is tough as nails and probably quite long.

In general, I don't believe in hanging game birds. Big game improves through aging at controlled temperatures, but this is done after it is gutted. Fowl, particularly if it has been penetrated by shot pellets, is a fragile meat. Perhaps someday I'll change my mind about this, but right now I think birds are best cleaned immediately after being killed.

To skin or not to skin is a common argument that takes place in our household where pheasants are concerned. If the bird has been badly ventilated by shot, I say skin it. If it has not been riddled badly, I'm all for plucking. For roasting or cooking whole, a plucked bird will hold its natural juices and end up tasting far better. Skinning, however, is quick after a long and bone-tiring day afield. Cut off the head, feet and first joint of the wings and slip the skin off like a glove. The warmer they are, the easier they skin. If you intend to skin the bird, it's also a good idea to remove the entrails in the field. The bird cools faster.

Plucking can also be done in the field if you begin the job before the body heat dissipates. The feathers pull out easier. But don't do it in a farmer's front yard or lane. That's a sure way not to be invited back. Carry a paper bag for the feathers. If you wait until you get home, a pail of boiling water is needed. Immerse the whole bird for no more than ten seconds, sloshing up and down a few times, and all the plumage will strip off easily. Remove the entrails and wash the cavity thoroughly. Then wipe the bird clean and refrigerate or freeze.

Birds of the year are best for the roasting recipes. With pheasants, I'm especially fond of using the quick-cooking Broiled Pheasant Breasts and Sautéed Pheasant Breasts. Try them, and I think you'll agree. The rest of the bird can be used in any of the other recipes.

## WINES

The overused rule that says "White meat, white wine; red meat, red wine" doesn't necessarily apply to pheasant. At least, it shouldn't apply all of the time. Wild pheasants are abundantly flavored and some of the delicious sauces used with them are even more so. For that reason, light, fruity, white wines don't have the character or body to hold up well. A rich, French Burgundy is ideal with any wild bird that is served with a formidable sauce. A roasted bird or grilled breast with few, if any, condiments comes out best with the clean but distinctive taste of one of the California Pinot Noirs (call them California Burgundies if you must). With game-farm birds or with recipes that call for cut pieces of pheasant mixed with other ingredients such as noodles or mild vegetables, a dry white or Beaujolais would be suitable.

## SHERRIED ROAST PHEASANT

**2 whole pheasants (with skin)**          **½ cup butter**
**sausage dressing**                              **½ cup dry sherry**
**2 tablespoons currant jelly**

Wash and dry pheasants and place on a buttered rack in a shallow oven-proof pan. Stuff with the dressing. Tie legs together and wings to the body, if necessary. Coat the birds with butter and roast in a 325° oven, basting every 30 minutes with more butter. After 1½ hours, pour mixture of sherry and jelly over the birds. Baste with the pan drippings every 10 minutes for another 30 minutes or until birds are tender. The carver should add a dollop of pan drippings to each slice of meat as it is removed from the birds.

## Sausage Dressing

½ pound pork sausage
2 tart apples, peeled, cored and chopped fine

¼ cup chopped parsley
1 beaten egg

Mix well and stuff 2 pheasants. Serves 4 to 6.

# HICKORY ROASTED PHEASANT

2 pheasants (with skin if possible)
celery dressing

hickory-smoked bacon strips

Stuff the pheasants with dressing and tie the legs together with string. Place in a roasting pan and arrange an ample amount of bacon strips over the birds. Cover and roast in a 325° oven for 1½ hours or until done.

## Celery Dressing

1 tablespoon chopped onion
½ cup chopped celery
1 tablespoon butter
¼ teaspoon salt

dash pepper
dash sage
dash poultry seasoning
1½ cups bread cubes

½ cup chicken bouillon

Sauté onion and celery in butter until tender. Add rest of ingredients and mix. Stuffs 2 pheasants. Stuffing should be moist to help keep the birds from drying out. Serves 4 to 6.

# BROILED PHEASANT BREASTS

4 pheasant breasts
1 cup salad oil
½ cup red wine

¼ teaspoon garlic salt
¼ teaspoon fresh ground pepper
butter

1½ teaspoons Worcestershire sauce

Mix marinade of the salad oil, wine, Worcestershire sauce, garlic salt and pepper. Place the breasts in the marinade for 4 hours, turning often. Wipe dry with paper toweling. Place on a broiler pan 4 inches from the heat source. Rub the breasts with butter and broil 15 minutes in total, 5 minutes on each side and 5 minutes straight up. Salt the breasts at the table. Makes 4 *ample* servings.

*Note:* The meat will be pink and moist—totally unlike any other pheasant you've eaten. My penciled note on this recipe is "Excellent."

## SAUTÉED PHEASANT BREASTS

| | |
|---|---|
| 1 large pheasant breast, boned into 2 fillets | freshly ground pepper |
| | 1 cup sliced mushrooms |
| 2 tablespoons soy sauce | ¼ cup sliced or slivered almonds |
| 2 tablespoons wine vinegar | ¼ cup butter |
| ¼ cup cooking oil | ¼ cup dry vermouth |

Marinate the pheasant fillets in soy sauce, vinegar, cooking oil and pepper for about 8 hours in the refrigerator. Sauté the mushrooms and almonds in a heavy skillet in the butter until they are lightly brown. Fry the pheasant fillets quickly in the hot skillet, about 5 minutes on a side. Just before serving, add the vermouth. Cut each fillet into thin slices with a fillet knife. Serve with the mushroom-almond mixture. The meat will be medium rare—just pink on the inside. This is an excellent treatment for old, tough birds. Serves 2.

*Note:* Penciled on recipe, "Superb."

## CREAMED PHEASANT

| | |
|---|---|
| 1 pheasant, cut into serving pieces | ⅓ cup port |
| flour seasoned with salt and pepper | 1 cup heavy cream |
| 2 tablespoons butter | ½ pound mushrooms, sliced |
| 1 tablespoon cooking oil | ¼ teaspoon crushed rosemary |
| 1 cup chicken stock | |

Douse pheasant pieces in seasoned flour and brown lightly in the butter and oil. Add the port and cook over high flame until it has cooked down, turning the meat in the wine. Add cream, mushrooms and rosemary. Cover and simmer until the pheasant is done. Remove the pieces to a heated platter and cook the sauce down until it is reduced by half. Serve with buttered rice, spooning the sauce over the rice and the pheasant. Will serve 2; double the recipe for 4 people.

*Note:* "Super" is my rating for this.

# PHEASANT IN TOMATO SAUCE

2 pheasants, cut into serving pieces
flour
2 tablespoons olive oil
1 onion, finely sliced
3 cups chopped tomatoes

1 garlic clove, finely chopped
1 teaspoon salt
½ teaspoon pepper
½ cup dry white wine

Douse meat in flour and lightly brown in hot olive oil. Add onion and cook until onion is transparent. Add tomatoes, garlic, salt and pepper. Cover and simmer for about 1 hour, until the meat is tender and tomatoes are reduced to a thick sauce. Add wine and cook another 15 minutes. Serves 4.

# PHEASANT AND SOUR CREAM

2 whole pheasants, rinsed and dried
6 sprigs parsley
¼ teaspoon thyme
½ cup butter
salt and pepper

1 cup chicken bouillon
¼ cup dry sherry
1 tablespoon flour (quick-mixing type)
½ cup sour cream
¼ teaspoon nutmeg

Place half the parsley and thyme in each bird's cavity. Melt the butter in a pan large enough to hold the pheasants. Brown the birds on all sides. Sprinkle with salt and pepper. Add bouillon and sherry to the pan. Lower heat, cover and simmer (turning once) until the birds are tender, about 1 hour for young pheasants. Remove birds to a heated platter. Add the flour to the pan juices and cook until slightly thickened. Add sour cream and nutmeg, mix and dole a little sauce on each bird. The rest can be served in a sauce boat to be spooned over rice or noodles. Serves 4.

*Note:* Penciled on recipe, "Great."

# PHEASANT CACCIATORE

1 pheasant, quartered
2 tablespoons olive oil
1 large onion, sliced
1 clove garlic, minced
½ green pepper, cut in strips
1 can tomatoes (1 pound, 12 ounce)

¼ teaspoon salt
¼ teaspoon pepper
1 bay leaf
¼ teaspoon basil
½ teaspoon oregano
¼ cup white wine

watercress or parsley sprigs

Heat oil in a heavy Dutch oven and brown the pheasant quarters on all sides. Remove meat. Add onion and garlic and cook until tender. Stir in rest of ingredients and bring to a boil. Put pheasant back in, cover and simmer until done (1 to 1½ hours). Serve on a bed of rice. Cook the sauce down until thickened. Dollop a little sauce over the rice and meat and serve the rest in a bowl. Garnish with watercress or parsley sprigs. Will serve 2.

*Note:* Penciled on recipe, "Very good."

## PHEASANT WITH SHERRY

| | |
|---|---|
| 2 pheasants, cut into serving pieces | ½ teaspoon thyme |
| ¼ cup butter | 1 cup chicken bouillon |
| salt and pepper | ¼ cup medium-dry sherry |

Brown meat pieces in the butter. Add rest of ingredients to the frying pan, cover and simmer until the birds are tender (about 1 hour). Remove to a heated platter. Serve with wild rice and sherry sauce. Serves 4.

## Sauce

| | |
|---|---|
| 1 tablespoon butter | 1 cup liquid; pan juices with enough light |
| 1 tablespoon flour | cream to make a cup |
| | ⅛ teaspoon nutmeg |

In a small saucepan, heat butter. Blend in flour and then 1 cup liquid and nutmeg. Stir until thickened and serve wtih pheasant and rice.

*Note:* "Good, fruity taste."

## BRAISED PHEASANT

| | |
|---|---|
| 2 pheasant, cut into serving pieces | 1 cup chicken bouillon |
| flour | 1 package dried onion soup mix |
| 1 tablespoon butter | ½ cup sliced mushrooms |
| 1 tablespoon cooking oil | ½ teaspoon tarragon |

Roll pheasant pieces in flour. Brown on all sides in butter and oil in a heavy skillet. Add rest of ingredients to the pan, blend and simmer for 1 hour or until tender. Will serve 4.

# HUNGARIAN PHEASANT

4 pairs of pheasant legs
flour with salt, pepper and paprika added
3 tablespoons cooking oil
1 cup chicken broth

½ cup medium-dry sherry
1 cup sour cream
2 tablespoons fresh, chopped parsley
2 teaspoons paprika

Coat pheasant legs with the seasoned flour. Brown in hot cooking oil on all sides. Remove legs from pan and add chicken broth and sherry to the pan juices, mixing well. Return legs to pan, cover and simmer until done, about 1½ hours. Remove legs to a heated platter with a mound of hot buttered noodles in the center. Add sour cream, parsley and paprika to the pan and heat until it is almost boiling. Pour sauce over noodles and pheasant legs and serve. Will serve 4.

*Note:* Penciled on recipe, "Good."

# PHEASANT POT PIE

4 to 6 pheasant legs
1 onion
1 stalk celery
½ teaspoon vinegar
2 cups diced potatoes
3 large carrots, diced

2 onions, chopped
1 tablespoon quick-mixing flour
1 teaspoon parsley
½ teaspoon thyme
½ cup sliced mushrooms (optional)
piecrust

Place pheasant legs in water to cover with the onion, celery and vinegar. Cook until tender. Set aside to cool, then cut into bite-sized pieces. In 2 cups of the pheasant broth, cook the potatoes, carrots and chopped onions. Thicken the broth with flour and add the pheasant pieces, parsley, thyme and mushrooms. Top with your favorite piecrust and place in a 400° oven for 15 minutes. Turn the oven down to 350° and bake another 20 minutes or until the casserole is bubbly. Serves 4.

# Quail

The bobwhite quail has always seemed like a glamour bird to me. It beckons up memories of the stories I read as a youngster, of our country's privileged few who trekked to their favorite Southern plantation once a year for a week or two of quail hunting. It all seemed so proper and civilized—the horses, the long gowns, the dogs, the Purdey shotguns—and so much fun. Those images were a far cry from the quail hunting I came to know later on, when invariably, a covey would flush as I was on my hands and knees crawling under a jungle of green briars. Can you imagine Stewart Alsop on his hands and knees while pursuing quail?

The plantation-type hunting that existed at the turn of the century is about gone. There still is fair hunting over most of the range, but because of clean-farming practices, many of our Southern quail have become a bird of the thick, scrubby woodlots that border farms and open fields. They do well, however, on tree farms where controlled annual burning takes place.

One of the most difficult things to accept is that you cannot stockpile quail. They have an annual 70 to 80 percent mortality rate whether they are hunted or not. A two-year-old wild quail is ready for Social Security. Habitat is all-important to this spunky little game bird. It cannot survive when food and cover are destroyed. Conversely, if the habitat improves, a pair of quail are capable of producing up to eighteen young in one season to take advantage of the new territory.

Some hunters believe that quail are more sporting now than they used to be because of hunting pressure. They think the bird has "learned" to be wary. There is another theory that the birds merely react to immediate danger but don't actually learn anything. These sportsmen feel that selective breeding has produced changes in our quail—that only the strongest, fastest and wariest live to breed. I'm not sure what they were like in the "good old days," but I sure know that they are capable of reducing me to a bundle of shakes when they catapult into the sky from between my legs. Just once, I'd like a little announcement from them, like "Here come de birds!" but I'd probably still miss them.

Like many of our native birds, the bobwhite was market-hunted in the 1800s. Around 1855, quail could be bought in city markets for 50 cents a dozen. It sounds amazingly cheap now but I'll bet it was a steep price in those days. But as much fun as they are to stalk, and delicious as they are on the table, they still have to be cleaned at the end of the hunt. There are many opinions on when to dress quail. I think it's better to leave the entrails in until after they have been plucked or skinned. Plucking is the best way to clean quail, since the tiny birds need the protection the skin affords. However, after helping to pluck twenty quail last fall at one sitting, I can sympathize with anyone who says "No way." The skin tears very easily when dry-plucking. If you use the water method of loosening the feathers, it is easy to immerse them too long in too hot water and slightly cook the skin. With all this in mind, I still like to pluck quail but half of my following recipes will work beautifully with skinned ones.

After the quail has been skinned or plucked, remove the head and cut off the legs at the first joint above the foot. The wings should be removed at the first joint from the breast. Open the body cavity and remove the entrails. Rinse quickly under cold water or wipe the cavity with a damp cloth. If you wish to split the bird, game shears are safer and much easier to use than a knife. With small quail such as bobwhite, blue and Gambels, you will want to serve two for each healthy appetite. With a larger bird such as the mountain quail, one will be adequate.

## WINES

Unlike other game birds, the delicate but easily identifiable flavor of quail can be overpowered by a rich, red wine. Some of the light whites can be delightful with roasted or grilled quail. The German Rieslings, if not too sweet, can be perfect. The California Chardonnays are excellent quail wines and so are some of the light French reds of Beaujolais persuasion.

## ROAST QUAIL

8 quail (with skin)
5 tablespoons butter

1½ teaspoons tarragon
salt and pepper

Have the quail at room temperature. Put ½ tablespoon butter and a sprinkling of tarragon in each cavity. Place the birds on a piece of buttered foil in an ovenproof dish. Rub with more butter, sprinkle with salt and pepper and place in a preheated 450° oven. Roast for 25 minutes, basting once with butter. Place on a heated platter and let sit for 5 minutes. They will continue to cook. Will serve 4.

*Note:* I have penciled "Super" on this recipe.

## QUAIL WITH CREAM SAUCE

8 quail
¼ cup flour
salt and pepper
¼ cup butter
⅛ teaspoon savory

⅛ teaspoon chervil
½ cup dry white wine
1 tablespoon minced onion
½ cup chopped fresh mushrooms
2 egg yolks

½ cup light cream

Tie the legs of the quail to the body with string to make a neat bundle. Mix the flour, salt and pepper and liberally douse each bird. In a hot skillet, brown each quail in the butter. Sprinkle the birds with the savory and chervil. Add wine, onion and mushrooms to the pan and stir. Cover and simmer for 25 minutes. Remove the quail to a heated platter. Reduce the pan juices to ½ cup. Blend the egg yolks and cream into the juices with a dash of salt and pepper. Heat and stir until thickened, but don't boil. Spoon the sauce over the quail. Serves 4.

*Note:* Penciled on recipe, "Simply great."

## SHERRIED QUAIL

4 quail, split in two
flour, salt and pepper
¼ cup butter

1 tablespoon minced green onion
shake of marjoram
½ cup sherry

Douse quail well in the mixture of flour, salt and pepper. Heat the butter in a frying pan. Brown the quail on all sides with the onion and marjoram.

Transfer the birds to a roasting pan. Place the sherry in the frying pan, bring to a boil and pour over the birds. Cover and roast in a 350° oven (preheated) for 35 minutes. Serve the birds on a heated platter garnished with watercress or parsley. Ladle a generous helping of sauce over each bird. Serves 2.

*Note:* Penciled on recipe, "Excellent."

## Sauce

| | |
|---|---|
| ½ cup jelly, such as currant, raspberry or elderberry | 1 tablespoon lemon juice |
| | ¼ teaspoon lemon rind |
| 1 tablespoon orange juice | ¼ teaspoon orange rind |
| ¼ teaspoon dry mustard | |

In a pan, melt jelly, add juices, rinds and mustard and bring to a boil.

## BARBECUED QUAIL

| | |
|---|---|
| 6 quail, split in two (with skin) | ¼ cup catsup |
| ¼ cup chopped onion | ½ teaspoon dry mustard |
| ¼ cup chopped green pepper | ¼ cup dry red wine |
| ¼ cup butter | ½ teaspoon salt |
| ¼ cup water | parsley or watercress sprigs |

Sauté the onion and green pepper in the butter. Add liquids and seasonings and simmer for 10 minutes. Preheat oven to 450°. Butter a shallow baking dish and arrange quail, skin side up, in the dish. Brush some butter on the quail and add a dollop of barbecue sauce to each bird. Place in the oven for 25 minutes, basting with the sauce once during the cooking time. Serve birds on a heated platter surrounding a bed of hot buttered rice. Ladle the pan juices over the rice and garnish with sprigs of parsley or watercress. Serves 3 or 4.

*Note:* Penciled on recipe, "Good."

## STUFFED QUAIL

| | |
|---|---|
| 8 quail (with skin) | ¼ cup butter |
| 1 onion, chopped | 1½ cups chicken livers |
| ½ green pepper, chopped | 2 cups cooked long-grain rice |
| 1 cup chopped celery | ½ cup chicken bouillon |
| ½ cup port wine | |

Sauté onion, pepper and celery slowly in butter until the vegetables are tender. Add livers and simmer for 5 minutes. Mix the vegetables and livers with the cooked rice and stuff the quail with the mixture, about ½ cup per bird. Rub the birds with butter and place in a shallow roasting pan. Heat the bouillon and port to the boiling point and pour over the birds. Place in a preheated 450° oven and roast for 30 minutes, basting with the pan juices during the cooking. Serves 4.

*Note:* Penciled on recipe, "Good."

## BRAISED QUAIL WITH CELERY

8 quail
flour with salt and pepper added
¼ cup butter
1 cup chopped celery

1 clove garlic, minced
2 tablespoons flour
½ cup chicken bouillon
½ cup milk

parsley sprigs

Roll the quail in the flour with a little salt and pepper added. Brown in butter on all sides and remove from pan. Add celery and garlic to the pan and sauté, adding more butter if necessary. When the vegetables are tender, add the 2 tablespoons of flour, then bouillon and milk. Stir until smooth. Return the quail to the pan, spooning the sauce over them. Cover and simmer for 25 to 30 minutes, turning often in the sauce. Place the quail on a hot platter surrounding a bed of noodles. Pour pan juices over the noodles. Garnish with parsley. Serves 4.

## BROILED QUAIL

4 quail, with skin
olive oil
seasoned salt

pepper
8 pieces of buttered toast
parsley sprigs

Clean quail and split in two halves with poultry shears. Brush birds with oil. Sprinkle with salt and pepper. Place on a piece of greased foil on a broiler pan. Broil in preheated broiler, 4 inches from the heat, for 8 to 10 minutes. Serve on toast, garnished with parsley. Will serve 4 at a luncheon, with a salad.

## QUAIL IN THE ASHES

8 quail
2 cups cooked wild rice

salt and pepper
thyme (optional)

8 thin slices fat salt pork

Rinse and dry quail. Fill cavities with wild rice and close with small skewers. Sprinkle with salt and pepper. Wrap each in a slice of fat salt pork.

Place on heavy-duty aluminum foil, large enough to completely enclose 2 or 4 quail, depending on size. Enclose a sprig of thyme in each package. Using the drugstore wrap, close packages. Bury in hot coals or ashes in fireplace or outdoor campfire. Let roast for 35 minutes and check for tenderness. Cook another 10 minutes if necessary. Keep the birds piled with hot coals throughout the cooking. Serves 4.

*Note:* This recipe came to me from Trenton, N. J. Scout Leader Joe Tryba. He uses it frequently on weekend camp-outs.

# Woodcock

Our black Labrador retriever loves woodcock hunting. Samantha has been with us for eleven hunting seasons now and she is used on all kinds of upland game as well as waterfowl. She performs to our satisfaction on all species, but woodcock seem to be a special passion—a close second to ducks and geese. They must have a stronger smell, for Sam never quarters with more style than she does in a swamp full of woodcock droppings. When her gun-toting companions miss one, there is a long, searching look at the shooter and then on to find the next bird.

Woodcock hunting as a sport is comparatively new, dating back to the early 1800s, probably because it was considered wasteful to use up powder on a bird weighing less than a half a pound. There were accounts of 100 to 150 birds per man at that time, and with black-powder weapons at that. But later in the 19th century bags of 20 were more usual. There wasn't much market-hunting for the timberdoodle. In the North, grouse were the big cash crop and in the South, the glamour bird in the grocery shops was the quail.

Because of the long beak that was often buried in swampy soil, some old-timers used to think the bird never ate anything solid but sucked liquid from boggy ground. They even nicknamed them "bog suckers." They do subsist mainly on earthworms and that wetland habitat is essential to their survival. Many good woodcock hunting grounds have turned out to be a home owner's headache: a constantly wet basement. How much better off we would have been to have left the swamp alone!

With no help at all from the male, the female woodcock has amazing success brooding her usual four eggs. Some timberdoodle watchers think she's able to hatch almost every egg because she never leaves the nest during the daylight hours, therefore effectively shielding them from ultraviolet rays. There is a theory that these rays may harm eggs of game birds and fish which are simple cells. Woodcock raise only one brood a year, usually early in the spring, so the offspring are ordinarily adult-size by hunting season.

The woodcock in the game bag is mostly breast meat, the dark breast meat of a long-distance flyer. Some have likened its taste to that of liver. I disagree. I know it is popular to ask, if you have never eaten a particular species before, "What does it taste like?" The other person is then put on the spot to come up with an intelligent answer. There is none. If someone asked what pork tasted like, what would you answer? It doesn't taste like beef or chicken or lamb. It simply tastes like pork. And woodcock tastes like woodcock.

The meat on the legs and wings of the woodcock is white and delicious if you want to go to the bother of using the whole bird. There is really very little meat on these pieces. The bird's breast is the only thing many hunters keep. As with doves, I like to pluck the bird even if I'm only saving the breast. That extra protection pays off in the kitchen, especially if a broiling recipe is used.

Sometimes it takes several weeks of hunting to provide enough birds for a hungry family. The best way to freeze these little birds is in water. It prevents freezer burn. Open up the top of an empty half-gallon cardboard milk container, wash well and stuff the woodcocks into it, cover the birds with cold water and freeze immediately. When serving, count on two birds (or breasts) per person.

## WINES

The woodcock calls for the richest and most powerful-tasting red wines that could ever be enjoyed with game. To their everlasting credit, no sauce or extra ingredient will ever completely hide the earthy aroma and taste of woodcock. Eating a brace of woodcock with a chunk of hard bread and a bottle of a robust Bordeaux red, or claret, as the British choose to call it, is a rare taste sensation. For those who prefer the viny bouquet of French Cabernet Sauvignon (the dominant grape of red Bordeaux), this bird was made for them. The fine California Cabernets (perhaps their best wines) will be equally complementary. This is not an attempt to straddle the international fence since the two wines, even though they are made from the same grape with a common ancestor in the vine root, do not come out of the bottle tasting the same. A fun thing to do with a meal of woodcock is to buy a bottle of medium-priced French Bordeaux and a bottle of equally priced California Cabernet and see which you like best. After all, wine likes and dislikes are personal things.

## BRANDYWINE BAKED WOODCOCK

8 woodcock (or breasts)
1 small onion, chopped
½ cup sliced mushrooms
2 tablespoons butter

½ cup apple juice
½ cup light cream
1 bay leaf
salt and pepper

Sauté the onion and mushrooms in the butter until tender. Add apple juice, cream, bay leaf and salt and pepper to taste to the vegetables. Bring just to the boiling point. Preheat oven to 350°. Place woodcocks in a roasting pan or casserole. Pour sauce over top, cover and place in oven. Roast for 50 minutes, turning the birds a couple of times in the sauce. Will serve 4.

*Note:* Strong woodcock flavor delicately penetrates the sauce. I've penciled "Very good" on this recipe.

## RARE ROASTED TIMBERDOODLE

8 birds, plucked
1 cooking apple

3 tablespoons butter
½ cup port

Preheat oven to 450°. Place a slice of apple in the cavity of each bird. Rub the birds with butter and place in a roasting pan. Pour a little heated port over each bird and roast for 25 minutes, basting with the rest of the port and pan juices. Serves 4.

*Note:* Penciled on recipe, "Excellent."

# GRILLED WOODCOCK

8 woodcock
1 cup dry red wine
3 tablespoons lemon juice
4 tablespoons minced onion
3 bay leaves, broken

10 peppercorns
¼ teaspoon fennel seed
fine bread crumbs
butter
black raspberry jam

Mix marinade of wine, lemon juice, onion, bay leaves, peppercorns and fennel seeds. Marinate the woodcocks, turning often, for 3 hours. Just before broiling, remove the woodcocks and roll in the bread crumbs, coating well. Grease a piece of foil with melted butter and place on a broiler pan. Dot the birds with butter and place on the foil. Broil 4 inches from the heat, 4 minutes on a side. Cooking time total will be 8 minutes. Serve on a heated platter with a sauce made of melted butter and black raspberry jam (half and half). Will serve 4.

*Note:* Penciled on recipe, "Good."

# BRAISED WOODCOCK LOUISE

8 woodcock breasts (or whole birds)
½ cup chopped celery
3 tablespoons butter
flour with salt and pepper added

¼ teaspoon tarragon
¼ teaspoon chervil
1 cup beef bouillon
5 juniper berries (optional)

Sauté celery in butter for a couple of minutes. Douse birds in seasoned flour and add to the frying pan. Brown on all sides. Give each bird a light shake of tarragon and chervil. Add bouillon and berries to the pan. Cover and simmer for 35 minutes, turning the birds often. Serves 4.

*Note:* A good recipe for those who don't like woodcock rare. I serve it with rice, fresh spinach with browned butter and a good-quality lettuce dressed with oil and vinegar.

# BROILED WOODCOCK

8 woodcock
salt and pepper
¼ teaspoon marjoram

¼ teaspoon minced parsley
bacon slices
melted butter

Sprinkle each woodcock with salt and pepper, marjoram and parsley. Wrap each bird in a slice of bacon and secure with a toothpick. Place on a buttered piece of foil on a broiled pan. Pour a little butter over each and broil (4 inches from the heat) for 8 minutes on each side. Serve immediately. Will serve 4.

*Note:* Penciled on recipe, "Truly great."

# Ruffed Grouse

The varying subspecies of ruffed grouse range in vastly different habitats from central to northwest Alaska and from Maine to the state of Washington. It's an old-timer in the United States, having lived here at least 25,000 years.

As with our other game birds, grouse chicks are susceptible to wet weather and predators during their first few weeks of life. The youngsters that don't heed the "gathering" call or the "stay put" command don't live to reproduce, thus guaranteeing survival of birds that are on the bright side.

Ruffed grouse chicks feed almost exclusively on insects (older birds like them too) so clear-cuts and slashings are important to a healthy continuing population. The adult birds are fond of high-quality tree buds, especially apple. At one time, in the mid 1800s, this selectivity led to bounties on grouse in some of the orchard counties of the New England states. Wouldn't it be great to live in a time when a grouse was considered a pest? Unfortunately (or fortunately), the bounties were discontinued before I was born.

The ruffed grouse's short, blunt wings are built for the quick burst of speed that serves it so well in escaping predators. Its flush is usually noisy but can be quiet if it isn't startled. The bird is a genius at using trees to camouflage its escape and at making its way through thick underbrush at a fast clip. However, its flight is short, averaging only a couple of hundred yards.

When I was growing up in north-central Pennsylvania, the only bird hunting we had was for grouse. It was fairly good hunting in a still young, second-growth, hardwood forest. One of the earliest memories I have is of staying with a baby sitter while Mother and Dad went grouse hunting. They always returned with birds in hand, carrying their shotguns heavily (Mother hunted with a .410), with a tired setter bringing up the rear. The trio gave off that woodsy odor that comes only after a long, brush-busting day. I could hardly wait until I was old enough to do special things like hunting. These days I undoubtedly hunt more often than Mother ever did, but I'm not the shot she was and I sure don't use a .410.

As much as Mother liked to hunt grouse, she detested cleaning them. Dad would pluck and gut them and then she would stand at the sink for what seemed like hours with a knife and pull each and every minute pinfeather out. One of my rebellions as an adult is in cleaning game. I figure a feather or two never hurt anyone (forgive me, Mother). I also found out that pinfeathers come out a heck of a lot easier after the bird has been frozen and then thawed.

The ruffed grouse is about midway in size between a quail and a pheasant, averaging from a pound and a quarter to a pound and a half. One bird per person is a good serving. The forest thunderbird is also midway between the quail and pheasant in the flavor-power column.

## WINES

As with pheasant, roasted and broiled grouse breast can be aided by a not-too-dry white wine. The German Moselles with their delightful fruitiness make an interesting combination. But for a real change of pace I like a bottle of Sebastiani Green Hungarian. When grouse are subjected to a rather strong herb, say rosemary or curry, then I'd just as soon go along with a more flavorful red Burgundy.

## GROUSE WITH SAUERKRAUT

| | |
|---|---|
| 4 grouse | 2 pounds sauerkraut |
| butter | bacon strips |

Dry birds thoroughly, rub with soft butter and brown under broiler. Place the birds on a large piece of heavy-duty aluminum foil. Stuff each with some wet sauerkraut and place the rest around the birds. Lay a couple of bacon strips over each breast. Seal foil and bake in a 325° oven for 1 hour. Serves 4.

*Note:* Penciled on recipe, "Excellent."

## ROAST GROUSE

| | |
|---|---|
| 4 whole grouse | ⅛ teaspoon chervil |
| ⅛ teaspoon marjoram | butter |
| | ¼ cup red wine |

Rub grouse with butter and sprinkle with marjoram and chervil. Place the birds on a large sheet of heavy-duty aluminum foil. Add the wine to the package and seal. Place in a roasting pan. Put in a preheated 400° oven and roast for 45 minutes. The birds may be browned under the broiler after roasting. Serves 4.

*Note:* Penciled on recipe, "Great."

## BROILED GROUSE

| | |
|---|---|
| 3 grouse, cut into serving pieces | 4 tablespoons cooking oil |
| 1 small bottle steak sauce (5 ounces) | |

Marinate grouse pieces in the oil and sauce for 3 hours, turning the pieces occasionally. Place pieces on broiler pan, 4 inches from the heat. Broil 5 to 7 minutes on one side. Turn, baste with sauce and broil another 5 to 7 minutes. Heat sauce and serve with the birds. Will serve 4.

My penciled note says "Moist and pungent, very good."

## BAKED GROUSE

| | |
|---|---|
| 3 grouse, cut into serving pieces | salt and pepper |
| flour | 1 cup light cream |
| 2 tablespoons butter | 1 cup dry red wine |
| 2 tablespoons cooking oil | ½ cup sliced mushrooms |
| | ¼ teaspoon tarragon |

Dredge grouse pieces in flour and brown in a heavy skillet using the butter and oil. Add salt and pepper. Place browned pieces in an oven-proof casserole. Add cream, wine, mushrooms and tarragon to the frying pan.

Bring this mixture to a boil and pour over the meat. Bake, covered, 1 hour in 350° oven. Serve the sauce in a gravy boat to be ladled over rice and grouse. Serves 4.

*Note:* Penciled on recipe, "Great."

## TROPICAL GROUSE

2 grouse, split in two
flour flavored with salt and pepper
2 tablespoons butter
2 tablespoons olive oil

1½ cups white wine
½ cup orange juice
½ teaspoon rosemary leaves
½ teaspoon dry mustard
pinch of ground red pepper

Douse the birds with seasoned flour and brown in the butter-oil mixture. Add wine, orange juice, rosemary, mustard and pepper to the pot, cover and simmer for 1 to 1½ hours. I use a Dutch oven for the browning and the cooking. Serve with mushroom sauce and rice. Serves 2.

### Mushroom Sauce

2 medium onions, chopped
¼ cup butter

1 cup fresh mushrooms, finely chopped
quick-mixing flour

Sauté onions lightly in butter. Ladle 1 cup of broth from the grouse pot to onion mixture and simmer for 5 minutes. Add mushrooms and cook another 2 minutes. Thicken with flour and serve over grouse and rice.

# Mourning
# Dove

The mourning dove is as good in the pan as it is sporting in the field. These darting little game birds are equally adaptable to today's world. They flourish in spite of all we do to destroy game bird habitat. In fact, the mourning dove population in the United States is increasing because the birds are able to select excellent nesting sites in our expanding suburbs. Other game birds such as pheasants and ducks find nesting habitat an increasing problem as we continue to practice clean farming and drain our wetlands.

A pair of doves will bring off several broods during a summer. But because the mortality rate is high, the birds will average about four offspring a year. The normal time between egg laying and the fledgling leaving the nest is only one month. Incubation takes 14 days. The amazing growth of the offspring (thirtyfold in 2 weeks) occurs because both parents are able to nourish the young birds with liquid secreted by glands in their crops known as pigeon milk. According to experts, doves and pigeons are the only male creatures in the world that "lactate" for the purpose of feeding extremely young offspring.

Although mourning doves are hunted in two-thirds of the contiguous states, dove hunting is far more of a tradition in the South and West than it is in the northern states. One of the reasons could be the migratory instinct in most mourning doves. Northern gunners eagerly look forward to opening day, usually the first of the hunting seasons, around Labor Day. They may have several days of good sport and then whiz-bang, a heavy frost hits the area and most of the doves move out overnight. In the South, a cold snap brings more northern flight birds and hunting opportunities increase.

I like dove hunting for selfish reasons. The weather is warm and pleasant here in Pennsylvania during the best of the season (early September). Second, our hunting hours don't open until noon each day so there is none of the break-of-dawn nonsense. And then I don't have to walk my legs off or crouch in a cold, wet blind. What isn't easy for me is hitting those little bullets. Their normal cruising speed is between 30 and 40 miles per hour and they have been clocked up to 55 mph. If speed weren't enough, even the young of the year quickly learn to zigzag, go into a fast dive or change directions in an instant upon spotting potential danger. Come to think about it, it's a wonder I down my usual average, which is a poor one out of eight.

Most dove hunters don't bother to pluck their birds. They simply lift the skin off the breast, pull the breast up and cut it from the body. If you're only going to save breasts, I think it is worth a couple of extra seconds to pluck the feathers from the breast and leave the skin intact. It pays off in the pot. And if you're really feeling ambitious, try plucking the whole bird. Those little wings and legs are delicious. While the birds are warm, plucking the feathers is fairly easy. After the birds have cooled, you may wish to slosh them for a couple of seconds in a pail of very hot water to loosen the feathers.

Like that of other migratory birds, the dove's breast meat is dark, rich and full of flavor. Many cookbooks consider one or two dove breasts a serving. Perhaps two doves would be enough if the whole bird is served, but when cooking only the breasts, I find that three or four per person is a nice helping. When serving whole game birds, invite only those friends who aren't afraid to use their fingers. It's a crime to see legs and wings of game birds go to waste because they are difficult to cut into with knife and fork.

## WINES

These little migratory birds are extremely flavorful, but they can be somewhat neutralized by powerful wines. A nice, young Beaujolais is a fine selection and I might opt for a rosé wine if it were not too sweet. Besides, those rosé wines look so nice in the glass, when sitting beside a platterful of dark-meated dove breasts.

One of the easiest ways to cook doves or dove breasts is to coat them with flour seasoned with salt and pepper and brown on all sides in a heavy skillet in two tablespoons of butter. When brown, lower the heat, add half a cup of dry white wine, cover and simmer for forty-five minutes to one hour. Add a little water if necessary during the cooking.

Fried doves are good when using this simple recipe: Cut the doves in two with poultry shears (or use the breasts). Dip the pieces in an egg wash—one egg beaten with a tablespoon of milk. Then roll in finely ground Italian-seasoned bread crumbs. Fry *slowly* in butter, turning often, until the doves are tender, about 25 to 30 minutes. Drain well on paper toweling and serve.

I always seem to end the season with a few dove breasts in the freezer. Not enough for a dinner but too many to throw into the stew pot with other odds and ends of game. A favorite way to utilize these half dozen or so choice pieces of meat is in spaghetti sauce. I add them in the last forty minutes of simmering. They are thoroughly cooked, lightly flavored by the powerful sauce and still retain their characteristic taste.

Both of these next recipes are favorites in our household, gourmet treatments for a sporty little game bird.

## DOVES MARIE

| | |
|---|---|
| 12 to 16 doves, whole birds or breasts | ½ teaspoon oregano |
| ¼ cup chopped onion | ¼ teaspoon basil |
| ½ cup chopped celery | salt and pepper to taste |
| 1 cup quartered mushrooms | 1 tablespoon soy sauce |
| 2 tablespoons butter | 1½ cups light cream |
| parsley sprigs | |

Arrange doves in a buttered, shallow baking dish. In a frying pan, gently sauté the onion, celery and mushrooms in the butter for 5 minutes. Add the seasonings, soy sauce and cream. Bring to the boiling point. Pour over the doves, cover the baking dish and bake in a preheated 350° oven for 1 hour. Twice during the cooking, remove the dish from the oven and turn the birds in the sauce. Cook some wild rice in plenty of salted water for 40 minutes. Drain and butter. Arrange on serving platter. Place doves around the rice and spoon sauce over both. Garnish with parsley. Serves 4.

## DOVES AMANDINE

| | |
|---|---|
| 12 to 16 doves or dove breasts | ⅓ cup chopped onion |
| salt and pepper | 1 cup Madeira |
| flour | 1 cup water |
| giblets (optional) | 4 tablespoons almonds (blanched and |
| 4 tablespoons cooking oil | slivered) |
| parsley sprigs | |

Season doves with salt and pepper and roll in flour. If giblets are used, parboil the heart and gizzard for 30 minutes, then roll them and the liver in flour. Brown doves and giblets in the hot oil. Add onion and sauté briefly. Add Madeira, water and almonds. Cover and simmer for 45 minutes. Serve on a bed of hot buttered noodles with parsley as garnish. Spoon the sauce over the doves and noodles on the serving platter. Will serve 4.

# Wild
# Turkey

The wild turkey is the largest, most intelligent and most prized game bird in North America. Our rather dumb, tame turkey of Thanksgiving fame probably didn't originate totally from these crafty wild birds but from a subspecies domestically grown by the Aztec Indians of Mexico and shipped from there to Spain. They were then introduced to the rest of Europe and came back to North America with early colonists. Experts suspect there was much cross-breeding after this reintroduction so the tame variety is a mixture of the Mexican subspecies and the North American wild turkey. We probably wouldn't recognize the wild turkey of colonial days because of its lack of fear of man. Like other game birds, the wary ones survived and the tame ones supplemented the colonists' meager diet.

Turkeys were relatively scarce during my growing-up years in north-central Pennsylvania and the first time I saw one was a frightening experience. My brother, father and I were brook-trout-fishing one early summer day on a favorite small run. We had spread out in order better to cover the little stream and not get in each other's way. Dad walked farther up the streamside path than Ted and I did. Suddenly we heard him shout and start running full-blast toward us. "Run, run," he yelled, waving his arms over his head, fending off a huge bird that kept flying at him, beating its wings at his head.

The three of us must have sprinted a quarter of a mile before we decided that the hen had given up the chase. Dad plopped down on the ground and told us about accidentally strolling between the mother hen and her newly hatched brood. They weren't able to fly and she was frantic. A more protective mother you'll never find!

We waited a full hour before venturing back up the trail to retrieve fly rods and scattered tackle. Dad laughed about the incident when he relayed it to others, but at the time, all three of us were scared of that big bird. And we had reason to be respectful. A 10 to 12 pound hen turkey can do a lot of damage.

Turkeys have the best eyesight and are the most cautious game birds that I know of. One example of this was demonstrated after turkeys had been widely restocked in Pennsylvania and were more plentiful in our neck of the woods. Jim and I then lived at Greystone Lodge at the foot of Denton Hill in Potter County. One of the nice features of our 40 acres was a healthy spring with an even flow, winter and summer. Area wild turkeys were attracted to the seep during the winter as a source of water, grit and a bit of green. Our house was within a hundred yards of the spring and we watched the turkeys every day from the kitchen window. But they never got used to our appearing on the back porch. One little movement and they would disappear for several hours. This happened for the five years we lived there. They never became accustomed to us.

Because Jim and I have never been seriously bitten by the turkey-hunting bug, turkeys to cook have been scarce in the Bashline household. I'll give you my tested two recipes; the other three are from good friends who are more productive turkey hunters. Do keep in mind that the wild turkey was not bred for its breast meat like the tame version. Some people are disappointed in the amount of breast meat.

## WINES

Wild turkeys represent a noble meal. Once a year is all most of us can manage so why not pull all stops here and serve champagne? Select a fine French label if you're so inclined. Mumm, Taittinger, Piper-Heidsieck in the brut (dry) persuasion would be delightful. But don't sell the American sparkling wines short. California's efforts are first class with Korbel, Kornell, Almadén, Christian Brothers and others doing an excellent job of making the "bubbly." New York State's Great Western label is also well worth trying. While champagne is a bit too costly for most people to drink often, it has a democratic taste when served with all sorts of wild game and fish. For that matter, it tastes good with almost any meat.

## ROAST TURKEY WITH PEANUTS

| | |
|---|---|
| 10- to 14-pound wild turkey | ½ cup dry white wine |
| 1 cup butter | ½ cup chicken bouillon |
| | salt and pepper |

Rub the bird with butter, sprinkle with salt and pepper, and stuff it with peanut dressing. Use skewers to close the body opening. Place the bird in a roasting pan and cover completely with cheesecloth. Mix the rest of the butter, the wine and bouillon together and use to baste the turkey every 25 minutes until you can baste with pan juices. Place in a 350° oven for the first hour, lower to 325° for the remaining time. Roast the bird for 20 to 25 minutes per pound.

*Note:* Penciled on recipe, "Super."

### Peanut Dressing

| | |
|---|---|
| 2 stalks celery, chopped | 2 eggs, beaten |
| 1 onion, finely chopped | 1 cup chicken bouillon |
| 3 teaspoons butter, melted | ½ cup white wine |
| 3 cups roasted peanuts | ½ teaspoon sage |
| 4½ cups dry bread crumbs | pepper to taste |

Sauté the celery and onion in the butter. Chop the peanuts coarsely and mix all ingredients together. The dressing should be quite moist to help the turkey keep its moisture intact. This should be enough dressing for a 12-pound wild turkey.

## ROAST WILD TURKEY

| | |
|---|---|
| 1 10- to 14-pound turkey | 1½ quarts dry bread crumbs |
| salt and pepper | 1 teaspoon salt |
| 1 pound pork sausage | ¼ teaspoon pepper |
| 1 onion, chopped | 4 tablespoons parsley, minced |
| 2 apples, peeled, cored and chopped | chicken bouillon |
| | butter |

Sprinkle dressed turkey with salt and pepper. In frying pan, cook sausage and onion for 10 minutes. Add apples, bread crumbs, salt, pepper and parsley and mix well. Add enough bouillon to make a moist dressing. Stuff the turkey. Place it in a roasting pan and cover with a double thickness of cheesecloth, soaked well in butter. Roast in 325° oven for 20 minutes per pound. Keep basting with butter, then pan juices. A 10-pound turkey will serve 5–6.

Shirley Grenoble, an outdoor writer who is actively involved with both the state and national Wild Turkey Federations, is an avid turkey hunter. Her recipe for roast turkey follows:

## ROAST TURKEY WITH BREAD DRESSING

| | |
|---|---|
| 1 wild turkey | turkey giblets (diced) |
| 1 cup diced onion | 1 cup melted butter or margarine |
| 1 cup finely chopped celery | 15 cups stale bread cubes |
| salt and pepper to taste | |

Sauté onion, celery and giblets in butter. When almost tender, reduce heat to very low, add bread cubes, salt and pepper and cover. Let mixture steam, turning occasionally until bread cubes are moist. Makes enough for a 15-pound turkey.

For variation, ½ cup chopped apples, raisins or almonds may be added to the dressing.

Stuff turkey with dressing, skewer and truss. Place turkey in roaster, add 3 cups hot water and cover. Roast at 250° approximately 20 minutes per pound.

The late Roger Latham, former outdoor editor of the *Pittsburgh Press* and author of the *Complete Book of the Wild Turkey,* cooked many wild turkeys. He passed on this advice:

"One delightful variation for cooking the wild turkey, in case you get tired of roast wild turkey all the time, is to quick-fry the breast meat. When the turkey is still uncooked, remove the meat from each side of the breast in one large fillet. Then lay each piece of white meat on a table or board, skin side down. Carefully cut thin steaks about a third of an inch thick. Salt the pieces, let them stand a few minutes in a pile, and when good and moist, dust each with flour. Shake off the excess and drop in a sizzling frying pan of hot butter or margarine. Brown quickly on one side, flop them over and brown the other side. This should only take a very few minutes, and the meat should not be overcooked. Fry it fast like you would a good steak, and it will almost melt in your mouth. The meat will be juicy and delicious, and bear little resemblance to the same meat when roasted."

Sounds great to me; I can hardly wait to try it on our next wild turkey.

Rob Keck of the National Wild Turkey Federation, and a champion turkey caller, also likes to quick-cook the turkey breast meat. His recipe makes my mouth water.

## "SHAKE 'N' BAKE" TURKEY WITH RUNNING GEAR GRAVY

This epicurean treat first hit the skillet back in the early 1950s by sheer accident when a tired and hungry turkey hunter was searching for a quick and easy evening meat at camp. Little did he know that he was "greas'n the pan" of a craze which occurs regularly in a rural Pennsylvania county known as "Shake 'n' Bake" (not to be confused with the commercial variety). It has since been adapted to grouse, quail, ringneck and venison. As this grandaddy of turkey hunters and cookers stated at one of our spring hunt meals, "We've been living high on the hog, but this is on top of the world."

The bird should be skinned rather than plucked. White breast meat is filleted from the bone. Remove the one main tendon from the breast. Skinning and cut-up time is approximately 15 minutes. All appendages are disjointed. Cold-water soaking may be necessary if excessive blood appears.

Breast fillets are cut across the grain about ¼ inch thick, 3 inches long and 1½ inches wide (about the size of a large oyster). When feeding a crowd, thinner and smaller pieces may be cut.

A mixture of 2 cups of milk and 3 beaten raw eggs is placed in a mixing bowl (more if needed).

Into a second bowl pour ½ pound of bread crumbs (bread crumbs have proven superior over most other types of breading for this treat).

With a meat fork immerse the fillet into the eggs and milk, then into the bread crumbs and repeat the same process for a double breading. The double breading seems to seal out excess grease from the meat.

A deep fryer or iron skillet may be used. Heat your oil to 365°. Drop the turkey into the heated oil and turn it one time in the required 10 minutes. (When you drop any amount of cold meat into hot oil, it cools the oil; make sure the oil remains hot to set the breading. In the deep fryer I use 3 gallons of oil so there is no significant cooling.)

Extract the fried meat from the skillet or fryer, place it in a paper-towel-lined pan to soak up the excess grease and place in a warm oven until all is fried.

A thick gravy is made from the neck, back, giblets and legs and thighs.

Most of that meat coming from the latter gives it the name "Running Gear Gravy" in that meat is cooked, browned, seasoned, cut up and added to the thickened broth. This gravy goes well on top of the fried meat as well as potatoes or rice (a 15-pound bird easily feeds eight).

Leftovers, if there are any, can be refrigerated after it cools, but you better put a lock on the refrigerator door.

# Game-Farm
# Birds

Hunting opportunities on public and private land decline each year as we lose habitat. More hunters with limited time, a bit more money in their pockets (and perhaps friends or clients to entertain) are heading for a regulated shooting ground. Some, having never hunted in the wild, advance to the licensed areas from the trap and skeet fields. Others have hunted extensively but may find themselves living in an urban area during their productive work years where the only sport hunting is on private ground. There are many types of regulated shooting areas. Some accept only groups; others encourage individual hunters. The price at times includes a midday meal, dogs and a handler. A few will allow you to bring your own dog (if it's controllable). There is sometimes a small extra fee connected with the cleaning of birds. Other times, it is part of the packaged deal.

At approximately 70 percent of these areas the game you take home is frozen and not the actual birds you killed that day. This is done for two reasons: First, most hunters are tired after several hours in the field and even the speediest game cleaning does require some waiting. Second, prefrozen birds keep better on the trip home, especially if it is more than an hour or so. About 50 percent of the game farms in this country now vacuum-bag their birds. This means the air is excluded within the heavy plastic bag. This serves two purposes: It saves space and it helps prevent freezer burn. The other 50 percent also bag in heavy plastic, pushing out as much air as possible by hand. The grounds operators have various methods to protect the game for the trip, with most utilizing either heavy cardboard boxes and newspaper or Styrofoam containers.

When the birds leave the regulated shooting grounds they are almost always in excellent condition. They have been plucked, much of the skin is intact and the entrails have been removed. What the hunter does with those birds from then on determines whether he enjoys several dinners of succulent game or is told to never bring that "stuff" home again.

It is essential to prevent the frozen birds from thawing or keep the others cold. Most tired hunters walk in their back door, toss their day's bag into the freezer and head for the shower. The first birds that are eaten may be fine but the longer they are in the freezer, the greater the chance for deterioration. One layer of protection is not enough for more than a week in the deep freeze. It can be punctured. I recommend using a good-quality freezer wrap over top of the shooting ground's plastic bag. Use ample paper, wrap well, seal with freezer tape and use a marking pen to label the package with species, number of servings and date. Then it's into the deep freeze and you have a fighting chance at having a good bird even if you keep it a year.

The duck and quail recipes that appear elsewhere in this book will serve the household chef well when he or she cooks a regulated-shooting-grounds bird. However, the shooting-area pheasant has lived an easier life than its wild counterpart and it's fun to use some different recipes on these birds which have a layer of fat that comes from ample food and little running and flying.

Chukar partridges are delicious little game birds that few of us have a chance at bagging in the wild, unless we live in certain parts of the Midwest or Idaho. I fell in love with the flavor of these swift flyers when experimenting with these recipes. I think you'll like them too.

When deciding how many birds to cook for a meal, here is my rule of thumb for the healthy appetites in my family: 2 quail per person; one chukar partridge per diner; one large duck will feed 2 people; a pheasant will serve 2 (or 3 if it's over 3 pounds).

## WINES

My wine choice for the rich taste of wild chukar partridge would be a red Burgundy or, if you follow the generic grape labeling, a Pinot Noir. Two other California specialties that do well with chukars or other heavily flavored game birds would be Barbara and Petite Sirah. They are both moderately dry with an interesting, spicy overtaste.

Game farm or preserve birds, be they quail, pheasants, chukar or Hungarian partridges, often do not offer the robust flavor of the wild individuals. The milder Chablis-type wines or even the sweeter Rieslings are usually a better choice with these more civilized fowl.

## LUCKY ROAST PHEASANT

2 pheasants with skin (2-pound birds)  
3 tablespoons butter

¼ teaspoon tarragon leaves  
fatty bacon slices

Thoroughly dry the pheasants with paper toweling. Rub with butter and place 1 tablespoon of butter and some tarragon in each cavity. Place on a greased rack inside a shallow roasting pan. Put the birds on one side and cover the upside with bacon slices. Place in a preheated 375° oven for 30 minutes. Turn the birds, cover with bacon and roast another 30 minutes. Cut the birds right down the middle and serve a half to each diner. If the skin isn't brown enough, stick the birds under the broiler for a few minutes.

*Note:* My penciled notation on this recipe: "Super, nice and juicy."

## CORKY'S PHEASANT

1 pheasant (3-pounder was tested)  
¼ cup apple juice  
¼ cup butter  
¼ cup dry vermouth

¼ teaspoon tarragon leaves  
cornstarch  
apple slices  
parsley or watercress

salt and pepper

If you wish, stuff bird with a favorite bread dressing. Rub the outside of the bird with butter and place in a shallow baking dish. Place under the broiler and brown, turning until all the skin is a delicate color.

Turn the oven down to 300°. Heat the apple juice, butter, vermouth and tarragon and baste the bird with the mixture at 20-minute intervals. Roast for 1½ to 1¾ hours, turning the bird a couple of times during the cooking time. The bird will be tender and the meat still juicy because of the slow cooking temperature. Will serve 2 or 3 (2-pound bird will serve 2).

Remove most of the fat from the roasting pan and thicken the rest of the juices with a little cornstarch mixed with cold water. Add a little extra water if necessary. Serve the pheasant garnished with apple slices and parsley or watercress. Add salt and pepper and a dollop of sauce to each serving at the table.

# BRAISED PHEASANT

1 large pheasant (3½-pounder was
   tested)
1 can beer
seasoned flour (salt and pepper)

3 tablespoons butter
½ teaspoon chervil
1 chicken bouillon cube
1 cup sliced mushrooms

Cut pheasant into serving pieces. If the bird is a large one, the breast should be cut in two chunks, crosswise. Marinate the pieces in the beer for 4 hours, turning occasionally. Dry the pheasant on paper toweling and douse well with the seasoned flour. Brown the pieces in the butter in a heavy skillet. Sprinkle with chervil, add the bouillon cube and 1 cup of the beer marinade. Cover and simmer for 1 to 1¼ hours. Add the mushrooms for the last half hour. More marinade can be used if necessary.

Serve over a bed of hot buttered noodles or rice-shaped pasta. Serve the juice in a bowl to be ladled over the pieces of pheasant and the pasta. A large bird will serve 3 people.

*Note:* "Very good. Bird I used was a little old. It would have been dry without sauce."

# PHEASANT HORS D'OEUVRES

1 pheasant breast, cut into bite-sized
   pieces
3½ tablespoons butter

salt and pepper
¾ tablespoon lemon juice
¼ teaspoon minced parsley
shake of tarragon leaves

Sauté the pieces of pheasant breast quickly in 2 tablespoons of the butter for no more than 3 to 4 minutes. Salt and pepper lightly to taste. Serve on toothpicks with a dip made of the rest of the butter, lemon juice, parsley and tarragon. Serve while warm. Serves 4.

*Note:* "Just plain great—so juicy."

# CHUKARS IN MADEIRA

2 partridges
seasoned flour (salt and pepper)
1 orange, peeled and halved
¼ cup butter

2 green onions, finely chopped
½ cup sliced mushrooms
½ cup giblet broth
¼ cup Madeira

Dust the birds with seasoned flour and place half an orange in each cavity. Melt the butter in a large, heavy skillet. When sizzling hot, brown the chukars on all sides. Remove them from the pan. Add onions and mushrooms and simmer until soft. Stir in giblets, giblet broth and Madeira and bring to the boiling point. Put the birds back in the pan and spoon juice over them. Cover tightly and simmer for ½ hour, turning and basting twice during the cooking. Serve on wooden platters with sharp knives. Serves 2.

*Note:* Penciled on recipe, "Excellent."

## Giblet Broth

partridge giblets
salt and pepper

onion slice
celery leaves

Cook giblets in water to cover with a little salt, pepper, a slice of onion and a couple celery leaves until they are done, about 1 hour. Remove from broth, cool and chop into small pieces. Cook the broth down until you have ½ cup.

## OUTDOOR-BARBECUED CHUKAR

4 chukar partridges
½ cup butter, melted
1 tablespoon steak sauce
1 crushed garlic clove

1 teaspoon seasoned salt
1 tablespoon lemon juice
¹⁄₁₆ teaspoon red pepper
½ teaspoon tarragon

¾ cup white wine

With poultry shears, cut each bird down the backbone, leaving the breast connected. Wipe the cavity with paper toweling. Mix all remaining ingredients in a shallow dish to make a sauce. Place the birds in the sauce for 1 hour, turning often. Let your charcoal fire burn down to hot coals. Place the birds, skin down, on the hot grill. If the fire flares up, control it with a plant mister or a water pistol. Turn a couple of times during the cooking, basting frequently with sauce.

When I first tried this recipe, cooking time was 30 minutes, but outdoor cooking varies with the day. Test thigh meat with a fork. It should penetrate without much probing. Before the testing, all turning should be done with tongs to avoid moisture loss. Heat rest of sauce and serve with meat. Breast can be sliced with knife and fork. Legs should be picked up and eaten by hand. Serves 4.

*Note:* "Good flavor—breast meat a bit dry without sauce."

## CHUKAR WITH WILD RICE

4 chukar partridges
3 tablespoons butter
1 large onion, sliced
1 tablespoon chervil

¼ teaspoon marjoram
2 dashes Tabasco sauce
1 cup sour cream
wild rice

Truss each bird into a neat bundle and tie with string. Brown them in hot butter on all sides. Place them in an oven-proof casserole. Sauté the onion in the remaining butter. Add seasonings and cream to the pan and heat until very hot. Pour over the birds, cover and place in a preheated 350° oven. Bake, basting twice with pan juices, for 50 minutes. Serve the birds over a bed of hot, buttered wild rice.

If you serve the birds on wooden platters with a well on one end (and I suggest that you do), place a little of the baking-dish juice in each guest's well. The white meat of the partridge can be a bit dry. It is much enhanced by dipping in the cooking juices. Serves 4.

*Note:* Penciled on recipe, "Very tasty."

# Rabbit

Many youngsters in the United States had their first hunting experience with cottontail rabbits. Their dad or grandpop probably kept a few beagles. Today, just hearing the baying of those compact trailers rekindles happy memories of days past.

One reason for the cottontail's popularity among sportsmen is that it thrives in nearly all cultivated and wild areas. It is also good on the dining table and fun to hunt. The only place where the rabbit doesn't flourish is on today's "clean" farms. Each year, fewer hedgerows, thickets and weed patches are allowed to remain for habitat. Cottontails love brush piles. Trimmed trees and bushes should be stacked against a fence or a pile of rocks or logs instead of being burned. Rabbits will use the twigs for food and the pile for cover.

The rabbit population quickly adjusts each year to the carrying capacity of the range because of its breeding capabilities. It is during this breeding season that the normally docile cottontail may become a violent bundle of fur. Does have been known to seriously wound and even kill an amorous admirer. Bucks will leap over their rivals and deliver a deadly kick with the hind legs while in midair.

As one of the gnawing animals, rabbits play a part in nature by turning grass into flesh in order to feed many predators. Because of their huge appetites, they're pure pain to those of us who love to garden. A rabbit will eat practically everything you don't want it to. Because it is a vegetarian, I've tried sprinkling dried blood around as a repellent. It works, but rain will wash it away and it's expensive. The best garden protection comes from a short, small-mesh fence firmly installed in the ground. I recently lost three small apple trees to rabbits. I had protected them for three feet up their trunks with extra-heavy-duty aluminum foil. What I hadn't counted on was an unusual amount of snow that made it simple for the rabbits to gnaw the bark above the wrapping.

Since the rabbits in our neck of the woods have slowly evolved into nocturnal creatures, they are often the by-product of a bird-hunting trip rather than the prime target of a hunt. But they are welcome as an alternate, both in the field and on the menu.

When time permits, I usually clean a rabbit in the field. The meat cools faster and there is less weight to carry in the game pocket. I carry a wad of paper toweling to clean the cavity and some moist towelettes for wiping my hands after the cleaning chore. The entrails and toweling should be buried or hidden under a large rock to be recycled into the soil. It's best not to feed the entrails to your dog. They could transmit tapeworms.

If you don't have a chance to field-dress, it is better to skin the rabbit at home before gutting. Cut a slit in the skin across the back at a right angle to the spine. Insert two fingers in each side of the slit and pull equally in both directions until the skin is over the neck and legs. Sever the legs at the lower joint and the head at the neck. With most recipes, you'll probably want to cut the rabbit into pieces before cooking. A quick wash under cold water finishes the cleaning chore with most cottontails. It is not necessary to soak them in salt water. If a piece of meat is a bit mangled, cleanse it under the water faucet, probing with a sharp knife for shot, bits of bone and blood clots.

The way rabbit is prepared in most American kitchens is pan-fried, similar to chicken. It's easy and has lasting appeal because the meat from most rabbits is tender and flavorful. The pieces of rabbit are doused in seasoned (with salt and pepper) flour and browned on all sides in cooking oil. Add a little water to the frying pan, a shake or two of marjoram (or another favorite herb), turn the heat to simmer, cover and cook until tender. Simple but delicious. One rabbit will usually serve three.

Note: Rabbit should always be well cooked because of the possibility of tularemia. However, modern drugs are effective against the disease and there have been few cases in the last 10 years.

## WINES

Unlike most other game animals, rabbit flesh has a delicate taste. It's not nearly so mild as tame rabbit but decidedly so when compared with squirrel, venison or waterfowl. For that reason, the wines selected for a rather simple meal of fried rabbit should be on the light side. A young Beaujolais usually works out fine and, if your tastes lean to the German Moselle types, those too are perfectly acceptable.

As a matter of fact, considering the Teutonic preference for rabbit, a Rhine or Moselle or a California of the Riesling persuasion seems almost traditional. The exception to the milder wines would be any recipe that "doctors up" the bunnies. Rabbit done in some sort of spicy tomato sauce would be better served with a medium Italian red, say a Bardolino.

The next rabbit recipe is one of the best I've ever eaten. The man who gave it to me says that he bones his rabbit first. I am lazy and don't. I don't think it makes a difference, but you may want to try it boned. It would be easier to serve.

## STUFFED RABBIT, GERMAN STYLE

| | |
|---|---|
| 1 whole rabbit | 3 whole red potatoes, washed |
| stuffing | 3 whole carrots, scraped |
| 4 tablespoons butter | ¾ cup chicken bouillon |

Dry rabbit and fill chest cavity with stuffing. Close opening with toothpicks and string. Force the rabbit into a round ball and truss with additional string. Brown on all sides in butter in a Dutch oven. Add potatoes, carrots and bouillon to pot and cover. Put in 350° oven for 2½ hours. Turn the rabbit over after 1½ hours. Serve on a heated platter. Mix 2 tablespoons of flour with 1 cup of water and add to pan juices. Heat, stirring constantly, until mixture boils and thickens. Serve as gravy. Serves 3.

### Stuffing

| | |
|---|---|
| ½ pound pork | salt and pepper |
| ½ pound veal | 1 clove garlic, minced |
| 6 slices bacon | 1 teaspoon parsley, minced |

Grind pork, veal and bacon together. Add salt and pepper, garlic and parsley and mix well. Stuff rabbit.

# BUNNIE IN A BAG

1 or 2 rabbits, cut in serving pieces
¼ cup flour
½ teaspoon salt
¼ teaspoon pepper

1 onion, sliced
1 stalk celery, sliced
2 tablespoons butter
½ cup dry red wine

1 teaspoon Kitchen Bouquet

Shake flour, salt and pepper in a 10" × 16" oven cooking bag and place in a roasting pan. Add rabbit and shake to coat meat. Then move the pieces around so they lie on the bottom of the bag in contact with the roasting pan. Add onion, celery, butter, wine and Kitchen Bouquet. Secure the bag with a tie and make 6 slits in top of bag. Bake at least 1 hour (or until rabbit is tender) in 350° oven. Each rabbit will serve 3.

*Note:* I tried this with two rabbits, one young and the other a large, old one. The young one was done in 1 hour and the old rabbit was still chewy after 2 hours.

# ENGLISH HEARTY PIE

1 rabbit
salt and pepper
bay leaf
celery leaves
⅜ teaspoon thyme
1 medium-sized onion, chopped except
    for 1 slice

1 beef bouillon cube
3 parsley sprigs
½ cup sliced mushrooms
2 tablespoons butter
2 tablespoons flour
¼ teaspoon parsley flakes
2 hard-boiled eggs, quartered

piecrust

Simmer rabbit in water to cover, with salt and pepper, bay leaf, celery leaves, ¼ teaspoon thyme, beef bouillon cube, slice of onion and parsley sprigs until meat is very tender. Remove rabbit and strain and reserve 1½ cups of stock. Arrange bite-sized pieces of rabbit meat and egg quarters in 1 large or 3 individual casseroles. Brown chopped onion and mushrooms lightly in butter. Stir in flour and add stock. When the stock is thick, add remaining thyme, parsley flakes, salt and pepper and mix well. Pour the mushroom mixture over the meat and eggs. Cover the dish(es) with your favorite piecrust and bake in a preheated 425° oven for 20 to 25 minutes, until the crust is brown and the contents bubbly. Will serve 3 or 4.

# HASENPFEFFER

2 rabbits, cut into serving pieces
3 tablespoons butter
½ teaspoon salt
1 medium onion
4 cloves
12 black peppercorns

1 teaspoon chopped parsley
½ teaspoon thyme
1 bay leaf
¼ cup lemon juice
1 cup port
2½ cups beef bouillon

Sprinkle rabbit pieces with salt and pepper and sauté in the butter until brown on all sides. Place in a 3-quart casserole. Add salt, onion stuck with cloves and a cheesecloth bag with the peppercorns, parsley, thyme and bay leaf tied inside. Also add the lemon juice, port and bouillon. Cover and bake for 1½ hours at 350°. Ten minutes before it's done, remove the cheesecloth bag. The broth can be thickened to use as gravy. Will serve 5.

*Note:* I served with rice, spinach salad and currant jelly. "Super."

# NELDA'S HOPPERS

2 rabbits, cut into serving pieces
4 onions, sliced
cooking oil
salt and pepper

1 garlic clove, minced
¾ cup red wine
1 cup tomatoes
½ teaspoon tarragon leaves

Sauté the onions in oil until soft. Add the rabbit and brown on all sides. Add rest of ingredients, cover and simmer until the meat is tender—1 to 1½ hours. Will serve 6.

# BARBECUED RABBIT

1 rabbit, cut into serving pieces
¼ cup flour

¼ teaspoon salt
2 tablespoons butter

barbecue sauce

Dry rabbit pieces on paper toweling. Dust with seasoned flour and brown in butter. Pour barbecue sauce over the rabbit and simmer until done, 1 to 1½ hours. Serves 3.

## Barbecue Sauce

3 tablespoons beef bouillon
3 tablespoons chili sauce
1 teaspoon steak sauce
3 tablespoons catsup

2 tablespoons wine vinegar
½ teaspoon salt
¼ teaspoon pepper
1 tablespoon brown sugar

1 small onion, chopped

Combine all ingredients and heat thoroughly.

## RABBIT LINGUINE

1 rabbit
chicken stock or bouillon
1 stalk celery, chopped
1 medium onion, chopped
3 tomatoes, chopped, seeded and juiced
   (or 1 1-pound can, drained)
¼ cup chopped parsley

1 clove garlic, minced
2 tablespoons olive oil
1 teaspoon basil
1 15-ounce can tomato sauce
1 6-ounce can tomato paste
⅛ teaspoon red pepper
pinch of oregano

1 6½-ounce can minced clams, drained

Cook the rabbit in chicken broth until done. Cool and cut into bite-sized pieces. Sauté the celery, onion, tomatoes, parsley and garlic in oil until they are tender. Add rest of ingredients (except clams) and simmer until well married—about 45 minutes. Add rabbit and clams and heat. Serve over hot linguine. Pass Romano cheese at the table. Serves 4.

*Note:* Penciled on recipe, "Super."

## RABBIT CURRY McGINNIS

1 rabbit
chicken broth
2 tablespoons butter
1 cup finely chopped, pared apples
1 cup chopped celery

½ cup chopped onion
½ cup sliced mushrooms
2 tablespoons cornstarch
1 teaspoon curry powder
¼ teaspoon salt

2 cups milk or light cream

Cook rabbit in chicken broth until tender. Remove rabbit and let cool, then bone and dice meat. Reserve ¾ cup broth. In a saucepan, melt butter and sauté until tender the apples, celery, onion and mushrooms. Mix the cornstarch, curry powder and salt and add the rabbit broth. Stir this mixture into the onion mixture. Add the milk and cook slowly until it thickens. Add the diced pieces of cooked rabbit meat. Serve with rice. Makes 4 servings.

## MARTHA'S RABBIT RICE CASSEROLE

1 rabbit
chicken bouillon
¼ cup butter
¼ cup flour
2 cups light cream

3 cups cooked long-grain rice
¼ cup sliced mushrooms
⅓ cup chopped green pepper
½ teaspoon salt
paprika

parsley sprigs

Cook rabbit in bouillon until tender. Let cool, then remove rabbit from broth, reserving liquid, and skin and dice meat. There should be 3 cups of rabbit meat and 1½ cups of the broth. In a large saucepan, melt the butter and blend in the flour. Slowly add cream and broth and cook, stirring constantly, until thick. Add rice, diced rabbit meat, mushrooms, green pepper and salt. Mix and pour into a greased 2-quart casserole. Bake in a 350° oven for 40 minutes. Sprinkle with paprika and garnish with sprigs of parsley. Serves 4 or 5.

## CARL'S RABBIT CASSEROLE

1 rabbit, cut in serving pieces
1 clove garlic
4 tablespoons cooking oil

4 tablespoons flour
½ teaspoon salt
⅛ teaspoon pepper

½ teaspoon marjoram

Rub frying pan with the cut side of the garlic clove. Add cooking oil to the pan and brown rabbit pieces. Remove meat, add flour and blend. Slowly add 2 cups of water and bring to a boil. Add salt, pepper and marjoram and mix. Place rabbit pieces in a casserole. Pour gravy over the meat, cover and Bake in 350. oven for 1 to ½ hours, until rabbit is tender. The rabbit can be basted once during the cooking. Serves 3.

## RUFFING'S RABBIT POT PIE

1 or 2 rabbits, cut in pieces
2 onions, sliced
2 tablespoons vinegar
2 tablespoons cooking oil
2 carrots, sliced

2 potatoes, cubed
2 stalks celery, diced
flour
salt and pepper to taste
1 double-crust pastry recipe

Boil rabbit in water to cover with 1 sliced onion and the vinegar for 15 minutes. Remove rabbit and dry on paper toweling. Brown the rabbit in the cooking oil in a frying pan. Add the second onion and a little water. Simmer for 30 minutes. At the same time, simmer the carrots, potatoes and celery in water to cover in a saucepan for 25 minutes. Remove rabbit from frying pan, add vegetable water to pan and thicken with flour to make gravy. Line the bottom of a casserole dish with half of your favorite pastry recipe. Cut the rabbit from the bone and dice in bite-sized pieces. Add to the vegetable mixture and pour it all in the casserole. Cover with gravy and adjust the salt and pepper to taste. Cover with top crust, secure on the sides and cut slits in the top. Bake in 350° oven for 1 hour. Serves 4 to 6.

## HERB'S RABBIT CASSEROLE

| | |
|---|---|
| 1 or 2 rabbits, cut in serving pieces | 1 clove garlic, pressed |
| flour seasoned with salt and pepper | ½ cup dry white wine |
| ⅓ cup cooking oil | ⅓ cup meat broth |
| 1 tablespoon rosemary leaves | 1 teaspoon wine vinegar |

Dredge the rabbit pieces in the seasoned flour. Put oil, rosemary and garlic in a frying pan and heat. Brown the meat in the mixture. Place the rabbit in an oven-proof casserole. Add the wine, broth and vinegar to the frying pan and bring to the boiling point. Scrape the pan and pour all juices over the rabbit. Cover and bake in a preheated 350° oven for 1 hour. One rabbit will serve 3.

*Note:* Very good with buttered noodles since the juice makes an excellent gravy.

## RABBIT WITH RAISINS

| | |
|---|---|
| 1 to 2 rabbits, cut into serving pieces | 4 whole cloves |
| ¼ cup wine vinegar | 9 peppercorns |
| ½ teaspoon salt | 2 bay leaves |
| ¼ teaspoon marjoram | ½ cup raisins |
| 1 small onion, chopped | 2 tablespoons brown sugar |
| 1 garlic clove | flour |

Place rabbit in a pot and cover with water. Add vinegar, salt, marjoram and onion. Place garlic, cloves, peppercorns and bay leaves in a cheesecloth bag and tie tightly. Add this to the pot and bring all to the boiling point. Cover and simmer until rabbit is almost done (about 1 hour). Remove the cheesecloth bag and add raisins and sugar. Continue simmering until the meat is tender. Place the rabbit on a heated platter and thicken pan juices with flour mixed with a little cold water.

*Note:* Hot buttered noodles are great with this dish. A Waldorf salad is perfect with the spicy rabbit.

# Gray
# Squirrel

The gray squirrel is an old-timer on our continent, having migrated here over the land bridge that once linked Asia and Alaska. It has been said that the early American backwoodsmen took squirrels with their flintlock rifles by aiming at the bark of the tree just beneath the squirrel's head. According to the tale, the concussion of the ball killed the animal without leaving a mark.

As a youngster, I lived in northern Pennsylvania where black squirrels, a color phase of the gray, were common. They were much prized by downstate hunters who would carefully transport a particularly handsome specimen home to be mounted. I always considered the gray to be more valuable because it looked bigger. Of course, this was an optical illusion caused by the lighter color but they still looked bigger and, therefore, more desirable for the table. The black phase of the gray squirrel seems to have followed the edge of the glacier during the last ice age, with few blacks seen south of the line.

Our home turf for the past three years is blessed with lots of nut trees, hickory, black walnut and butternut. As a result, we have a regular bushytail bonanza. Jim and I do our level best to take as many of these busy nut hoarders as possible during the gunning season. We have two reasons for this war on squirrels: They are excellent in the pot and, later on in the winter, they would drive us crazy by hogging our bird feeders.

A friend recently overheard me complaining about having to skin all those critters and asked how I had been doing it. I answered that I first cut off the head, then the four feet at the first joint, and the tail (carefully, so my fly-tying husband could use it). Then I cut a wide slit in the middle of the back skin and, inserting both hands in the slit, pulled the skin in opposite directions until it came off the front and back legs, hopefully at the same time.

My friend declared that I was doing it the hard way, that I should remove the legs and tail and then cut the skin all the way around the neck. Place the head on the ground, step on it hard, grasp the neck skin in both hands and pull. This advice made good sense. The way I was doing it, I had to pull against myself. His method was one straight pull. But then I tried it and found that to cut all the way around the neck consumed more time than the whole skinning process did in my old way. All this really illustrates is that one method is right for one person and another may suit someone else. In cleaning game, nothing is black and white except the final product, a completely cleaned animal. One thing I'm sure of: it is much easier to skin a warm squirrel than one that has been allowed to cool. The entrails are removed after the skinning and the carcass is then washed under a stream of cool water.

I cut a squirrel into five serving pieces. The carcass is cut behind the front legs and again, just ahead of the hind legs, to separate the saddle. Then each set of legs is separated. Squirrel is more likely to become freezer-burned than many other game animals because of the small size. One of the best ways to freeze squirrel pieces is in milk cartons filled with water. My freezer space is limited, however, so I double- and sometimes triple-wrap them— first in Saran wrap, then in aluminum foil, and finally in freezer paper. The plastic and aluminum foil force the air from the package and the outside layer reinforces it all.

Compared to a rabbit's average age of less than a year, a squirrel has fewer diseases and enemies and therefore normally lives to at least eighteen months. To the cook, this means that a squirrel is more apt to be tough since some individuals live several years. Most of the recipes in this chapter take this into account, suggesting that you check for tenderness after a certain cooking time.

Squirrel is one of the best-tasting game animals, which makes sense when you consider all the good things a squirrel eats. If you like game as much as my family does, you should figure on almost one squirrel per person when cooking a meal. For our family of four, I usually serve three of them.

## WINES

I think that Zinfandel is just about the perfect wine for squirrels. It is spicy but not too much so to prevent the flavor of the squirrel from shining through. Most white wines don't have enough body for squirrel. Squirrel stew is perfect with Zinfandel too, although one of the inexpensive California jug Burgundies will also do the job nicely.

## CURRIED FRIED SQUIRREL

3 squirrels, cut into serving pieces
1 onion, chopped
2 tablespoons butter
2 tablespoons olive oil
parsley sprigs
flour, seasoned with salt and pepper
½ teaspoon curry powder (more if you wish)
1 cup port wine

Lightly brown onion in the butter/oil mixture. Douse the meat pieces in the seasoned flour and brown. Sprinkle the curry on each piece of squirrel. Add wine, cover and simmer for 1 hour or until the meat is tender. Serve on buttered noodles with a sprig of parsley. Serves 3 or 4.

*Note:* Penciled on recipe, "Very good."

## BUCK RUN SQUIRREL

3 squirrels, cut in pieces
flour
salt and pepper
3 tablespoons butter
1 cup beef bouillon
1 stalk celery, chopped
3 tablespoons steak sauce
1 tablespoon minced parsley
1 small onion, sliced
1 clove garlic, pressed or minced
2 bay leaves

Dredge squirrel pieces in flour that has been seasoned with salt and pepper. Brown in butter in a Dutch oven or similar oven-proof dish. Add remaining ingredients, heat, cover and place in a 375° preheated oven for 1 to 1¼ hours, or until the squirrel is tender. Serves 4.

*Note:* Penciled on recipe, "Succulent."

## FRICASSEED SQUIRREL

3 squirrels, cleaned and cut into serving pieces
½ teaspoon salt
⅛ teaspoon pepper
¼ cup flour
1 cup beef bouillon
3 slices of bacon, cut in small pieces
1 small onion, sliced
1 chunk of celery top with leaves
2 teaspoons lemon juice
½ teaspoon thyme

Rub the squirrel pieces with salt and pepper and roll in flour. Fry in heavy skillet with bacon pieces until brown on all sides. Add rest of ingredients, cover and simmer for 1 hour or until tender. Serve with rice, using the broth as a sauce. Serves 4.

## FRIED SQUIRREL

3 squirrels, cut in serving pieces  
½ teaspoon salt  
8 peppercorns  
2 bay leaves  
flour  
2 tablespoons butter  
2 tablespoons cooking oil

Simmer squirrel pieces in salted water with peppercorns and bay leaves for 1 hour or until tender. Thoroughly dry the squirrel with paper toweling. Coat with flour and brown pieces on all sides in the butter/oil mixture in a hot skillet. Serve on a heated platter. Will serve 4.

## SAVORY SQUIRREL

3 squirrels, cut into serving pieces  
½ teaspoon salt  
¼ cup port wine  
¼ cup heavy cream  
⅛ teaspoon savory  
⅛ teaspoon fresh ground pepper  
1 teaspoon Kitchen Bouquet  
cornstarch

Simmer the squirrels in water to cover with the salt until done. It may take 2 hours if the squirrels are old and tough. Place the meat on a heated platter and reduce the liquid to 1 cup by boiling at a high temperature. Add the port, cream, savory and Kitchen Bouquet. Thicken with a little cornstarch mixed with cold water. Serve the sauce ladled over hot rice and the squirrel pieces. Will serve 4.

*Note:* Penciled on recipe, "Good."

## SLATE RUN SQUIRREL STEW

3 squirrels, cut in serving pieces  
flour  
4 tablespoons butter  
2 large onions, sliced  
2 large tomatoes, chopped (2 cups)  
2 cups beef bouillon  
½ teaspoon salt  
¼ teaspoon tarragon  
dash of red pepper  
3 carrots, sliced  
2 stalks celery, chopped

Douse squirrel pieces in flour and brown in butter in a Dutch oven. Add onions and sauté for a few minutes. Add tomatoes, bouillon, salt, tarragon, and pepper and simmer, covered, for 30 minutes. Add carrots and celery, cover and simmer another 40 minutes or until meat and vegetables are tender. Serves 4.

*Note:* Serve with plenty of hot, crusty bread to soak up the delicious juice.

## BRUNSWICK STEW (MODERN VERSION)

3 squirrels, cut in serving pieces
2 tablespoons butter
½ cup chopped onion
1 cup bread crumbs
¾ teaspoon salt
¼ teaspoon pepper

3 chicken bouillon cubes
1 10-ounce package frozen whole-kernel corn
1 10-ounce package frozen baby lima beans
1 teaspoon minced parsley

In a Dutch oven, brown the squirrel pieces, a few at a time, in the butter. Sauté the onion for a few minutes in the pot. Then return all the squirrel pieces to the pot along with the bread crumbs, bouillon cubes and 3 cups of water. Bring to a boil, cover and simmer about 45 minutes, depending on how tough the squirrels are. Stir occasionally. Add the corn and beans together with the salt and pepper about 15 minutes before the dish is to be served. Sprinkle with parsley. Serves 6.

*Note:* Great with hot biscuits and a salad.

## BARBECUED SQUIRREL

3 squirrels, cut in serving pieces
flour seasoned with salt and pepper

2 tablespoons cooking oil
barbecue sauce

Dredge squirrel in seasoned flour and brown in oil. Cover with barbecue sauce and simmer for 45 minutes to 1¼ hours. Serves 4. *Note:* The squirrels I tested were young. They cooked in 45 minutes. An excellent recipe—great-tasting sauce.

## Barbecue Sauce

½ cup chili sauce
½ cup water
1 tablespoon steak sauce
2 tablespoons lemon juice

½ teaspoon salt
pepper
3 tablespoons minced onion
1 tablespoon brown sugar

2 drops Tabasco sauce

Mix well, heat and use on squirrels in above recipe.

## SQUIRREL AND BROCCOLI CASSEROLE

3 squirrels, cut in serving pieces
1 chicken bouillon cube
1 bay leaf
2 carrots, sliced
1 small onion, sliced
½ teaspoon salt
2 10-ounce packages frozen broccoli
⅔ cup mayonnaise

1 cup grated cheddar cheese
1 teaspoon lemon juice
1¼ cup light cream
⅓ cup milk
1 teaspoon parsley flakes
⅛ teaspoon basil
bread crumbs
butter

Cook the squirrels in water with chicken bouillon and bay leaf. When done, cool, bone and cut into bite-sized pieces. Cook the carrots and onion with salt in water until almost done and drain. Cook the broccoli slightly and place on the bottom of a buttered 9" × 13" baking dish. Top with squirrel, carrots and onion. Mix mayonnaise, cheese, liquids and seasonings together and spread over the top. Top with buttered bread crumbs. Bake in preheated 350° oven for 45 minutes, until bubbly. Serves 5 or 6.

*Note:* Penciled on recipe, "Good."

## SQUIRREL CAKES

2 squirrels
salt
1 small onion, minced

1 teaspoon parsley flakes
½ cup crushed cornflakes
1 can golden mushroom soup (undiluted)

butter

Parboil squirrel in salted water until tender (from 20 to 30 minutes). Remove the meat from the bones and cut into very fine pieces or put through a grinder or food processor. Mix with onion, parsley and cornflakes. Moisten with enough soup to shape into small, flat cakes. Fry in hot butter until well browned on both sides. Heat the rest of the soup. Serve the cakes with a spoonful of soup over each helping. Will serve 2 or 3.

*Note:* Unusual dish—good.

## BIGLERVILLE SQUIRREL

3 squirrels, cut in pieces
flour
salt and pepper
4 tablespoons butter
1 small onion, chopped

½ cup sliced mushrooms
1 cup dry white wine
½ teaspoon marjoram
2 tablespoons chopped parsley
1½ tablespoons quick-mixing flour

1 cup light cream

Douse the squirrel with the seasoned flour and brown in butter in a heavy skillet and remove from pan. Sauté onions and mushrooms in skillet and return squirrel to pan. Add wine, marjoram and parsley, mix well, cover and simmer until squirrel is tender, 1 to 1½ hours. Add water during simmering if pan juices get low. Let squirrel cool and remove meat from the bones. Add enough water to pan liquid to make 1 cup. Add cream and squirrel to the pan and bring to the boiling point. If the liquid is too thin, add a little quick-mixing flour. Serve over hot biscuits or toast. Serves 4.

*Note:* Absolute great—my favorite squirrel recipe. Doubly good the second day, if there's any left over.

## LOUISIANA SQUIRREL

3 squirrels, cut in serving pieces
salt and pepper
2 tablespoons cooking oil
1 onion, chopped
1 stalk celery, chopped

½ cup chopped green pepper
1 tablespoon chopped parsley
⅛ teaspoon red pepper
¾ cup uncooked long-grain rice
1½ cups water

Dry squirrel pieces on paper toweling and sprinkle with salt and pepper. Brown in cooking oil in a heavy skillet. Add onion, celery, green pepper and parsley and sauté until vegetables are wilted. Put the squirrel back in the pan and dust with red pepper. Cover and cook slowly for about 1 hour, until squirrel is tender. Add water and rice. Stir, cover and cook until rice is tender—30 more minutes. Adjust salt. Serves 4.

*Note:* Excellent—rice is bitey.

# Ducks

Waterfowl management has been highly refined in the past few years. Through banding and life history studies, biologists can give the less common ducks, like the redhead and canvasback, the protection they need while permitting liberal regulations on more common species. This causes a problem with those duck hunters who continue to think that all ducks are alike. To become a more thoughtful hunter and to foil the antihunting movement, all waterfowlers should learn to identify species. A particularly good guide has recently been published by the U. S. Fish and Wildlife Service; their new edition of *Ducks at a Distance* is a must for today's waterfowler. Still, nothing takes the place of hunting with a knowledgeable companion. One of the encouraging aspects of the many Ducks Unlimited chapters is their counsel to young waterfowlers, both male and female, under their Greenwing program.

Duck hunting has a rich tradition in the United States. A misty morning, wet wool jacket, hard-working retriever, camouflage boat and a string of decoys all add up to one of hunting's elite, the waterfowler. It's also one sport that can be enjoyed before the working day begins in most communities, since the best hunting is usually at dawn.

Unfortunately, after the hunt comes the cleaning chore. Unless a duck is badly shot up and you'll be using it in a casserole, it is essential that it be plucked. The protection of the skin and the underlaying layer of fat is of great value in the cooking process. Most experts dry-pluck their birds. *Pluck* is probably the wrong word. They really rub the body feathers off with a rolling motion of their thumbs and forefingers. If you do decide to dry-pluck, save the resulting down for use in clothing or sleeping bags.

I usually strip the feathers off via the wet method. It works well for me and I have less trouble with feathers floating around the garage for days after the cleaning. I bring a pail of water to the boiling point, add a couple of drops of detergent, then slosh the duck up and down in the pail for about ten seconds (six seconds for small ducks). This will penetrate the feathers but not cook the skin. Remove the breast feathers first, then the back, wing and legs. Cut the wings and legs off at the first joint when you've plucked to that point. After severing the head, gut the bird and thoroughly wash the cavity under cool running water, being sure to remove all traces of lung (pink, spongy material). Singeing over a gas flame will remove residual hair and pinfeathers. If you freeze the bird, pinfeathers will be easier to remove after thawing.

"Strong gamey taste," "fishy smell," "too greasy," are some of the terms used to describe waterfowl by those who have never eaten it or have had an unpleasant first experience. The diving sea ducks do have a high percentage of animal matter in their diet, which makes them less desirable as food than the puddle ducks or even the freshwater divers whose diet is mainly vegetarian. Use my recipe for brant on these sea ducks and I think you'll find them delicious.

Because wild ducks have a much shorter life span than wild geese, the cook has a better chance of acquiring a tender one. I prefer to cook ducks fast and hot, and end up with rare meat. But I've included other tested methods in the following recipes.


## *WINES*

With rare, broiled duck breast, I'd throw caution and expense to the wind and serve a bottle of the best Cabernet Sauvignon I could afford. A well-aged bottle of French Bordeaux from the Médoc region would be elegant. An equally acceptable choice would be a fine California red from one of the houses which specialize in the cabernet grapes. Some good ones are Beaulieu, Charles Krug, Louis Martini and Stony Hill (if you can find it).

# RARE ROAST DUCK

2 large ducks (or 4 small ones)
2 carrots, chopped
2 stalks celery, chopped
1 dozen ripe olives, chopped
1 onion, chopped
2 tablespoons cornstarch

olive oil
½ cup port wine
½ cup chicken bouillon
salt and pepper
½ cup ripe olive juice

Have ducks at room temperature. Sauté carrots, celery, olives and onions in oil for 10 minutes. Place mixture in the bottom of a shallow roasting pan. Put the ducks on top of the vegetables after brushing them with olive oil. Heat the port and bouillon until almost boiling and pour over the ducks. Sprinkle with salt and pepper. Place in a preheated 425° oven for 35 to 40 minutes, basting twice with pan juices during the roasting. Place ducks on a hot platter to keep warm. Strain the pan juices. Blend cornstarch into the olive juice and thicken pan juices. Serve the sauce ladled over the duck slices.

*Note:* Penciled on recipe, "Great."

# STRUBLE LAKE ROAST DUCK

2 large ducks (or 4 small ones)
½ cup chopped onion
½ cup butter
2 tablespoons chopped parsley
thyme

1 cup bread crumbs
½ teaspoon sage
½ teaspoon salt
dash of freshly ground pepper

Have ducks at room temperature. Sauté the onion in the butter until tender but not brown. Add rest of ingredients except thyme. Stuff ducks. Rub the ducks with butter and sprinkle each with a little thyme. Place in a roasting pan. Preheat broiler and place ducks about 3 inches from the heat to brown for 5 minutes. Turn oven down to 350° and roast for 55 minutes. The birds will be just beyond the pink stage but not overcooked. Small ducks will take 40 minutes at 350°. Serves 4.

*Note:* "Excellent"—good recipe for those who aren't sure if they'll like rare ducks.

# REMINGTON MALLARDS

2 large ducks
2 tablespoons dry sherry
1 teaspoon celery salt
1 teaspoon onion salt
1 teaspoon celery seed

½ teaspoon curry powder
2 teaspoons salt
½ teaspoon pepper
1 onion, chopped
1 stalk celery, chopped

Place the ducks in a roasting pan, breast up. Sprinkle each with a tablespoon of sherry. Mix together the next 6 ingredients and shake over the ducks. Let the ducks stand in the dry marinade about 1 hour. Then add ¼ to ½ inch of water and the vegetables to the pan and roast at 500° (preheated oven) for 20 minutes. Turn the ducks over (breast down) and bake another 20 minutes. Turn the heat down to 300°, cover the pan and bake another hour. Will serve 4.

*Note:* "Good"—an excellent recipe for those who like the well-done treatment on waterfowl.

## TAPPLY'S BARBECUED DUCK

2 large duck breasts (or 4 small ones)
2½ tablespoons prepared mustard
1⅓ tablespoons catsup
1⅓ tablespoons steak sauce

4 tablespoons port wine
4 tablespoons butter
salt and pepper
paprika

Blend the mustard into the catsup. Add ½ cup water, steak sauce, wine and butter and heat slowly in saucepan. Cut the whole breast (with bone) from ducks. Dry and sprinkle with salt and pepper and paprika. Place on heavy-duty aluminum foil on a broiler pan. Broil breast (4 inches from heat) for 10 minutes. Remove from oven. Using a turkey baster, remove the excess fat from the foil. This will help avoid flame-ups in the oven. Ladle some sauce on the breasts and return to the broiler for another 10 minutes (a little less for small ducks), basting every few minutes with the sauce. Place the ducks on a heated platter and scrape the drippings into a sauce bowl with any leftover sauce. Serve the breasts, cut in thin slices, with sauce ladled over each piece. They will be medium rare and beautifully juicy. Will serve 4.

*Note:* "Super." Use rest of ducks to make the soup recipe that follows.

## STEAMED DUCK SOUP

legs, thighs and wings from 2 ducks
1½ teaspoons salt
¼ teaspoon MSG

Use duck left over from the Tapply's Barbecued Duck recipe. Put duck, salt, MSG and 6 cups of water in the top of a double boiler and simmer for 4 hours—until duck is tender. Remove meat and chill broth until the fat congeals. Scoop it off, reheat the broth slightly and pour through a dish towel to remove meat particles from the consomme. Just before serving, bring the broth and duck pieces to the boiling point. Serve with one piece of meat in each bowl of clear soup. Makes 6 servings as a first course.

*Note:* "Unusual and elegant dish."

## BRANT PARMIGIAN

| | |
|---|---|
| 1¼ pounds thinly sliced (¼-inch) brant breast meat | 1 egg, beaten |
| 3 tablespoons butter | 1 8-ounce can tomato sauce |
| ½ cup crushed cornflakes | ¼ teaspoon basil |
| ¼ cup Parmesan cheese | ½ teaspoon oregano |
| salt and pepper | ¼ teaspoon sugar |
| | 3 slices mozzarella cheese |

Melt butter in a baking dish. Combine cornflakes, cheese and salt and pepper. Dip breast fillets in egg and then in cornflake mixture. Place in baking dish. Bake in a hot (400°) oven for 40 minutes or until tender, turning once during the baking. Heat the tomato sauce, herbs and sugar. When meat is tender, pour the sauce over it and drape a piece of cheese over each fillet. Return to the oven until the cheese is melted. Serve with buttered noodles. Serves 4.

*Note:* Penciled on recipe, "Great."

## *LEFTOVERS*

Duck (and goose) meat is so flavorful that I never waste leftover wings, giblets, backbones, etc. They are saved in the freezer until there is enough to cook. Everything is then dumped in a roasting pan with water to cover, 2 beef bouillon cubes, 1 bay leaf, 1 sliced onion, 1 stalk of celery and salt and pepper. It is simmered until all is tender. The meat is drained, cooled and cut into bite-sized pieces. The broth is strained. Both are used for the following recipes.

## DUCKETTI

| | |
|---|---|
| 2 cups cut-up duck meat (cooked) | 1 cup sliced mushrooms |
| 1¼ cups spaghetti, broken into 2-inch pieces | 1 cup duck broth |
| ¼ cup diced pimento | ¾ cup light cream |
| ¼ cup chopped green pepper | ½ teaspoon salt |
| ¼ cup chopped onion | 1¾ cups grated sharp cheddar cheese (½ pound) |
| ⅛ teaspoon pepper | |

Cook spaghetti as directed on the package. Drain. Place duck, pimento, pepper, onion and mushrooms in greased 1½-quart casserole. Add broth, cream, salt, pepper, 1¼ cups cheese and spaghetti. With 2 forks, toss lightly until all is well mixed and coated with sauce. Sprinkle remaining cheese on top. Cover and bake in 350° oven for about 45 minutes, until bubbly throughout. The dish can be made and held in the refrigerator until baking time. Serves 6.

*Note:* "Succulent."

## DUCK SOUP MELVILLE

2 to 3 cups cooked duck meat (bite-sized pieces)
5 cups duck broth
2 cups cut-up tomatoes (or 1 16-ounce can)
1 large onion, sliced

½ teaspoon salt
2 cups sliced carrots
1¼ cups sliced celery
½ cup chopped green pepper
⅔ cup quick cooking barley
3 tablespoons minced parsley

1 teaspoon chervil

Place all the above ingredients except the cooked duck meat in a Dutch oven. Bring to a boil and simmer for 45 minutes, covered. Add meat and heat thoroughly. Serve in bowls.

Can also be thickened with flour and heated for a stew.

## DUCK DEVON

2 cups cubed duck meat (cooked)
⅓ cup chopped onion
½ cup chopped celery
⅓ cup chopped green pepper
¼ cup sliced mushrooms
3 tablespoons butter

3 tablespoons flour
1½ cups duck broth
6 drops Tabasco sauce
2 egg yolks
3 tablespoons dry vermouth
salt and pepper

parsley sprigs

Sauté the onions, celery, green pepper and mushrooms in the butter until tender. Add flour and gradually stir in the broth and Tabasco. Remove from the heat, add a little of the sauce to the egg yolks, mix and return to the pan, adding slowly and stirring thoroughly. Add vermouth and duck meat and add salt and pepper to taste. Serve on rice or hot buttered toast. Garnish with parsley. Serves 4.

*Note:* Penciled on recipe, "Good."

# DUCK HASH

2 cups cooked duck meat, diced
2 tablespoons butter
1 large onion, diced
2 large potatoes, steamed, peeled and
    diced

½ teaspoon salt
¼ teaspoon freshly ground pepper
1 teaspoon marjoram
1 teaspoon caraway seeds
parsley sprigs

Use a heavy iron skillet for this dish. Heat the butter in the skillet and sauté the onion until it is cooked but not brown. Add the duck meat, potatoes, salt, pepper, marjoram and caraway. Cook over moderate heat, turning occasionally with a spatula until the mixture is heated thoroughly and begins to brown. When it is sizzly, sprinkle a few parsley sprigs over the top for color and bring the pan directly to the table.

The hash will be a little dry for some tastes, so Worcestershire sauce may be offered. Serve with coleslaw and hot bread. Serves 4.

*Note:* Penciled on recipe, "Good."

# Geese

More than a million geese are bagged annually by our nation's hunters, and the goose population is growing every year. The young birds are especially prized for their tender, lean, dark meat, but the older ones are also tasty if they're treated right in the kitchen. It is the game bird that I receive the most inquiries about. It seems that more hunters are bringing home their first goose and the cook in the family hasn't the foggiest notion what to do with the large bird.

Since I live on the Atlantic Flyway, Canada goose is a large part of our annual game bag and it has fast become one of my preferred meats, if not the favorite. The meat is so flavorful that it is difficult to fail with a goose recipe. It has that added "umph" that is missing in a lot of birds that are born, mature and die within a year. They just don't have a goose's character. (Some of that extra flavor is also shared by the other migratory birds. Ducks, woodcock and doves all have the same characteristic dark breast meat that comes from traveling long distances.)

With a large number of geese to test, I think I now understand more fully the limitations under which we must work when cooking a goose. One of the most important is the age factor. Unlike other game birds, geese can range from less than 1 year up to 25 and it's difficult to tell a bird's age from looking at it. Skin is sometimes a clue since the tougher it is, the older the bird. Size is of no help since the eleven subspecies of the Canada goose range from duck size (cackling Canada) to over 20 pounds (giant Canada). At times, a very old goose is small and a very young one is large.

Because of these differences, most of my new favorite goose recipes feature a medium-rare cooking time. I usually plan to serve only the breast, even if the whole bird is cooked. The breast of the average 5 to 6 pound dressed goose we capture in the Atlantic Flyway today will serve four. If the cooked goose turns out to be young, the wings, legs and thighs are an extra bonus to feast on at dinner. If they are tough (as they are much of the time), I use them later in the week in a casserole, meat pie, Goose Stroganoff or Goose with Curry and other recipes given in this chapter. The breast meat, when thinly sliced (with a Rapala fillet knife), is easy to manage even if it is a bit tough. Cutting against the grain solves the problem—it's like serving London broil. However, much as I enjoy rare goose, I've included some traditional goose recipes in this chapter. One of my favorites for a confirmed old-timer is Brandied Goose. Another great one for a tough goose is Braised Goose.

*Tip:* Tapply's Barbecued Duck (see previous chapter) is an excellent cooking method to use with geese. Simply increase the broiling time from 20 minutes to 27.

Clean the goose much as you would a duck; plucking is preferred. However, I do include one recipe for broiling the breast without the skin so if plucking is a problem, not to worry. Do save the hearts and livers. They are unbelievably good and I've included a recipe for each. I'll bet many are wasted each year and it's a shame.

## WINES

The rich taste of geese demands a robust wine with plenty of aroma. A powerful Burgundy is the perfect choice and even some of the hard-hitting Spanish reds would not be out of place. California's Pinot Noir wines are also excellent goose mates but they usually are a bit subdued when compared with the French wines made from the same grape. If wine is not your thing, a hearty pitcher of ale is not bad with most goose recipes.

# RARE-ROASTED GOOSE

1 5- to 6-pound goose (with skin)
1 cup cooked sauerkraut

1 apple, cored, peeled and quartered
¼ cup butter, melted
½ cup dry red wine

Have the goose at room temperature. Heat the sauerkraut and apple to the boiling point. Preheat the oven to 500°. Place the roasting pan with half the wine (¼ cup) in the oven to heat. Stuff the goose with the sauerkraut and apple mixture. Rub the bird with butter and place in the heated roasting pan. Place in the oven and baste every 5 minutes with the rest of the wine and butter. Roast for 30 minutes for rare or 35 minutes for medium-rare stage. Place on a wooden platter and slice thinly. Serve the pan juices in a heated serving bowl and ladle generously over the goose slices. Will serve 4.

*Note:* If the goose is a bit old, the legs and thighs will be a little tough. Save them for a meat pie or casserole by parboiling the carcass with a beef bouillon cube and a bit of onion and celery.

*Note:* Penciled on recipe, "Great."

# RICE-STUFFED GOOSE

1 young goose
½ teaspoon salt
¼ teaspoon pepper
3 tablespoons butter

1 onion, coarsely chopped
2 bay leaves
1 teaspoon marjoram
rice stuffing

Brown bird on all sides under broiler, if it has skin. Omit this step if the bird was skinned when cleaned. Stuff the goose with rice stuffing and place in a foil package in a roasting pan. Before you seal the package, add the salt, pepper, butter, onion, bay leaves and marjoram. Roast for 1¾ hours at 350° (2 hours or more for a large bird). Will feed 4 to 6.

## Rice Stuffing

2 tablespoons minced onions
2 tablespoons minced celery

2 tablespoons minced carrots
4 tablespoons butter
2 cups cooked wild rice

Slowly sauté the vegetables in the butter and add the rice when they are tender. Mix well and stuff goose.

# YOUNG ROASTED GOOSE

| | |
|---|---|
| 1 4-pound goose | 1 large onion, quartered |
| 2 apples, cored and quartered | butter |
| | ½ cup dry red wine |

Stuff goose with apples. Place the onion in a roasting pan. Butter the goose and place it in the pan. Pour the wine over it and place it in a hot oven (400°) for 25 minutes. Reduce heat and cover. Roast at 350° for 2 hours. Serves 4 to 6.

*Note:* Penciled on recipe, "Good."

# SYLVIA'S WILD GOOSE BREAST

| | |
|---|---|
| 1 goose breast, skinned and boned (2 fillets) | ¼ cup soy sauce |
| | ¼ cup cooking oil |
| ½ cup dry red wine | ¼ teaspoon fresh ground pepper |

In a shallow dish combine the wine, soy sauce, oil and pepper. Marinate the skinned and boned goose fillets for 2½ hours, turning often. Remove from marinade and place on foil on a broiler pan. Preheat the broiler and place the fillets 5 inches from the heat for 10 minutes of broiling on each side (20 minutes total cooking). Place on a wooden carving board and slice each fillet thinly, diagonally against the grain. Ladle a bit of sauce over each slice of meat. Serves 4.

*Note:* Penciled on recipe, "Super."

## Sauce

| | |
|---|---|
| ¼ cup black raspberry jelly | 1 teaspoon soy sauce |
| ¼ cup water | ½ teaspoon steak sauce |
| 1½ tablespoons Dijon-type mustard | ¼ teaspoon ground caraway seeds |
| 1 teaspoon lime juice | ½ teaspoon salt |
| | ⅛ teaspoon pepper |

Combine ingredients, heat and serve in a heated gravy boat.

# BRAISED GOOSE

| | |
|---|---|
| 1 large goose | ½ teaspoon sage, crushed |
| salt | 2 cloves garlic |
| freshly ground pepper | 2 cups dry white wine |
| | 5 cups beef stock or bouillon |

Wash and dry goose, inside and out. Rub the cavity with salt and pepper. Put the bird into a roasting pan and place in oven so the meat is about 4 inches from the heat. Brown on all sides under the broiler, turning frequently (total broiling time will be 15 to 20 minutes). Add sage, garlic, wine and bouillon to the pan. Bring the liquid to a simmer, cover and place in a 350° oven for 2½ hours. Turn goose twice while cooking. Goose is done when the leg moves easily at joint. Serves 6 to 8.

*Note:* Penciled on recipe, "Very good."

## BRANDIED GOOSE

| | |
|---|---|
| 1 *old* goose, cut into pieces | ⅛ teaspoon marjoram |
| flour | ¼ teaspoon salt |
| 2 tablespoons butter | pepper |
| 2 tablespoons cooking oil | 2 bay leaves |
| 3 cups bouillon (1 beef and 2 chicken) | 3 tablespoons cornstarch |
| 2 tablespoons steak sauce | 1 pound-can sweet cherries (pitted) |
| 3 tablespoons dry sherry | 2 tablespoons brandy |

Roll pieces of goose in flour and brown in butter and oil in a Dutch oven or other oven-proof pan. Brown just a few pieces at a time. Add bouillon, steak sauce, sherry, marjoram, salt, pepper and bay leaves to the pan. Heat. Return goose to pan, cover and place in 325° oven for at least 2½ hours, until tender. Remove goose pieces from the pan. Mix cornstarch with cherries and add to the pan juices with the brandy. Stir and heat over low flame until the sauce is slightly thickened. Return meat and baste with sauce. Simmer for 15 minutes, basting several times. Place goose on a heated platter and spoon a little sauce over each piece. Serve rest of sauce in a gravy boat to be ladled over hot goose and rice. Serves 6 to 8.

*Note:* Penciled on recipe, "Excellent."

## GOOSE WITH CURRY

| | |
|---|---|
| 2½ cups cooked goose meat (bite-sized pieces) | ¼ cup dry vermouth |
| | 1 clove garlic, finely minced |
| 1 large onion, sliced | 2½ tablespoons seedless raisins |
| 2 tablespoons olive oil | ½ apple, peeled and chopped |
| 1 teaspoon to 1 tablespoon curry powder | ¼ teaspoon thyme |
| 1½ tablespoons flour | 1 bay leaf |
| 1½ cups goose stock | salt and pepper |

Simmer onions in oil for 10 minutes until they are tender but not brown. Add curry (the amount depends on your fondness for this spice—I use 1 teaspoon). Blend in the flour and then the goose stock. Add vermouth, garlic, fruit, herbs and salt and pepper. Simmer for 30 minutes, adding more goose stock if it becomes too thick. Add goose meat before serving and heat to the boiling point. Serve ladled over hot, long-grain rice. The dish may be prepared the day before, reheated and served over fresh rice just before dinner. Will serve 4.

*Note:* Penciled on recipe, "Excellent."

### Goose Stock

goose legs, wings and carcass
1 beef bouillon cube
        celery leaves
salt and pepper
1 slice onion

Cook goose parts in water to cover with bouillon cube, salt, pepper, onion and celery leaves until tender. Cool the meat and remove from bones. Use the stock in the above recipe and/or for soup.

## GOOSE STROGANOFF

1½ to 2 cups cooked goose meat
1 cup sliced fresh mushrooms
1½ tablespoons butter
1½ tablespoons flour
1½ cups goose broth
1½ teaspoons prepared mustard
1 cup sour cream
salt and pepper to taste
paprika
parsley sprigs

Sauté mushrooms in the butter until tender. Add flour and then broth slowly. Heat, stirring constantly, until broth is thickened. Add goose meat, mustard, sour cream and salt and pepper and bring to the boiling point. Serve on buttered rice with a dash of paprika and a sprig of parsley. Makes 3 to 4 servings.

*Note:* Penciled on recipe, "Great."

### Cooked Goose Meat

leftover goose parts
salt
    1 beef bouillon cube
1 onion, sliced
celery leaves

Cover goose parts left over from Rare-Roasted Goose with salted water. Add onion, celery leaves and bouillon cube and simmer until meat is tender. Cut meat into bite-sized chunks and strain broth.

# GOOSE LIVER SPREAD

½ pound goose livers
celery leaves
1 egg, hard cooked and chopped
1 small onion, finely chopped
3 whole mushrooms, finely chopped

1 tablespoon butter
salt and pepper
2 tablespoons minced parsley
1 tablespoon brandy
2 tablespoons soft butter

cooking liquid

Drop the goose livers into boiling seasoned water to which a few celery leaves have been added. Simmer until the livers are tender. Drain and cool. Sauté the onions and mushrooms in the 1 tablespoon of butter. Blend the chopped livers, egg and onion and mushroom mixture into a fine paste. Add the parsley, brandy, soft butter and enough of the cooking liquid from the livers to make a spreadable consistency. Correct the seasonings. Serve with bland crackers.

*Note:* Penciled on recipe, "Great."

# GOOSE HEARTS

goose hearts
bay leaf

salt and pepper
onion slices

vinegar

Boil hearts in water with salt, pepper, onion and bay leaf, about 35 minutes (until tender). Drain, cool and slice thinly. Put in half-water, half-vinegar mixture (enough to cover). Add more salt and pepper if necessary. Refrigerate overnight. Use heart slices (dried) as appetizers or for sandwiches.

*Note:* Penciled on recipe, "Super."

# *Deer*

In our household, killing a deer starts a lengthy sequence of pleasant events. As delicious as the smaller game birds and animals are, there is something special about arriving home with a big game animal. You are really "bringing home the bacon." You are providing a stack of meat for the freezer because of your skill in the woods. It's a good feeling.

When I prepare for a deer hunt a few extra items go in my coat pockets besides ammunition, a thermos and lunch. I like to be ready to dress my deer (a bit of positive thinking). A sharp knife is essential. A wad of paper toweling is handy, and a couple of self-closing plastic bags are perfect for transporting the heart and liver. Once your deer has been downed, tag it (if required by law) and drag it to a convenient dressing location. Ideally, it should be on a slope with the head a bit higher than the hindquarters. This allows for better drainage of the carcass.

Even if it is cold, strip off your hunting jacket but keep that blaze orange hat on. Roll up your shirt sleeves and remove any jewelry, stashing it in a pocket. You're going to be working inside a large, warm, but rather messy animal. It's easier to clean your hands and arms when they are free of encumbering ornaments.

## DRESSING AND SKINNING

Many hunters remove the scent glands (the dark patch at the hind leg joint) first, fearing that they will taint the meat. The problem is handling them to cut them off. You get the scent on your fingers and spread it to the meat you're trying to protect. Better to leave them totally alone, remembering not to touch them as you roll the deer over or heave it around. You can remove these glands after the rest of the dressing is finished.

To field-dress, make the first cut around the anus. Using a sharp, narrow-bladed knife, you'll find that this operation is easy, and not unlike coring an apple. There is a natural, bone-lined opening here. Next, if the deer is a male, cut beneath the penis and testicles and the tubes leading to the abdomen. They lead back to the anal opening. Do not cut through these tubes, but merely free them with some careful cutting. Now go to the abdominal wall near the center of the deer's belly. Make a small cut into the hide, pulling the skin up to avoid cutting into the stomach or intestines. Sticking a finger beneath the hide, guide the point of the knife to the rear, being careful to miss the intestines. Then cut forward through the breast bone to about the second or third rib.

Everything inside wants to fall out at this point. Reach up into the forward part of the chest and cut the windpipe loose. This will free the lungs and heart. Cut through the wall separating the forward part of the chest from the rear portion. This is the diaphragm. It must be cut on both sides of the chest right up to the backbone. When this is loose, most of the body cavity contents will fall free. A minor cut here or there will do it. Separate the heart and liver from the rest of the contents and, if there is snow on the ground, toss them on a pile of clean snow to cool before putting them in the plastic bags.

The testicles, penis, and anal sheath will pull out through the opening cut between the hams. With this method, it is not necessary to separate the pelvic bone. The meat on both hind legs (the round steak) will not be exposed to dirt or stomach contents if the animal has been gut-shot.

Wipe the inside of the body cavity with paper toweling and you're ready to drag the carcass from the woods. Don't worry about a little blood here and there. The final touches can be taken care of when you get home.

Once the deer is field-dressed, carry it home in the coolest, cleanest possible way. This means never placing it on the vehicle's front fender, next to the hot motor. The top of the car can also be a problem with road dirt and oil. If your deer must be transported this way, a large sheet of plastic will protect the carcass. One of the best places to carry a deer is in a trunk spread with clean newspapers or inside the back of a station wagon, with the heater off. If the whole deer won't fit into the trunk, let the feet hang out, not the head. Why offend nonhunters with the dead head and its tongue? The same is true for placing your deer on the top of the car; it only takes a few minutes to arrange the carcass so it doesn't upset anyone. However, check local regulations. Some states require that your deer be exposed.

If you have a clean, cool place to hang the deer, take the hide off as soon as you arrive home. It will never be easier to skin. Hang the deer by both hind legs with ropes through the leg tendons just above the "heel" joints. Spread them far enough to allow plenty of work room. Make a cut just beneath the tail but do not cut through the tail. Slit the inside of each leg to the heel joint and cut through the skin around both legs. Using the tail as a handle, pull on it, then on the leg skin—first one and then the other, until the hide begins to pull free. It's tough to get started, but once the hide begins to loosen it'll come easier. Pull, but cut sparingly between hide and the transparent layer between skin and flesh. Push with the heel of your hand and be careful not to cut through the hide. When you get to the front legs, skin them out by circling the knee joint and slitting the inside of each leg just as you did on the hind legs. Join the cuts with the belly cut, and the hide will peel down over the head in a neat manner. Continue to pull and cut until the hide is near the base of the skull. Cut through the neck meat and lop off the backbone with a meatsaw or hacksaw.

## BUTCHERING

If you wish to age your deer in a garage or outdoors, it's best to leave the hide on until it's time to butcher. The meat should be aged for about ten days if you can keep it at a temperature between 32° and 42° Fahrenheit. Sometimes it is possible to rent locker space, or perhaps a friendly butcher will help out. If the deer must be cut up soon after it is killed because of warm weather or other considerations, don't worry about it. I've had some fine venison that was not aged. The most important consideration is that you don't lose any of the meat from improper storage.

After skinning, the legs should be lopped off at the knee and heel joints. There is not enough meat on the lower extremities to worry about. Hang the carcass up by the hind legs and make sure the ropes or whatever you use are sturdy. Using a meat saw, or hacksaw if that's all you have, begin to saw lengthwise from between the ham to the base of the neck. The neck can be cut off as a cylindrical piece. Try to make the saw follow the exact center of the spinal column. If you get off to one side, it's tough to get back on track.

Search for the natural joint at the hams and cut them off (they look just like pork hams). Leave one ham whole, if you'd like, for a leg of venison roast, or cut them both into round steak. The round steak can be cut from both sides of the leg bone without sawing through the bone each time. It's a lot easier and takes less space in the freezer. If you don't get all of the meat off the leg bone, don't worry. The trimmings will make great stew meat or can be ground into venison burger.

From just ahead of the hind legs and on up to the middle of the rib cage, venison chops can be cut with nothing more than a meat saw, a knife and a sharp hatchet. Cut through the fleshy part, making the chops as thick as you want them. When you hit bone, saw through it and make the final cut with the hatchet in case the gristle is too tough for the knife.

Each shoulder can be cut into roasts or used as ground or stew meat. Removing the front legs of venison is interesting if you've never done it before. The front legs of a deer are not connected to the rest of the skeletal structure. They "float" on the side of the animal and are connected only by rather soft tendons. They can easily be cut free with a knife by following the contour of the shoulder. The upper part of each front leg can be roasted or trimmed for burger or stew meat.

This is but one way to butcher a deer. There are several variations, and most of them work well. For instance, if you desire double or "butterfly" chops, don't split the carcass. Remove the saddle or center part of the back and cut the entire section into slices with a knife and saw. If you want to "wow" friends with an entire saddle-of-venison roast, leave the piece intact. Some hunters and home freezers who are short on space prefer to completely bone the entire deer. This requires some clever knife work, but it can be done in less than two hours if you follow the muscle structure.

## COOKING

The liver is best eaten shortly after the deer is killed. In many hunting camps it is the traditional first evening's feast—one that's worthy of the tired and hungry hunters. A simple way to prepare it is sliced thin and sautéed in hot butter until it's nicely browned on both sides but still pink in the middle. The heart can also be served the same way, with a few fried onions on the side.

After much experimenting, I've found that the burger mix that pleases my family is three parts venison to one part fatty pork, all ground together. This mixture is excellent as burgers, in meat loaf, in Sloppy Joes, or in any one of a thousand burger recipes.

Steaks and chops can be fast-fried (or broiled) much as the liver can be. If they are done quickly and left medium-rare in the center, the meat will be tender and juicy. The ways to prepare venison are limited only by your imagination. However, usually the fat on venison is not the flavorful stuff we are used to in domestic beef, so it is often best to trim off all fat before freezing and then add some beef suet if you wish to use extra fat during the cooking.

We usually save one whole leg for an annual Venison-in-a-Pit cookout, a social time for family and friends to celebrate the good things that hunters are privy to in this country. At our annual cookout we try to get the guests involved all through the day. This way, we have help digging the hole, gathering the wood, starting the fire and tending it. Lots of raw clams and frosty beer make it a festive occasion. Our pit is usually about 30 inches deep, 50 inches long and 30 inches wide. If your soil doesn't hold heat well, it can be lined with rocks. Build a big hardwood fire in the pit and allow the fire to burn down to a four-inch-thick bed of coals.

Place a grill or a piece of hardware cloth over the coals and lay the venison roast, well wrapped in heavy duty aluminum foil, on the grill. Cover the pit with dampened burlap bags, anchored to the ground on the sides with rocks or dirt. The chief chef often opts to add aluminum-wrapped chicken quarters, baking potatoes, and corn to the pit at varying times during the cooking. The chicken will take at least an hour, the potatoes 1½ hours and the corn 45 minutes, all of course varying with their proximity to the coals. A venison ham roast should cook in approximately 3½ hours, but there are many variables such as age of the animal, size of the roast and heat of the coals. It could take longer than 3½ hours, so keep your guests happy with plenty of appetizers and refreshments. When the meat is cooking properly, you should be able to hear it sizzling in the pit.

## WINES

Most antlered game provides rich, red meat that cries out for an equally rich wine. As with ducks, the savory aroma of a venison chop or steak will be much favored by a good bottle of Cabernet Sauvignon. Unless you are well versed in reading French wine labels or have complete trust in your wine salesman, it's probably safer to stick with the California products. They are so consistent year after year that it's hard to go far wrong with one of them.

# VENISON IN A PIT

1 large (7–11 pounds) venison ham roast
   (or two small ones)
4 bay leaves
4 tablespoons butter

2 onions, sliced
1 stalk celery
1 teaspoon marjoram
4 slices bacon (optional)

Use a large sheet of the extra heavy aluminum foil. Place the ham in the center of the sheet and add the rest of the ingredients. If you wish, drape the bacon over the roast. Using the drugstore wrap, close the foil securely. To be sure the juice does not leak out, wrap again in a second sheet of foil. Cook in the pit on a rack. When the package is opened and the roast is done, save the juice. It can be thickened for gravy or saved for soup or broth. Serves 8 to 14. (See previous page for complete directions for pit cooking.)

# SADDLE OF VENISON

1½ pounds venison saddle (yearling deer)
garlic clove

butter
¼ teaspoon thyme

Have venison at room temperature. Rub the saddle with the cut clove of garlic. Amply cover with butter and sprinkle with thyme. Place in a roasting pan. Have oven preheated to 450°. Roast at that temperature for 15 minutes, rub with more butter and roast another 15 minutes at 400°. For an older deer and a thicker saddle, roast another 5 or 10 minutes. Cut the meat from the bone and serve as little medallions. Salt and pepper at the table. This roast served 4.
*Note:* "Great—best ever eaten."

# VENISON WITH CIDER AND HERBS

5- to 6-pound venison roast
1 tablespoon cooking oil
½ teaspoon salt
¼ teaspoon pepper
¼ cup flour

1 teaspoon marjoram
1 teaspoon thyme
1 teaspoon rosemary
1 clove garlic, crushed
1 cup apple cider

flour

Dry meat well and cut several deep slits in the roast. Rub the roast with oil. Combine salt, pepper, flour, marjoram, thyme, rosemary and garlic and add just enough water to make a paste. Rub it on the roast, pushing some of the paste into the slits. Place the meat in a shallow pan surrounded by the cider and 1 cup water. Bake uncovered in a 325° oven for 1 hour. Baste with the pan juices, cover and roast another 2 hours, basting every 20 minutes or so. Slice thin to serve. Thicken pan juices with flour for gravy. Serves 6 to 8.

## VENISON POT ROAST, HUNGARIAN STYLE

5-pound venison roast
several strips salt pork
2 cloves garlic
salt and pepper
flour
3 tablespoons olive oil
2 onions, coarsely chopped

2 carrots, sliced
1¼ teaspoons oregano
1 teaspoon minced parsley
1 stalk celery, chopped
½ cup beef bouillon
½ cup dry white wine
1 tablespoon Hungarian paprika

1 cup sour cream

Using a larding needle or a sharp, thin knife, push the strips of salt pork into the roast. Sliver the garlic cloves and push into slots cut in meat. Rub the roast with salt and pepper and roll in flour. Sear quickly on all sides in the olive oil in a Dutch oven. Add onions, carrots, oregano, parsley, celery, bouillon and wine to the pot, cover and simmer for 2 hours. Check doneness, add the paprika and more broth if necessary. When done, remove to a hot platter, add sour cream to the broth and heat until almost boiling. Serve the roast sliced with a dollop of sauce over each piece. Buttered noodles with poppy seeds go well with this dish. Serves 6 to 7.

*Note:* Penciled on recipe, "Great."

## VENISON IN A BAG

5-pound venison roast
salt and pepper
6 slices bacon
1 onion, sliced

2 bay leaves
2 beef bouillon cubes
1 small bottle of beer
flour

Salt and pepper the roast and place in an oven cooking bag. Lay the bacon on top of the roast. Add onion, bay leaves and bouillon cubes to the bag and then add the beer. Close the bag according to directions and roast in a 350° oven approximately 2 hours. Thicken pan juices with flour for gravy. Heavy aluminum foil can be used instead of the bag, but care must be used not to pierce the foil. Serves 6.

# BRAISED NECK ROAST

3½–5-pound venison neck roast
8 slices bacon
1 cup dry red wine
1 cup beef bouillon
1 onion, sliced
1 clove garlic, minced
¼ cup lemon juice
½ teaspoon freshly ground pepper

½ teaspoon salt
¼ teaspoon ground cloves
¼ teaspoon ground ginger
2 teaspoons Italian seasonings
1 tablespoon olive oil
2 carrots, pared
1 stalk celery
quick-mixing flour

Bone the neck roast with a fillet knife. You'll end up with 2 long strips of meat plus a couple of small pieces from underneath the neckbone. Boil the bacon in a pan of water for 5 minutes to remove the smoky flavor, then spread it on one strip of meat. Lay the other strip on top and roll the strips together. Using string, tie into a rolled roast. Marinate the roast in the wine, bouillon, onion, garlic, lemon juice and seasonings for 4 hours. Remove, pat dry and brown in a Dutch oven or heavy frying pan in the hot oil. When brown on all sides, add marinade and vegetables and simmer for 3 hours, or until tender. Make gravy with pan juices thickened with flour. Slice roast thinly and serve with a little gravy on each slice. Serves 4.

*Note:* Penciled on recipe, "Good."

# VIC'S VENISON ROAST

6-pound venison roast
1 ¼ cups light cream
1 teaspoon savory

salt and pepper
1 onion, sliced
1 cup sliced mushrooms

Lay roast on a large sheet of heavy-duty aluminum foil. Pour the cream over the roast, sprinkle with savory and salt and pepper and add onion and mushrooms. Using the drugstore wrap, seal the roast and place in a roasting pan in a 350° oven. Roast for about 2½ hours. Serves 8 to 10.

*Note:* Penciled on recipe, "Good."

# BARBECUED SHOULDER ROAST

4-pound venison shoulder roast                 2 tablespoons cooking oil

In a deep pan, brown roast in oil on all sides. Pour barbecue sauce over the roast, cover and bake for about 2 hours in a 350° oven. Slice thin and serve with sauce spooned over the meat. Serves 4 to 6.

## Barbecue Sauce

1 cup catsup
½ teaspoon salt
2 tablespoons steak sauce
¼ cup vinegar

1 tablespoon butter
⅛ teaspoon cinnamon
3 slices lemon
1 onion, sliced thin
⅛ teaspoon allspice

Mix all ingredients and simmer for 10 minutes before pouring over roast.

## PENNY'S POT ROAST

4-pound venison shoulder roast
flour with salt and pepper added
2 tablespoons butter
¼ teaspoon basil
½ teaspoon parsley
1 carrot, chopped

1 onion, chopped
1 celery stalk, diced
1 cup beef bouillon
1 cup dry red wine
4 potatoes, cut in quarters
4 carrots, cut in quarters
flour

Dust roast with seasoned flour and brown in a heavy Dutch oven using the butter. When brown on all sides, sprinkle the roast with basil and parsley and add the chopped carrot, onion, celery, bouillon and wine to the pan. Cover and simmer for 1½ hours, turning the roast several times. Add cut carrots and potatoes to the pot and simmer another 45 minutes. Thicken juices with flour and serve as gravy. Serves 4 to 6.

## BROILED VENISON CHOPS

8 small venison chops (or 4 large ones)
meat tenderizer

butter
salt and pepper

Have chops cut 1-inch thick. One-half hour before broiling, moisten the meat with a little water, sprinkle with meat tenderizer, and pierce in several places with a fork. Butter both sides of meat and place on a broiler rack, 4 inches from the heat. Broil 5 minutes on each side and serve immediately. Salt and pepper to taste at the table. Serves 4.

*Note:* Handle cooking chops with tongs to preserve juices. "Excellent."

# VENISON STEAK VICTOR

4 venison steaks
butter

1 tablespoon dry vermouth
salt and pepper

Cut the steaks 1-inch thick. Heat an ample amount of butter in a heavy iron skillet. Over a very hot fire, quickly fry the steaks, 3 minutes on a side. Add vermouth and serve on hot plates. Salt and pepper to taste at the table. *Note:* Penciled on recipe, "Great." Serves 4.

# SWISSED VENISON STEAK

4 venison round steaks
flour seasoned with salt and pepper
2 tablespoons cooking oil

2 onions, sliced
2 cups chopped tomatoes
1 teaspoon sugar

Douse steaks with seasoned flour. Heat the oil in a heavy skillet and brown the steaks on both sides. Add the onions and tomatoes and sugar. Cover, lower heat and simmer until tender, about 1¼ hours. Serves 4.

# VALLE'S VENISON STROGANOFF

2 pounds venison round steak, cut ¾
  inch thick
4 tablespoons butter
1 onion, chopped
¼ teaspoon basil
½ teaspoon salt

pepper
1¼ cups beef bouillon
1 cup sliced mushrooms
2 tablespoons flour
1½ teaspoons prepared mustard
1 cup sour cream

Remove fat from meat and cut meat into strips ¼ inch wide and 1½ inches long. Brown meat in 2 tablespoons butter in a skillet. Transfer to an oven-proof casserole and add onion, basil, salt and pepper. Heat bouillon in same skillet until it reaches the boiling point, scraping the bottom to loosen meat particles. Pour over the meat, cover and bake in 350° oven for 1½ hours, turning twice during the baking time.

Sauté mushrooms in 2 tablespoons butter until lightly brown. Stir in flour and then liquid from the meat. Stir constantly until the mixture cooks and thickens. Add mustard and sour cream and bring to the boiling point. Pour over the meat and serve over cooked rice. Serves 4.

*Note:* Penciled on recipe, "Really great."

## McGINNIS CHINESE PEPPER STEAK

2 pounds venison steak
2 tablespoons cooking oil
1⅓ cups beef bouillon
1 medium onion, coarsely chopped
1 green pepper, coarsely chopped
1 stalk celery, coarsely chopped

3 tablespoons cornstarch
2 tablespoons soy sauce
2 teaspoons sugar
pinch of ginger
1 16-ounce can Chinese vegetables
    (drained)

Partially thaw venison steak, cut into thin strips (⅛-inch slices) and brown in oil. Add bouillon and simmer for 10 minutes. Add onion, green pepper and celery and simmer another 10 minutes. Mix 2 tablespoons water, cornstarch, soy sauce, sugar and ginger and add to the pan. Cook until slightly thick and add vegetables. Serve with rice. Serves 5 or 6.

*Note:* Penciled on recipe, "Good."

## VENISON IN A WOK

2 pounds venison round steak
1 cup + 2 tablespoons cooking oil
¼ cup soy sauce
¼ teaspoon ginger
pinch of cayenne pepper
1 large onion, cut into chunks

6 large mushrooms, cut into chunks
1 stalk celery, cut into chunks
1 green pepper, cut into thin strips
½ cup chicken bouillon
¼ teaspoon ginger
¼ teaspoon dry mustard

cornstarch

Slice the steak into strips about $\frac{1}{16}$ inch thick, cutting against the grain with a sharp knife. Marinate the meat in a bowl with the 1 cup cooking oil, mixed with soy sauce, ginger and cayenne pepper. Place the bowl in the refrigerator for 3 hours.

Just before time to cook, prepare the vegetables (slicing and chopping). Heat the 2 tablespoons of cooking oil in a wok (375° if it is electric). Place the meat in the hot oil and stir-fry for 3 minutes. Push the meat up the side and add the onion. Stir-fry for 2 minutes, push up the side and add mushrooms, for 2 minutes of stir-frying. Next comes 2 minutes of stir-frying celery and last, 1 minute for the green pepper. Add to pan ½ cup of marinade, bouillon, ginger and dry mustard. Simmer for 2 minutes. Thicken pan juices slightly with a little cornstarch dissolved in cold water. Serve over hot rice. Serves 6.

*Note:* Penciled on recipe, "Excellent."

# VENISON RAGOUT

2 pounds venison leg meat
1½ cups red wine
¾ cup sliced carrots
¾ cup chopped celery
4 green onions, chopped
12 juniper berries, crushed
1 tablespoon olive oil

1 teaspoon salt
½ teaspoon marjoram
⅛ teaspoon fresh ground pepper
1 bay leaf, crushed
flour
3 tablespoons butter
1 cup beef bouillon

Cut leg meat into strips 1 inch thick and 3 inches long. Place the wine, carrots, celery, onions, berries, oil, seasonings and 1 cup water in a bowl and add the meat. Add more water if the meat is not covered. Refrigerate, covered, for 5 hours. Remove the meat with a slotted spoon, then drain the vegetables, reserving the marinade. Dredge the meat with flour and brown in the butter in a skillet. Transfer meat to an oven-proof casserole and brown the vegetables in the skillet, adding more butter if necessary. Add marinade and bouillon to skillet and boil for a minute. Transfer all to the casserole and cover. Place in 325° oven and bake for 2 hours, adding a little water if it becomes dry. Correct salt and pepper and serve with a green vegetable, salad and rolls. Serves 6.

*Note:* Penciled on recipe, "Great."

# HILDA'S VENISON AND NOODLES

1½ pounds venison stew meat, cubed
1½ tablespoons cooking oil
1½ cups beer
2 beef bouillon cubes
1 onion, sliced
1 tablespoon horseradish
2 teaspoons steak sauce

3 drops Tabasco sauce
½ teaspoon thyme
½ teaspoon dill weed
¼ teaspoon allspice
salt and pepper
quick-mixing flour
buttered noodles

parsley

Brown the venison cubes in the oil in a heavy skillet. Add the rest of the ingredients, correct the seasonings, cover and simmer for 2½ hours. Thicken the liquid with a little flour and serve over a bed of buttered noodles with a sprig of parsley for garnish. Serves 4.

*Note:* Excellent—German-type sweet and sour.

# HUNTER'S STEW

1½ pounds venison stew meat, cubed
flour
½ teaspoon salt
⅛ teaspoon pepper
2 tablespoons cooking oil
1 onion, coarsely chopped
1 clove garlic, minced
¾ cup dry red wine
1 beef bouillon cube

6 carrots, cut in 2-inch strips
2 stalks celery, cut in 2-inch strips
1 cup fresh or frozen cranberries
1 teaspoon sugar
1 tablespoon steak sauce
2 teaspoons Hungarian paprika
4 juniper berries (optional)
2 whole cloves
1 bay leaf

cornstarch

Dredge stew meat in flour seasoned with salt and pepper and brown in the hot oil in a Dutch oven with the onion and garlic. When brown, add wine, 2 cups water, and bouillon cube and bring to a boil. Cover and simmer for 1¼ hours. Add carrots, celery, cranberries, sugar, steak sauce, paprika, berries, cloves and bay leaf. Cover and simmer another 45 minutes until vegetables are tender. Thicken to taste with cornstarch mixed with a little cold water. Serves 6. Great with hot biscuits.

# VENISON MOUSSAKA

1½ pounds venison burger
2 cups cooked green beans
1 8-ounce can tomato sauce
½ teaspoon garlic salt
⅛ teaspoon cinnamon

2 eggs, slightly beaten
1½ cups cream-style cottage cheese
2 tablespoons ripe olive juice
⅓ cup grated Parmesan cheese
4 ripe olives, sliced

Place green beans in a buttered casserole. Brown meat in a skillet and drain off excess fat. Add tomato sauce, garlic salt and cinnamon. Spread the meat mixture over the beans. Combine eggs, cottage cheese and olive juice and spread over the meat mixture in the casserole. Sprinkle with Parmesan cheese. Bake in a 350° oven for 30 minutes. Garnish with olive slices. Makes 6 servings.

*Note:* A favorite.

# BLACK FOREST VENISON RIBS

4 to 6 pounds venison ribs
1 part vinegar/3 parts water solution
2 bay leaves

2 tablespoons salt
1 sliced onion
melted butter

Marinate ribs for 48 hours in vinegar/water solution to cover with bay leaves, salt and onion. Refrigerate. Dry pieces and put in a shallow baking or roasting pan. Brush with melted butter and roast in 450° oven, basting twice, for 30 minutes. Turn oven temperature down to 350° and baste meat at 15-minute intervals with the sauce (coating well) until the ribs are tender, 1 to 1½ hours. Serves 4.

*Note:* If there is any left over, remove meat from bones, trim all fat and cut meat into very thin strips. Heat in a frying pan with some catsup and serve in warm hamburger rolls. A delicious barbecue venison sandwich.

## Sauce

| | |
|---|---|
| 1 cup chili sauce | 2 tablespoons lemon juice |
| ¼ cup steak sauce | ½ teaspoon chili powder |
| ½ teaspoon salt | |

Combine the ingredients in a saucepan with 1½ cups water and heat until it comes to a boil. Use to baste ribs.

## VICKSBURG VENISON MEAT PIE

| | |
|---|---|
| 3 cups leftover venison roast, cut in bite-sized chunks | ½ pound mushroom caps |
| 2 carrots, sliced thin | 2 tablespoons butter |
| salt and pepper | leftover gravy |
| | pastry for single crust |
| ⅛ teaspoon savory | |

Cook carrots in a little water seasoned with salt and pepper. Sauté mushrooms in the butter. Add both to the leftover meat and gravy. Add more salt and pepper if necessary. Make your favorite pastry crust, adding the savory to the flour. Place the meat mixture in a well-buttered 1-quart casserole and cover with the crust, sealing the dough to the sides. Slit the top to allow the steam to escape. Bake in a preheated 425° oven for about 15 minutes until the crust begins to brown. Turn the oven down to 350° for another 15 minutes or so until the meat pie is bubbly hot. Will serve 4.

*Note:* "Delicious."

## VENISON SPREAD

| | |
|---|---|
| leftover venison shoulder roast | salt and pepper |
| bread and butter pickles | garlic salt |
| mayonnaise | |

Put meat through the meat grinder, using the coarse blade, with enough of the pickles to make a nice spread. Use pickles to help push the dry meat through the grinder. Add seasonings to taste and enough mayonnaise to make the mixture of spreadable consistency. Serve on bread or crackers for lunch or appetizers.

## PICKLED VENISON HEART

| | |
|---|---|
| 1 venison heart | 1 small onion, sliced |
| salt | 3 parts water/1 part vinegar mixture |
| 2 bay leaves | pepper |

Place heart in a large saucepan. Add water to cover, a little salt and the bay leaves. Bring to a boil, lower heat and simmer (covered) until it is tender. It will take longer than a beef heart but there is no set time. (It depends on the age of the animal and how hard it had to work. The last one I cooked simmered for about 4 hours.) Drain when tender, cool and then slice thin. Place the slices in a bowl with the onion and the water/vinegar mixture (enough to cover the heart slices). Add salt and pepper to taste. Soak in refrigerator for several hours. Dry and use in sandwiches with mustard (like a roast beef sandwich) or as appetizer material. Place a dab of mustard on a rye cracker, top with a piece of heart and a tiny piece of parsley.

*Note:* "Great with beer."

## SUGAR RUN VENISON LIVER

| | |
|---|---|
| 1 venison liver, sliced thin | 2 tablespoons butter |
| salt and pepper | 2 tablespoons cooking oil |
| 1 small onion, chopped finely | flour |
| 5 mushrooms, finely chopped | ¼ cup dry vermouth |

Sauté onion and mushrooms in butter/cooking oil mixture until the vegetables are tender. While they are cooking, dredge the liver slices in the flour, seasoned with salt and pepper. Push the onion and mushrooms to the edge of the frying pan and add the liver slices. Sauté for about 8 minutes, 4 minutes on a side. Just before serving, add the vermouth and mix with the pan juices. Place the liver slices on a heated platter and cover with mushroom/onion mixture. Serve immediately.

*Note:* Penciled on recipe, "Super."

# Other
# Big Game

"I shot an antelope in Wyoming last fall and am not pleased with the flavor of the meat," states a letter from a Western hunter. He went on to describe several incidents that occurred during the hunt and wonders "if they could possibly have affected the meat." The animal didn't drop immediately and wasn't recovered until after a lengthy chase. Then the hunter accidentally cut into the stomach, allowing the contents to seep out for a half hour before the final dressing. Topping this were abnormally warm temperatures during the days following the kill.

I strongly suspect the slitting of the stomach caused the major problem, but all three probably contributed and there is another possibility. The animal could have been eating something strongly flavored. Antelope at times will feed on enough sage to affect the meat taste. Some people mind it and others don't.

When I was a child, our family raised rabbits during the summer. My dad would feed them scraps from the vegetable garden as well as their regular food and then butcher them in the fall. One September he had a surplus of cabbage leaves (left over from a sauerkraut project) that were devoured by the rabbits. Shortly afterwards the animals were killed, cleaned and frozen. You guessed it, they not only smelled like cabbage while being cooked but tasted the same way. It was almost impossible to disguise the flavor.

Luckily, most wild animals don't get into anything as strong as cabbage, but at times you'll come across a piece of game that has an unusual flavor. That's when you use all those recipes that call for elaborate marinades, soakings and sauces to cover up the "gamey" flavor. That is the *only* time when it is acceptable to turn an entire large game animal into burger, sausage or bologna. The rest of the time you can reduce me to tears by describing how you had your butcher make burger out of the tenderloin of your elk.

For the most part, game should be treated exactly as you would the most expensive cuts from the meat market. There is no gameyness to disguise, only that particular animal's unique flavor. Usually, game is more environmentally sound to eat than commercial meat since it isn't pumped full of chemicals. Dieters find its leanness an extra bonus. Many of the recipes under the venison chapter will score as well using elk, antelope, moose or caribou meat. Just keep in mind, if the hunter bagged a trophy-sized animal it may need a slow cooking treatment to tenderize the meat. You can judge the rest of the meat from a good cut, cooked as simply as possible. Try one of the chops. Broil it or pan-fry it rare with a bit of butter and see how tender it is.

Caribou liver is the tenderest and most flavorful of all the liver I've eaten. Cut it thin and sauté it in butter. It needs nothing else to embellish its natural flavor. The steaks and chops are great, too. Use the quick-cooking venison recipes. One of the best stews I ever had was made from caribou front shoulder meat.

## CARIBOU STEW

1½ pounds cubed caribou stew meat
    (front shoulder)
flour seasoned with salt and pepper
3 tablespoons butter
2 onions, whole

1½ cups beef bouillon
4 potatoes, quartered
4 carrots, quartered
1½ tablespoons flour
¾ cup tomato sauce

Douse the stew meat with the seasoned flour and brown in a Dutch oven in the butter. Add onions and bouillon to the pot, cover and simmer for 1 hour. Add potatoes and carrots and cook until tender, another 30 to 45 minutes. Blend flour into tomato sauce and add to the stew. Bring to a boil, stirring until the broth is thickened. Serves 4. Delicious with hot, crusty Italian bread.

## BEAR

Bear meat is traditionally cooked slowly with moist heat to tenderize it. The flesh is usually better-tasting from a young one because the diet will contain more fruits and vegetables. "You are what you eat" is particularly true of bears and some of these critters do get into some awful-smelling "delicacies." Then the only solution is lots of marinades, powerful herbs and sauces. One of the best bear recipes I ever tasted was at a friend's house.

## TERRY BELL'S BEAR WITH BEER

8- to 9-pound bear roast
1 cup chopped celery
½ cup brown sugar
½ cup chopped onion

1 cup beer
½ cup apple cider
¾ cup soy sauce
1 bay leaf

Mix all ingredients except roast in a saucepan over low heat. Stir until smooth. Pour into a large pot, such as a Dutch oven. Place roast in the marinade. Cover and set in refrigerator for 48 hours. Turn occasionally to expose both sides of meat to marinade. Place pot in a 300° oven and simmer for 10 to 12 hours. Let stand in juice overnight. Serve cold, slicing thin. Serves 6 to 8.

## BEAR STEAK BRADFORD

2- to 3-pound loin bear steak
1 carrot, chopped
1 stalk celery, chopped
1 teaspoon paprika

½ cup orange juice
1 garlic clove, crushed
3 tablespoons butter
¼ cup tomato sauce

3 drops tabasco sauce

Cut steak into 4 servings. Mix carrot, celery, paprika, orange juice, garlic and ½ cup water, bring to a boil and simmer for 10 minutes. Let cool, place steaks in the marinade and refrigerate for 18 hours. Remove steaks from marinade and blot with paper toweling. Heat the butter in a heavy skillet and sear the steaks quickly on each side. Turn the heat down, add the tomato sauce and Tabasco and cook to the degree of doneness you wish. With a young bear, rare would be fine. An older one will need more time. Serves 4.

# MOOSE

## DEVILED MOOSE (OR ELK) STEAK

4 slices moose round steak, 1 inch thick    ⅛ teaspoon pepper
1½ teaspoons dry mustard                 2 tablespoons butter
½   teaspoon salt                        ½ cup beef bouillon
1 tablespoon steak sauce

Pound the dry mustard, salt and pepper into the steak slices with a meat mallet, using the mallet on both sides of the steak. Brown the meat in a heavy skillet in butter. Add bouillon and steak sauce, cover and simmer for 1½ hours, until tender. Serves 4.

# ANTELOPE

## ANTELOPE STEAK PAULINE

2 pounds round steak, cut ½ inch thick    2 tablespoons butter
stuffing                                ½ cup beef bouillon
flour seasoned with salt and pepper       ½ cup tomato juice
flour

Spread stuffing on steak, roll and secure with string. Roll in seasoned flour and brown in butter in a roasting pan. Heat bouillon and juice and pour over the rolled steak. Cover and bake in a 350° oven for 1½ hours. Thicken gravy with a little flour and serve with mashed potatoes and corn on the cob. Serves 4.

### Stuffing

¼ cup minced carrots               ¼ cup minced celery
¼ cup minced onions              4 tablespoons butter
2 cups soft bread crumbs

Sauté the vegetables in the butter until soft. Add the bread crumbs and mix thoroughly.

# Trout—
# Brook, Brown,
# and Rainbow

Trout have an interesting history in North America. The native brookies are small stream trout to most of us in the United States, but in Canada, where they exist in large rivers *and* are controlled with predation from walleyes, northern pike, char or lake trout, they grow to trophy size of four pounds and over. Brook trout seem to need both big water and density control to attain some size. The brown trout, a native of Europe, has fast become a favorite in the United States because it is more difficult to catch and is tolerant of environmental changes. The rainbow trout (another native) has been far more adaptable to distribution in different waters than the brookie. They are also able to withstand higher water temperatures than the brook and brown trout.

Small, wild trout were the lollipops of my childhood. Because my dad took the time to show a four-year-old how to coax them into taking a worm-baited hook on frosty mornings, they were my first successes in the outdoor world. At that time, opening day of trout season always occurred on April 15. Our ritual started the day before, with the spading of half-frozen garden soil in search of enough delectable angleworms to fill a Prince Albert can. Those tobacco cans were just the right size to fit into a jacket pocket. Dad always punched a few holes in the lid with a nail so the worms could breathe.

Opening day, activities began while it was still dark. A quick breakfast was the rule, since we were always too excited to eat much. Then came what seemed like an interminable car ride to Dad's favorite spot, Nelson Run. We drove as far as the road went, then walked the rest of the way. We could have fished closer to civilization but preferred solitude; if we were not the only anglers on our chosen section of the run, we would at least be the first to arrive.

Dad's advice was, "If you can see the trout, it can see you." So I approached the stream on all fours, dangling the worm on a short piece of line from an old bamboo fly rod. I almost always captured half a dozen 6- to 7-inch beauties, while Dad would limit out with 8-inch graybeards. In these acidic brooks, food was scarce and a 9-inch brook trout was a trophy.

By the time the sun peaked over the mountains, we were usually on our way back to the car, muddy but happy. Dad would clean the trout, change his clothes, and be off to work. I would relate the morning's adventures to my mother and later to my schoolmates. Often I had caught more than any of the boys—a heady thrill!

The culmination of the day was dinner: fried brook trout, of course. Mother was always careful to keep *my* trout separate so I could eat the ones I had caught. The small trout were prepared simply. The fish slime was wiped off with paper toweling. Mother often removed the heads, but leaving them on would help the trout to lie in the frying pan without curling. Each fish was liberally coated with flour laced with salt and pepper. Frying was done in a mixture of butter and margarine in an iron skillet. The little trout needed only a few minutes on each side to be done to perfection.

A rule of thumb for cooking fish is 10 minutes of cooking per inch of thickness. But trout less than ten inches long are not that thick; eight minutes is plenty. When trout are small, you can eat skin and all. In fact, my dad often ate everything, including the bones, of a 6-inch trout. On larger trout, the skin is less delicate and should be discarded after cooking.

Twelve- to fourteen-inch trout can be broiled with great success. Place them on a buttered piece of foil, brush with melted butter and leave under a hot broiler (four inches from the heat) for five minutes on each side. Check with a toothpick at the thickest part of the back after ten minutes. If the meat flakes easily, it is done. Remove to heated plates. Then, using a fork, lift the skin off one side, salt and pepper the meat and eat from the bones. After the meat is gone from the first side, the entire bone structure can be lifted out and, with the addition of a little more salt and pepper, you are ready to eat the second side. When cooking this size fish you'll find one trout per serving is adequate.

The same size trout is excellent grilled over coals on an open fire or charcoal grill. Clean the trout, roll in flour and then dip in melted butter. Place them in an oiled, hinged wire grill and cook about 5 minutes on each side, basting with additional butter. Don't let the trout get too close to the hot coals or the flesh will be overcooked.

Fancy restaurants make a big deal out of Trout au Bleu but the coloration happens automatically. The skin will turn blue provided the trout is cooked within a few minutes of being killed. Restaurants accomplish this with live tanks. You can do it in the field. All you need is a one-burner stove, a pan deep enough for trout and a few seasonings. It's a marvelous way to surprise your angling buddies on your next fishing trip.

## TROUT AU BLEU

| | |
|---|---|
| 4 12- to 14-inch trout | 1 bay leaf |
| vinegar | 1 teaspoon salt |
| 6 peppercorns | butter |

Put 3 parts water to 1 part vinegar (enough to cover fish), peppercorns, bay leaf and salt in a pot and bring to a rolling boil. Plunge the cleaned, fresh-caught trout into the water and simmer about 10 minutes until the meat flakes. The vinegar will turn the skin a bluish color. Serve with melted butter. Will serve 4.

## DICKIE HAAS'S HONEY BROOK TROUT

| | |
|---|---|
| 2 boneless trout, 14 to 16 ounces | 1 egg |
| ½ cup cornmeal | ⅓ cup milk |
| ¼ cup flour | 1 lemon, cut in half |
| ½ teaspoon salt | 4 tablespoons butter |
| ½ teaspoon pepper | 2 tablespoons honey |

Using a thin-bladed trout fillet knife, carefully remove the bones from the trout, leaving the back skin intact. Combine cornmeal with flour, salt and pepper. In another bowl, beat egg slightly and stir in milk. Rub each trout with half of the lemon. Dredge in the cornmeal mixture. Then dip into the egg wash and dredge in the cornmeal mixture again.

Have the frying pan and butter heated almost to the smoking point. Place the trout in pan with the meat side down. Cook until golden brown. Turn trout and spread honey across the top. Lower heat, cover pan and cook 3 to 4 minutes more. Serve these tasty fish with a wedge of lemon. Serves 2.

# TROUT ALMANDINE

4 12- to 14-inch trout
flour mixed with salt and pepper
4 tablespoons butter

¼ cup slivered, blanched almonds
¼ cup dry vermouth
parsley or chervil flakes

Dust the fish lightly with the flour, salt and pepper mixture. Fry in butter over moderately high heat for 5 minutes on a side (check with toothpick at thickest point for flakiness). Remove the fish from the frying pan and quickly brown the almonds lightly in the pan (add more butter if necessary). Keep the fish hot on a platter in a warm oven. Add vermouth to the pan, heat with the parsley or chervil and serve over the fish. Will serve 4.

*Note:* Penciled on recipe, "Excellent."

# BROACHED TROUT

*Good*

2 13-inch trout
½ cup dry vermouth
shake of celery salt
salt and pepper

1 tablespoon butter
½ cup mayonnaise
3 tablespoons Parmesan cheese
1 teaspoon steak sauce

¼ cup crushed cashew nuts

Poach trout in a large pan with 1 inch of water, the dry vermouth, celery salt and salt and pepper to taste. Simmer gently for 6 minutes (only on one side). Remove the fish with a pancake turner from the liquid, drain and place in a greased, oven-proof, shallow dish. Place butter in dish. Remove the skin and fins from the upside. Combine mayonnaise, cheese and steak sauce and spread over the trout. Sprinkle with the nuts. In a preheated broiler, broil for 6 minutes about 6 inches from the heat source. Check for flakiness and serve. Will serve 2.

*Note:* Penciled on recipe, "Very good."

# TROUT LISA

4 11- to 12-inch trout
flour seasoned with salt and pepper
1 egg, beaten

1 cup crushed, dried bread crumbs,
  Italian flavored
4 tablespoons butter

4 tablespoons olive oil

Clean trout, remove heads and dry thoroughly on paper toweling. Dust with seasoned flour. Dip the fish in the beaten egg and roll in the bread crumbs. Let rest for 5 minutes. Heat the butter and oil in a heavy skillet. When the pan is sizzling hot, add the trout. Brown for 4 minutes on one side; flop over and brown for 3 minutes on the other. Cover pan, reduce heat to medium and continue cooking for 3 more minutes. Check fish at the thickest place with a fork. If the flesh flakes, it's done. Serves 4.

*Note:* Penciled on recipe, "Excellent."

## SWISS BAKED TROUT

| | |
|---|---|
| 4 9-inch trout, cleaned | ½ cup butter, melted |
| 2 tablespoons minced onion | ¼ cup fine, dry bread crumbs |
| 2 tablespoons minced parsley | ¼ cup grated Swiss cheese |
| ⅓ cup finely chopped mushrooms | ¼ cup dry vermouth |
| salt and pepper to taste | paprika |

Line a greased shallow baking dish with the onion, parsley and mushrooms mixed together. Salt and pepper the dressed trout (inside and out) and lay on the vegetable mixture. Pour *half* the butter over them, cover with a lid or foil and place in a preheated 400° oven for 15 minutes. Take the dish from the oven, cover the trout with the crumbs and Swiss cheese. Sprinkle the crumb mixture with the rest of melted butter and the dry vermouth. Add paprika for color. Cover again and return to the oven for another 10 minutes. If you wish to brown the crumbs, slip the pan under the broiler for a few seconds just before serving. Will serve 2. This dish is good with fresh corn on the cob and sliced garden tomatoes.

*Note:* An excellent recipe for people who don't mind deboning small whole trout while they are eating.

## TROUT WITH CLAMATO SAUCE

| | |
|---|---|
| 6 10-inch trout | 1 onion, cut in quarters |
| 1 bay leaf | 1 stalk celery with leaves |
| | salt and pepper |

Make court bouillon by placing, in a heavy, deep frying pan, enough water to cover trout along with the bay leaf, onion and celery. Bring to a boil and simmer for 5 minutes. Add the trout, cover and simmer (after the water starts to boil again) for 10 minutes. Remove trout, drain and cool a bit. Butter a piece of aluminum foil. Remove the skin and bones from the fish and place warm chunks of meat on the foil. Keep in a warm oven until ready to serve. Divide the fish flesh between 4 plates. Mound the serving on each plate, add salt and pepper, and spoon clamato sauce over each. Serves 4.

# Clamato Sauce

⅓ cup finely chopped celery
¼ cup finely chopped onion
3 tablespoons butter
1 tablespoon cooking oil

salt and pepper
2 tablespoons flour
1 5½-ounce can Clamato juice
¼ cup heavy cream

1 tablespoon dry vermouth

Slowly sauté the celery and onion in the butter/oil mixture for about 10 minutes. Add salt and pepper to taste. Blend in flour, then juice, cream and wine. Serve over trout chunks.

# Lake
# Trout

The lake trout is one of the reasons Yankee anglers visit Canadian lakes year after year. The chance of that deep-bellied trophy is a powerful incentive. This largest of the char family inhabits deep, clear lakes from Labrador all across Canada and south into parts of the northern United States.

Lakers are most often fished for by trolling large spoons with deep-running wire line. That is considered the acceptable way to angle for them in many Canadian provinces. It is more interesting, however, to use lighter tackle and experiment with different depths. Lake trout are extremely sensitive to water temperature, but light tackle is more fun when used in a lake like Great Bear where there is no thermocline. Jim and I took many lakers (between 2 and 15 pounds) on trolled streamer flies at Great Bear not long ago. However, my largest lake trout, a 35-pounder, was caught on Stramond Lake in Quebec using a light graphite casting stick and a lure that was running slowly at about the 18-foot level, supposedly much too shallow for summer trout in this lake. During the 30-minute tug of war, I could feel every headshake and every surge just as if the trout were at my fingertips. A thrill like that is only possible with light tackle. A wire line separates the angler from the catch with too much hardware. It may be effective, but the challenge just isn't there.

Since the fat content of lake trout is high, the simple methods of cooking are the best. You do not fry lake trout. If you do, your taste buds aren't developed! Lake trout are best poached (or boiled), steamed, smoked, broiled or even baked.

The best lakers for eating are the small ones, 4 pounds and under. The bigger the lake trout, the stronger the flavor of the flesh. Also, the large trout are the breeders and should be returned to the lake unless you intend to have a trophy mounted.

While we were at Great Bear Lake, we prepared several shore lunches with lakers—simple meals with a minimum of equipment and condiments, but this fish is eminently suitable for such treatment.

All the methods would be equally easy to accomplish in the backyard on a grill or over an open fire. Have you ever noticed how good fish tastes when prepared in fresh air? It isn't all psychological. Part of it is cooking over wood or *real* hardwood charcoal. The real stuff is hard to find these days, but it does pay off in good-flavored food.

## GRILLED LAKE TROUT

1 large lake trout, cleaned and scaled | tartar sauce
butter | salt and pepper

Wipe the fish thoroughly with paper toweling. Rub the skin with soft butter. Place on a hot grill over charcoal. Timing is always a problem when you cook outside, but when things begin to sizzle, start timing. The fish should take 10 minutes per inch of thickness. About halfway through the grilling time, use a pancake turner to flop the fish over, being careful to retain as much protective skin as possible. When the flesh flakes, place the fish on a platter and strip off the skin. Season with salt and pepper. Serve with tartar sauce.

## Tartar Sauce

1 cup mayonnaise | 1 teaspoon chervil
½ cup bread and butter pickles, chopped | ½ teaspoon minced parsley
    fine | ½ teaspoon prepared mustard
2 teaspoons minced onions | ½ teaspoon dill weed
½ teaspoon tarragon leaves

Combine all ingredients and chill for at least 1 hour before serving.

# BAKED LAKE TROUT

1 large lake trout, cleaned and scaled
1 tablespoon lemon juice
⅛ teaspoon garlic powder
¼ teaspoon celery salt

¼ teaspoon onion salt
salt and pepper
butter
lemon wedges

Butter a large piece of heavy-duty aluminum foil. Place the trout in the center. Sprinkle with lemon juice and seasonings and add a large chunk of butter. Seal well and bake over hot coals, turning once, for about 20 minutes. Check fish for flakiness. If done, serve with lemon wedges. The skin will slip off easily and the meat will pull away from the bones with a touch of the fork.

*Note:* Penciled on recipe, "Great."

# WALLY'S FILLETS

4 large lake trout fillets
butter
salt and pepper
¼ teaspoon garlic powder

Tabasco sauce
1 onion, sliced thin
1 zucchini, sliced thin.
1 tomato, sliced thin

Butter an ample piece of heavy-duty aluminum foil. Place 2 of the fillets in the center. Sprinkle with salt and pepper, garlic powder and Tabasco. Top with onion slices, then zucchini and then the tomato. Add another layer of fish fillets, more seasonings and seal the package. Bake over hot coals for about 10 minutes on a side after the package begins to sizzle. Serve with just a little lemon juice. Serves 4.

*Note:* Penciled on recipe, "Super."

# TROUT WITH CUCUMBER SAUCE

4 large lake trout fillets
1 cup sour cream
1 tablespoon fresh dill weed
¼ cup minced cucumber
1 teaspoon minced onion

½ teaspoon dry mustard
1 teaspoon chervil
salt and pepper
lemon slices
parsley sprigs

Steam fillets by placing on a greased rack in a frying pan with a little boiling water in the bottom. Cover and simmer for 10 to 15 minutes, until the fish flakes. Chill fillets in the refrigerator. Arrange on a chilled platter. Mix the rest of the ingredients and spread over the fillets as a sauce. Decorate the platter with slices of lemon and sprigs of parsley. Serves 4.

## LAKE TROUT LOUISE

4 skinless lake trout fillets  
1 cup plain yogurt  
1 tablespoon wine vinegar  

1 teaspoon sugar  
2 teaspoons Dijon-type mustard  
5 drops Tabasco sauce  
salt and pepper

Place fillets in a well-greased baking dish. Make sauce of the rest of the ingredients and spread over fillets. Bake in 400° oven for 25 to 30 minutes, until fish flakes when probed with a fork. Serves 4.

## BROILED TROUT

4 skinless lake trout fillets  
2 tablespoons butter  

¼ cup dry vermouth  
½ teaspoon dill weed  
salt and pepper

Place the fillets on a broiler pan. Baste with a sauce made from the rest of the ingredients. Broil, 4 inches from the heat, for about 10 minutes, basting a couple of times during the cooking. Remove from the broiler when the fish flakes. Serves 4.

# Black
# Bass

Black bass, both largemouth and smallmouth, are members of the sunfish family. It seems the more popular a fish, the more regional names for it pop up. To this rule, the bass is no exception. There are at least forty-four names for the largemouth black bass, including some really far-out ones such as green trout and yellow pond perch. The largemouth black bass's range originally extended from Canada through the Great Lakes and Mississippi River systems on into Florida and Mexico. Because of its greater adaptability to warm, still water, the largemouth has been stocked extensively in ponds through most of the United States and parts of Canada, Central America, Europe and Africa. Typical habitat is weedy, mud-bottomed, sluggishly moving fresh water. The largemouth is distinguished from the smallmouth by the size of its mouth, which usually extends back past the eye.

The smallmouth black bass once had a range limited to the Great Lakes drainage system, but it is now found in practically every state and province of North America. Its favorite haunts are clean, cool lakes and large streams with little mud and vegetation.

If the bass fancier is interested in bringing home some fillets for the table, the fish to keep are those of three pounds and under. The flesh from the black bass is lean, with a delicate texture, especially in the small ones. Releasing the breeders is a good conservation practice.

Because the skin can be strongly flavored, it should be removed before cooking. Habitat does make a difference in flesh flavor. In general, you'll find more sportsmen raving over a sweet smallmouth fillet that was taken from a cool Maine pond than a river-bred largemouth from an industrial section of Florida.

I've heard anglers state flatly, "I don't like to eat bass." I'm willing to bet that the only bass they've ever tried were large ones that were fried in a ton of grease, or lunkers that were taken from polluted water or dehydrated from spending a hot day on a boat bottom. Bass fishing in most parts of the United States is primarily a warm-weather sport. If the air temperature is above that of the water from which the fish just emerged, deterioration of the flesh will start immediately, so careful treatment is important if you want an elegant meal.

When fishing from a boat, you can keep bass on a stringer in the water, and if you are careful, the bass will remain alive throughout the day. When moving to another spot, pull the stringer in and place it in the bait bucket or other pail of water. The stringer can be left in the water while you are rowing, but even slow motor speeds may kill the fish. If a fish dies on the stringer, remove it and place in an ice chest or in a shaded place with a wet cloth over it. Dead fish spoil more rapidly in water than out of it.

Anglers who fish from shore should have a chest cooler amply stocked with ice in a nearby car. If you prefer to dress your bass at stream or dockside, it is necessary to carry heavy plastic bags with you. Fish flesh that comes in contact with water becomes soft rapidly. Unless a fillet is actually "dirty," I usually don't wash it but instead wipe both sides with paper toweling immediately before cooking or freezing.

Deep-frying is a traditional way to prepare bass. It also may be one of the most misunderstood cooking treatments. It conjures up visions of fat-soaked fish flesh. Nothing could be further from the truth. If it is handled correctly, the cooking oil never reaches the fish. If the fish and batter are ice cold and the oil is piping hot, the batter cooks instantly when it hits the oil. The fillet is sealed inside and steam-cooks in a couple of minutes. Crisp and delicious!

# BEER-BATTER BASS   *Good*

1¼ pounds thin bass fillets
¼ cup lemon juice
salt and pepper

flour seasoned with salt and pepper
beer batter
cooking oil
tartar sauce

Cut fillets into 1- to 1½-inch strips and toss with the lemon juice and salt and pepper. Let mixture stand for half an hour in refrigerator. Drain the fillets, douse with the seasoned flour, and dip into the well-stirred beer batter. Deep-fry immediately in hot oil (I used peanut oil) at 360° for about 2 minutes. Drain on paper toweling. Keep fillets in a warm oven on a heated platter until all are cooked. Serve with tartar sauce. Will serve 4.

*Note:* I've tried this recipe with the mini deep fryers and found it worked perfectly. I set the temperature control at high and fried 2 strips at a time.

## Beer Batter

¾ cup flour
¼ teaspoon salt

dash of pepper
⅛ teaspoon dill salt
¾ cup beer

Sift flour, salt, pepper, and dill salt together. Blend in the beer. Let set, covered, in the refrigerator for 1 hour.

## CHEESY BASS FILLETS

1 pound bass fillets
3 tablespoons mayonnaise
1 teaspoon prepared mustard
2 teaspoons lemon juice

¼ teaspoon chervil
1 tablespoon grated Parmesan cheese
1 tablespoon bread crumbs
parsley sprigs
lemon wedges

Mix mayonnaise, mustard, lemon juice, and chervil together and spread over the fish fillets. Place the fillets on buttered aluminum foil. Sprinkle with cheese and bread crumbs. Broil 4 inches from heat for 6 to 10 minutes, until the flesh flakes. Thin fillets will take 6 minutes, thicker ones 10. Serve with parsley sprigs and lemon wedges. Serves 4.

*Note:* Penciled on recipe, "Great."

# BASS FLORENTINE

1½ pounds bass fillets
1 onion, sliced
4 tablespoons butter
1 pound fresh spinach
2 cups sliced mushrooms
¼ teaspoon thyme

⅛ teaspoon lemon pepper
½ teaspoon salt
⅓ cup dry white wine
1 tablespoon cornstarch
½ teaspoon salt
lemon wedges

In large skillet, cook onion in 2 tablespoons of butter until tender. Add spinach, mushrooms, and fillets. Dot bass with rest of butter. Sprinkle with thyme, lemon pepper, and ½ teaspoon salt. Add white wine. Cover and cook over low heat until fish flakes easily, 15 to 20 minutes. Place fish on warm platter. Combine cornstarch, ½ teaspoon salt and ¼ cup water. Stir into spinach mixture and cook until thickened and bubbly. Place spinach mixture on platter and cover with fillets. Garnish with lemon wedges. Serves 4.

*Note:* Penciled on recipe, "Excellent."

# ORANGE FILLETS UNDER BLACK-BUTTERED CREAM

1½ to 2 pounds skinless bass fillets
flour
butter
salt
freshly ground pepper
½ cup heavy cream
¼ cup Pinot Chardonnay wine

3 tablespoons finely chopped fresh
  parsley
2 teaspoons grated fresh orange peel
½ teaspoon fresh lemon juice
dash of Tabasco
1 orange, cut in wedges
parsley sprigs

Wipe fish dry. Dust with flour. Heat butter to a depth of ¼ inch in a frying pan, until it is hot. Add fillets and sauté quickly, turning once. When they flake, remove to a heated platter. Season with salt and pepper. Add or remove butter to make ⅓ cup in pan. Heat until it browns deeply. Add cream, wine, chopped parsley, orange peel, lemon juice and Tabasco. Cook over high heat, stirring, until slightly reduced. Pour over fish. Garnish with orange wedges and parsley sprigs. Serves 4.

*Note:* Penciled on recipe, "Super."

# BAKED BASS WITH MUSHROOM STUFFING

1 large (2-pound) bass, cleaned and
  scaled
salt and pepper
1 cup chopped fresh mushrooms
2 teaspoons minced chives or onion

2 tablespoons butter
2 tomatoes, peeled, seeded and chopped
2 tablespoons minced parsley
2 tablespoons lemon juice
Hollandaise sauce

Lightly salt and pepper inside of the bass. Sauté mushrooms and chives or onion in butter until nicely browned. Add tomatoes, parsley and lemon juice and heat thoroughly. Stuff the fish with the mixture and close the cavity with toothpicks or skewers and string (if necessary). Bake in an ovenproof pan in a preheated 400° oven for at least 30 minutes. Check with a toothpick, where the fish is thickest, to see if the flesh will flake before removing from the oven. Serve hot with Hollandaise sauce. Will serve 4.

## STEAMED BASS WITH HOT SAUCE

4 large bass fillets (or 8 small ones)
1 cup chili sauce
2 drops Tabasco sauce
2 tablespoons lemon juice
½ teaspoon salt

¼ teaspoon pepper
1 teaspoon steak sauce
1 teaspoon horseradish
1 tablespoon pickle relish
parsley sprigs

Steam the bass by adding a little water to the bottom of a frying pan or roasting pan. Grease a small rack and place it in the pan. The rack must sit above the water. Lay the fillets on the rack. Cover and steam about 10 minutes until the fish flakes when it is probed with a fork. Combine the rest of the ingredients (except parsley) in a saucepan and simmer for 5 minutes. Transfer the hot, steamed fish to a heated platter and pour a little sauce over each fillet. Serve the rest of the hot sauce in a bowl to be passed at the table. Garnish with parsley sprigs. Serves 4.

*Note:* Penciled on recipe, "Great."

## *LEFTOVERS*

The next three recipes utilize bass that is either left over from another recipe or has been steamed specifically for the dish. To steam bass, follow the directions in Steamed Bass with Hot Sauce.

## BASS SALAD

1½ pounds bass fillets, steamed
juice of ½ lemon
1 cup finely chopped celery
1 teaspoon salt

2 tablespoons paprika
mayonnaise
lettuce cups
4 sprigs parsley

Flake the cooked fish and chill. When cool, add lemon juice, celery, salt and paprika and toss lightly with enough mayonnaise to moisten. Arrange in lettuce cups and garnish with a sprig of parsley. Serves 4.

# NORMA'S FISH CHOWDER

1½ cups chunks leftover bass
½ cup diced celery
⅔ cup diced onions
½ cup diced green pepper
2 tablespoons butter
1 cup corn, cut from the cob (or frozen)
2 cups diced potatoes
½ cup diced carrots
½ cup finely chopped mushrooms
¼ cup crisply cooked bacon bits

2 hard-boiled eggs, chopped fine
1 teaspoon salt
pepper and garlic salt to taste
2 tablespoons minced parsley
½ teaspoon dill weed
1 tablespoon lemon juice
⅛ teaspoon fennel (optional)
2 cups fish broth
1 cup light cream
paprika

Sauté celery, onions and green pepper for 7 minutes in the butter in a large saucepan. Add all other ingredients except the fish, cream and paprika. Use water if fish broth is not available. Mix and then bring to a boil. Cover and simmer for 20 minutes. Test the vegetables. If they are tender, add more salt and pepper if necessary. Add fish and cream, bring just to the boiling point, simmer lightly for about 10 minutes and serve, sprinkling with paprika. Serves 6.

*Note:* "Best chowder I've ever had—simply great."

## BASS CANAPÉS

2 cups flaked, cooked bass
¼ cup mayonnaise
½ teaspoon steak sauce
salt and pepper to taste
¼ teaspoon dill weed

2 drops Tabasco sauce
24 small bread rounds
butter
1 large cucumber, peeled and chopped
        fine
pimiento

Mix bass, mayonnaise, steak sauce, salt and pepper, dill weed and Tabasco together well. Add more mayonnaise if needed to hold the mixture together. Spread bread rounds with a thin layer of butter and a layer of cucumber. Salt and pepper lightly. Mound with the fish mixture. Place under broiler (4 inches from the heat) for a few minutes to brown slightly. Decorate with a slice of pimiento and serve immediately.

## SEVICHE

1 pound bass fillets, skinned and cut into
        bite-sized chunks (uncooked)
½ teaspoon salt
1 medium onion, sliced

1 small green pepper, sliced
5 drops Tabasco sauce
1 garlic clove, minced
limes or lemons

Put the fish and the rest of the ingredients in a bowl and cover with fresh-squeezed lime or lemon juice. Cover and refrigerate overnight. Drain and serve with crisp melba rounds. As a first-course cocktail, this recipe will serve 4. As a snack, you may want to double it.

*Note:* At first glance this appears to be raw fish. However, the citrus juice "cooks" the fish. If you've never tried pickled fish, give it a whirl—it's low in calories.

# Northern
# Pike

There seems to be no middle-of-the-road opinion about the northern pike. It is either loved or hated. Where the northern is on the small side or where it is not the preferred species in a lake or river, the mere mention of its name brings a sneer. It is blamed for gobbling up many of the young of the "glamour" fish (and it does). Also, it is quick to grab the lure or bait that is meant for that same preferred fish. But the northern is often the salvation of many a fishing trip, in both the United States and Canada.

Few freshwater fish, pound for pound, battle harder, jump higher or strike with more gusto than the northern pike. I spent a week at a fishing camp in Labrador a few years ago. The headlined fish were large (4- to 6-pound) brook trout that frequented the Little Minipi River. We had lots of fun catching the big brutes but decided to take a day out in the middle of the week to try for some of the large northerns that preyed on the brook trout and lived in a connecting lake. Those large northerns, caught on fly rods with streamers, were supersport. Spectacular jumps, long runs and a battle right up to netting time made that day a highlight of the trip.

Yet our guides, although polite, were reluctant to touch the "snakes," as they called the pike. When we decided to keep one for camp food, it was the youngest guide who was assigned the task of filleting the beast. After eating fried brook trout earlier in the week, we found fried pike (not the preferred method of cooking pike, either) a delicacy.

What the guides didn't realize is that unless there is heavy predation from a voracious eater like the northern, brook trout just can't grow to a large size because there are too many of them for the food supply. The northern pike, which feeds only in the daytime, will eat practically anything that moves, including young birds, mice and muskrats. Because of this appetite, the pike is one of the fastest-growing freshwater fish.

The meat of the northern pike is sweet, white and firm. Poaching, baking and smoking are among the preferred cooking methods. I like to fillet most of my pike, but if you wish to bake a whole one, it is best to scale it. Because the pike is long for its weight, it will undoubtedly be necessary to cut the head and the tail off to fit it in (or on) a pan to bake or poach one whole. But no problem, you only lose the cheek meat on the head, and that head isn't particularly handsome on a fish platter anyway.

## BAKED PIKE

| | |
|---|---|
| 1 large pike, scaled and gutted | 2 bay leaves, crushed |
| butter | 1 cup milk |
| salt and pepper | parsley sprigs |
| onion salt | mustard sauce |

Cover a large cookie sheet with heavy-duty aluminum foil and turn up the edges. Butter the foil. Place the whole pike on the foil and brush with melted butter, inside and out. Sprinkle the fish with salt and pepper, onion salt and bay leaves. Heat milk and pour over the fish. Place the fish in a preheated 450° oven and bake about 12 minutes per pound or 10 minutes per inch of thickness. Check fish at the thickest place along the backbone. Remove to a heated platter, strip off the skin and garnish with parsley. Serve with mustard sauce. Count on 1 serving per pound of fish.

### Mustard Sauce

| | |
|---|---|
| 1 tablespoon butter | ½ teaspoon powdered mustard |
| 1 tablespoon flour | ⅓ cup grated Parmesan cheese |
| 1 cup milk | salt and pepper |

Melt butter in saucepan, blend in flour and then milk. Cook until thickened. Add rest of ingredients and serve with fish.

# POACHED PIKE

1 large pike, scaled and gutted
3 green onions
1 garlic clove

3 sprigs parsley
salt and pepper
⅛ teaspoon thyme
horseradish sauce

Place enough water to cover the fish into a large roasting pan with the onions, garlic, parsley, salt and pepper and thyme. Cover and simmer for 15 minutes. Add fish, bring to a boil, lower heat and simmer until the fish flakes when probed with a fork—about 10 minutes per inch of thickness. Drain and serve on heated platter with horseradish sauce. Count on 1 serving per pound of fish.

*Note:* Penciled on recipe, "Great."

## Horseradish Sauce

6 tablespoons butter
1 tablespoon lemon juice

1 teaspoon horseradish
1 tablespoon minced parsley
½ teaspoon savory

Melt the butter in a saucepan and add rest of ingredients. Serve with poached pike.

# BOILED PIKE

3 pounds pike fillets, cut into chunks
1 whole onion
2 tablespoons salt
20 peppercorns

2 tablespoons vinegar
2 tablespoons sugar
2 bay leaves
melted butter

Put onion, salt, peppercorns, vinegar, sugar and bay leaves into 3 quarts water and bring to a boil. Simmer for 15 minutes. Add fish, bring to another boil and cook for 10 minutes. Serve the chunks dipped in melted butter. Serves 6.

*Note:* Penciled on recipe, "Excellent."

# NORTHERN PIKE CREOLE

1 pound cooked pike, flaked
¼ cup butter
3 tablespoons chopped onion
½ cup chopped celery
3 tablespoons chopped green pepper
1 minced garlic clove

¼ cup flour
3 cups chopped tomatoes
1 bay leaf
½ teaspoon salt
⅛ teaspoon pepper
dash of red pepper

1 tablespoon sugar

Melt butter in a frying pan and add onion, celery, green pepper and garlic. Sauté for 7 minutes. Blend in flour. Add tomatoes, seasonings and sugar, mix and simmer for 20 minutes. Add fish, remove bay leaf and bring to a boil. Serve over hot rice. Will serve 4.

## CHARCOAL-BROILED PIKE FINGERS

2 pounds skinned pike fillet, cut into
    fingers
4 tablespoons butter
        orange sauce

1 onion, chunked
1 teaspoon oregano
½ teaspoon salt

Butter a large piece of heavy-duty aluminum foil and add fish, butter, onion, oregano and salt. Wrap and place on a hot grill over charcoal coals. Grill about 15 minutes, depending on how hot the coals are. Serve with orange sauce. Will serve 4 or 5.

### Orange Sauce

¼ cup melted butter
¼ cup fresh orange juice

½ teaspoon thyme
1 teaspoon minced parsley

Mix together and serve with pike fingers.

## PIKE BURGERS

2 pounds skinless small pike
2 eggs, beaten
1 tablespoon lemon juice
1 teaspoon minced parsley

6 drops Tabasco sauce
1 tablespoon minced onion
dried, crushed bread crumbs
butter

Small pike can be ground in the meat grinder (fine setting), bones and all. Mix the ground pike with the eggs, lemon juice, parsley, Tabasco, onion and enough bread crumbs to form balls. Fry patties in hot butter. Serves 6.

# Walleye

Wherever the walleye is found in abundance, it's considered a prime target by anglers. They are a school fish that bite readily and are also tasty in the pot. Unlike the northern pike, the walleye feeds primarily in the evening and at night and will be found on or close to the bottom of a lake or river. One of the favorite methods to angle for the walleye is to troll slowly across sandbars near a deep drop-off. The walleye is a slow, methodical feeder that likes to study its prey, mostly small fish. When trolling, the successful angler will either row or use an electric motor. When a school is located, a gentle, enticing twitch of the wrist and a superslow retrieve will usually take several of these delicious fish in a short time.

Walleye grow faster in the warmer states in the TVA impoundments of Tennessee and Kentucky than they do in Canada because they are sensitive to temperature and stop actively feeding when it gets cold. A record 25-pounder came from Tennessee.

In the early 1800s, the walleye was stocked in Pennsylvania. It flourished and was dubbed the Susquehanna salmon when it brought top dollar on the commercial market. The walleye, which is commonly miscalled walleyed pike, pickerel or jack, is actually a close relative of the yellow perch. This makes sense because it is difficult to decide which has the best-tasting flesh. The walleye is so versatile that there is no limit to the ways it can be cooked. It is one of the few fish that can be fried perfectly.

Three of my favorite walleye meals were prepared by guides and were such standouts that I have to share them with you.

Charlie, from Stramond Lodge in Quebec, believed in a hearty shore lunch. After the fire was roaring, several thick slabs of good Canadian bacon were fried. Thin slices of raw potatoes went in the huge skillet next. When the potatoes were tender, Charlie put them in some foil by the side of the fire and was ready to cook the fish.

After filleting the walleyes, Charlie would give them a quick wash in the lake water. He then put them in a plastic bag with a package of the Shake'n Bake mixture for fish. A couple of quick shakes and the fish was well coated and ready to fry in the hot bacon fat. Charlie turned them once, drained them on paper toweling and we were ready for our shore lunch feast. It was great.

Walleye is featured at the annual Voyageur Day Celebration held each July at Crane Lake, Boundary Waters Canoe Area in Minnesota. The billing says *World's Largest Outdoor Walleye Fish Fry* and I believe it. A whole row of guides line up to fry the fillets in gigantic skillets, half full of hot cooking oil over open fires (in July yet). They feed thousands in a few hours and the fish is delicious.

I sidled up to the Crane Lake natives in charge of coating the fresh fillets with a white substance, prior to the frying. What was in the coating? They simply smiled and went on with their work. Intrigued, I kept asking until one kind woman answered "It's only Aunt Jemima's pancake mix!" And so it was. When the natural flavor is as good as the walleye's, simple cooking can be the best.

Orville, from Saskatchewan, likes to involve others in his walleye preparations. For instance, my job at shore lunchtime was to crush the cracker crumbs (I used a Scotch bottle). Ordinary cracker crumbs were not good enough for Orville, they had to be finely powdered. The finished dish reflected his fussiness; it was superb!

## ORVILLE'S WALLEYE FILLETS

4 large skinless, boneless walleye fillets
1 egg
½ cup evaporated milk

1 cup *finely* powdered cracker crumbs
salt and pepper
cooking oil

Beat egg and milk together (at home, I use light cream). Coat the fillets thoroughly with the egg mixture and douse in cracker crumbs. Add salt and pepper to taste. Fry quickly over hot fire in a heavy skillet with hot oil. Serves 4.

## BROILED WALLEYE

4 large walleye fillets
⅓ cup sliced almonds, crushed
2 teaspoons lemon juice
1 tablespoon prepared mustard

1 teaspoon soy sauce
salt and pepper
1 teaspoon sugar
1 shake red pepper

¼ cup heavy cream

Place the walleye fillets on a greased broiler pan. Mix all the rest of the ingredients together and spread evenly over the fish. Broil, 5 inches from the heat, for about 10 minutes or until the fish flakes. Serves 4.

## WALLEYE VERONIQUE

1½ to 2 pounds walleye fillets
2 tablespoons minced onion
½ cup fish broth (or chicken broth)
¼ cup dry white wine

½ cup seedless green grapes, halved
salt and pepper
paprika
parsley sprigs

Place onion, broth and wine in a heavy skillet. Bring to a boil and add fillets to the pan. Cover and simmer for 5 minutes. Add grapes and simmer another 5 minutes or until the fish flakes when probed with fork. Use a pancake turner to remove the fillets to a heated platter.

Reduce the liquid in the pan to about ¼ cup and spoon over fillets with the grapes. Salt and pepper to taste and sprinkle with paprika. Garnish with parsley. Serves 4.

*Note:* "Simple but excellent."

# VEGETABLE-DRESSED WALLEYE

4 large walleye fillets
1 tablespoon lemon juice
vegetable stuffing

2 tablespoons butter
2 tablespoons dry white wine
lemon slices
parsley sprigs

Lay the fillets on a well-buttered shallow baking dish. Sprinkle the fish with lemon juice. Lightly cover with stuffing. Drizzle the wine over the stuffing and dot with butter. Cover the dish and bake in a preheated 350° oven for 20 minutes. Uncover and cook another 15 minutes or until the fillets flake when probed with a fork. Garnish with lemon slices and parsley. Will serve 4.

*Note:* Penciled on recipe, "Great."

## Vegetable Stuffing

½ cup chopped celery
¼ cup chopped onion
⅓ cup chopped green pepper
¼ cup thinly sliced carrot
¼ cup butter

1 cup soft bread crumbs
1 cup chopped tomato
1 tablespoon minced parsley
½ teaspoon dill weed
salt and pepper to taste

Sauté the celery, onion, green pepper and carrots in butter for 10 minutes. Add rest of ingredients and mix well.

## WALLEYES WITH CREAM

1½ pounds walleye fillets
1 carrot
½ small zucchini
½ cup dry vermouth

⅓ cup heavy cream
2 tablespoons minced green onion
salt and pepper
paprika

Cut the carrot and zucchini into very thin (matchstick-size) strips, about 4 inches long. Put the vermouth in a large, heavy skillet. Add the carrots and poach for 6 minutes, covered. Add zucchini and cook, covered, another 4 minutes. Put the vegetables on a heated platter, reduce the wine to a few tablespoons and add cream and onion. When hot, add walleye fillets, cover and simmer until they flake when touched with a fork. They may be turned while simmering if they are large fillets. Cooking time will be about 10 minutes. Place them on the heated platter, season with salt and pepper and surround with the poached vegetables. If the cream/wine mixture is too thin, reduce it over the heat slightly, then pour over the cooked fillets. Dust with paprika and serve immediately. Serves 4.

*Note:* "Succulent."

# ROBERT'S WALLEYES

4 walleye fillets
2 tablespoons dry vermouth
2 tablespoons butter
2 tablespoons flour
¾ cup milk

½ teaspoon horseradish
salt and pepper
⅓ cup soft bread crumbs
1 tablespoon grated Parmesan cheese
paprika
chopped parsley

Pour the dry vermouth in a shallow, buttered baking pan and place in a 350° oven for 7 minutes. While the wine is heating, make a white sauce by melting the butter in a saucepan, adding the flour and blending in the milk. Cook until the sauce is thick. Add horseradish and salt and pepper to taste. Place the fillets in the baking pan on the vermouth. Salt and pepper them. Spread the sauce over the fillets and place in a preheated broiler (4 inches from the heat) for 6 minutes. Remove from oven, sprinkle with bread crumbs and cheese. Broil for another 4 minutes or until the fish flakes when probed with a fork. Shake a little paprika over the cooked fillets and garnish with chopped parsley. Serve immediately. Will serve 4.

*Note:* Penciled on recipe, "Good."

# *Salmon*

Unlike other fish that have survived since ancient times such as the carp and pike, the salmon was not merely an edible food. Stone Age paintings indicate that primitive man considered the salmon gourmet fare. It never lost that respect through the years. In the Middle Ages in Europe, elaborately decorated platters of beautifully cooked salmon were shepherded to the food-laden tables with trumpets. It was the *pièce de résistance* amid the many meat courses.

This same kind of salmon mystique carries over to infect the angler. Once fishermen have had a running, slashing, jumping fireball at the end of the flyline, they are hooked for life. Some fish run farther, some jump higher, but none put it all together like the salmon, especially the sea-run varieties.

Like the shad, it is a puzzle why the sea-run salmon strikes at our flies when it enters fresh water. It could be reflex action or even anger, but whatever the reason, it will not swallow anything. Since the stomach of a salmon will be empty, if the salmon is going to be frozen, I suggest that it not be gutted until after thawing. Remove the gills only. There is nothing to spoil in that stomach. And the fish that has not been opened up will keep better in the frozen state.

Salmon caught in the United States can be the Atlantic or the three Pacific species, chinook, coho and sockeye. All four of them also occur as land-locked. At times, what the landlocked salmon feed on in the Great Lakes, or in other lakes, causes the flesh to be less desirable on the table than their sea-run counterparts. However, I have proved to my satisfaction that when you prepare all salmon with simple recipes, you will be rewarded with superb flavor.

Not long ago I cooked Lake Erie coho, using two different recipes, for a large number of Erie natives, many of whom either fished themselves or had someone in their families who consistently brought salmon home. I was astounded when they raved over the salmon, saying that they had never tasted better fish. One said she would never again give away the salmon her son caught. Imagine, giving away salmon! I should have asked what horrible cooking method had caused her to turn away from the fish. But I didn't. I was afraid she would answer "frying" and I would not be able to control my face. Salmon is an oily fish, as are mackerel, bluefish, and lake trout among others. Frying is at the bottom of the cooking methods for oily fish—in fact, it really shouldn't even be considered. As with all the oily fish, salmon can be smoked perfectly. Check the chapter on smoking for a good recipe.

The fish boil has been growing in popularity as a favorite method of cooking Great Lakes salmon. There are many formulas and fancy methods for mass production of the boil by communities along the lakes, but you can do it at home by simply bringing a pot full of salted water to the boiling point and adding chunks of salmon. Boil for 10 minutes, drain the salmon and serve with melted butter. It's a super way to treat Great Lakes salmon.

Poaching has to be my favorite cooking method for salmon. Once poached, the fish may be served either hot or cold with a simple sauce.

## POACHED SALMON

| | |
|---|---|
| 1 whole 6- to 12-pound salmon, cleaned | 3 bay leaves |
| ½ cup dry white wine | salt |
| 1 stalk celery | peppercorns |
| 1 scrubbed carrot | lemon slices, sprigs of parsley, slices of |
| 1 onion, cut into chunks | sweet red pepper, etc. |
| salmon sauce | |

Fill a large roasting pan to about the halfway point with hot water. Add wine, celery, carrot, onion, bay leaves, salt and peppercorns. Cover and bring to a boil. Simmer for 15 minutes to marry all the flavors. Wipe the salmon with paper toweling. The fish may be wrapped in cheesecloth to make it easier to lift it from the court bouillon or it may be placed in the bouillon and moved about with pancake turners. Add the fish to the bouillon and bring it to a boil again. Start timing when it reaches a boil. Simmer for 10 minutes per inch of thickness of the fish (measure at the thickest place on the back). Most salmon will take between 20 to 30 minutes. If the fish is not totally immersed in the water, it will have to be turned once during the poaching time. This is where the cheesecloth, with the ends dangling from the ends of the pan, is handy.

Before removing the fish from the liquid, check at the thickest place on the backbone with a fork. If the flesh flakes when it is probed, it is done. Remove the poached salmon to a heated platter. Carefully peel the skin from top side of the cooked salmon and decorate with colorful garnishes such as lemon slices, parsley and red pepper. If at all possible, the head and tail should be retained on the platter. The eye may be replaced by a small ripe olive. The small piece of cheek meat should be presented at the table to the guest of honor. Serve with a dollop of salmon sauce. Count on 1 serving per pound.

## Salmon Sauce

| | |
|---|---|
| 1 cup mayonnaise | 1 teaspoon steak sauce |
| ¼ cup prepared mustard | ½ teaspoon dill weed |
| 1 tablespoon lemon juice | ¼ teaspoon salt |
| | pepper |

Mix all ingredients together and serve with salmon, either hot or cold.

## BAKED WHOLE SALMON

| | |
|---|---|
| 1 large (4- to 6-pound) salmon, cleaned | 5 tablespoons butter |
| 2 onions, cut in thin slices | salt and pepper to taste |
| 1 small green pepper, cut in thin slices | 3 strips bacon (optional) |
| 1 small zucchini, cut in thin slices | melted butter |
| 1 small sliced tomato | lemon juice |
| 6 sprigs of parsley | chervil |

Preheat oven to 450° and line baking dish or large roasting pan with heavy-duty foil. Butter the foil. Place the cleaned salmon in the foil. Stuff the cavity of the fish with sliced vegetables, dot with butter and add salt and pepper. Secure the stuffing with toothpicks. If you wish to add bacon, place on the fish skin and close the foil package lightly. Bake about 10 minutes per inch of thickness of the fish after everything has heated to the cooking point, about 5 minutes. After 30 minutes (for a 4- to 6-pound fish) check the fish at the thickest point with a fork. If the flesh flakes, it is done. Place fish on a warm platter, remove top skin and garnish. Can be served with melted butter laced with a little lemon juice and chervil. Will serve 6.

## CHARCOAL-BROILED SALMON FILLETS

4 large salmon fillets (with skin)
½ teaspoon steak sauce
2 shakes bitters
½ teaspoon lemon juice
pinch of: thyme, basil, oregano, MSG

couple of shakes of: paprika, parsley flakes, chives, garlic salt, salt and pepper
1 tablespoon grated Parmesan cheese
¾ cup mayonnaise

Mix all spices and seasonings thoroughly with the mayonnaise and spread on fillets. Broil on a charcoal grill, skin side down, for 15 to 20 minutes (if the grill is medium-hot). Use a foil blanket to cover the fillets lightly. The mayonnaise mixture will brown and the herbs will soak into the fish flesh. Serves 4.

*Note:* Penciled on recipe, "Absolutely great recipe."

## GEORGE RIVER SALMON

4 salmon steaks, cut about 1 inch thick
3 tablespoons Dijon-type mustard
2 tablespoons olive oil

½ cup dry white wine
salt and pepper
parsley

Mix the mustard, oil, wine and salt and pepper together in a bowl. Add the salmon steaks to the sauce and marinate in the refrigerator for 2 hours, turning often. Place the steaks on a buttered piece of foil on a broiler pan. Preheat the oven broiler. Place steaks 4 inches from heat source and broil until they flake, about 10 minutes. Twice during the cooking, brush with some of the marinade. Serve garnished with parsley. Will serve 4.

*Note:* Penciled on recipe, "Excellent—pungent flavor."

## LUCKY SALMON

4 salmon steaks, cut 1 inch thick
¾ cup mayonnaise
3 tablespoons Dijon-type mustard
¼ teaspoon dill weed

⅛ teaspoon chili powder
½ teaspoon celery salt
pinch garlic powder
1 teaspoon lemon juice

Broil salmon steaks (4 inches from the heat) for 4 minutes on each side. Mix the rest of the ingredients and spread over the steaks. Place under the broiler again and broil until nicely brown, another 2 to 3 minutes. Check to be sure the fish is done by probing with a toothpick. Serves 4.

*Note:* Penciled on recipe, "Great."

# SALMON MOUSSE

1 pound boneless, skinless raw salmon  
2 egg whites (medium size)  
1 teaspoon sugar  
¼ teaspoon grated nutmeg  

¼ teaspoon pepper  
2 cups heavy cream  
wine sauce  
capers  

watercress or parsley

Crush fish in a mortar (or use a food processor) until it is completely pulverized. Add unbeaten egg whites and mix thoroughly. Keep the fish ice-cold. The easiest way to do this during the mixing is to place the bowl of pulverized fish in a bigger bowl containing ice. Season with sugar, nutmeg and pepper and mix thoroughly. Add the cream, a little at a time, and mix in with a wooden spoon until the fish has entirely disappeared. Oil 5 custard cups and divide the mixture between them. Set the cups in a pan containing *boiling* water and place in a preheated 375° oven to poach for about 30 minutes. Turn out onto small plates, serve with a dollop of wine sauce, a few capers and a sprig of watercress or parsley. Serves 5. "Simple but elegant."

*Note:* After the cream has been added, the bowl (still in the ice) can be held in the refrigerator a couple of hours until baking time. Mix again slightly, pour in custard cups and proceed with the steps.

## Wine Sauce

½ cup dry vermouth  
1 tablespoon minced onion  
¼ teaspoon crushed tarragon  

1½ tablespoons butter  
1 tablespoon snipped parsley  
dash of salt and pepper  

In a saucepan, combine the wine, onion and tarragon. Bring to a boil and simmer uncovered for 3 minutes. Remove from heat and add rest of ingredients.

# PICKLED SALMON

1-pound chunk of skinless, boneless
    salmon
5 parts of wine vinegar
1 part brandy
1 teaspoon salt

½ teaspoon rosemary
½ teaspoon freshly ground pepper
dash of: garlic salt, celery salt, dill weed,
    red pepper
3 drops Tabasco sauce

Mix all ingredients in a bowl and place the chunk of salmon in it. Cover and refrigerate for 48 hours, turning the salmon often. Slice thin and serve with crackers or rye bread. Serves 16 to 20.

## *LEFTOVERS*

The next three recipes utilize leftover cooked salmon—or you can poach a fillet or the tail section to use in the recipes. All three are favorites.

## SALMON QUICHE

baked piecrust shell
½ cup flaked, cooked salmon (firmed in
    the measuring cup)
3 large eggs
¼ teaspoon salt
pinch of nutmeg

pinch of pepper
heavy cream
1 teaspoon minced parsley
1½ tablespoons butter
capers
parsley sprigs

Place the salmon in the bottom of the baked piecrust. In a quart-sized measuring cup, break the eggs and beat. Add salt, nutmeg and pepper and enough cream to bring the liquid up to the 1⅓ cup mark. Mix. Pour the mixture over the salmon and sprinkle the minced parsley over the top. Cut the butter into chunks and drop on the top. Place the quiche in a preheated 375° oven and bake for 30 minutes. Check by inserting a knife in the center. If it comes out clean, custard is done. Remove from oven and let cool for 10 minutes. Serve in wedges as an appetizer, first course or luncheon dish. Decorate each piece with a sprinkling of capers and a sprig of parsley. Makes 6 to 10 servings.
*Note:* Penciled on recipe, "Excellent."

# MECATINA SALMON SALAD

2 cups cooked salmon, bite-sized chunks
2 hard-boiled eggs, cut in quarters
1 cup cucumber, bite-sized chunks
½ cup celery, bite-sized chunks
10 ripe olives, halved

2 tablespoons chopped green onion
1 tomato, cut in chunks
1½ cup lettuce chunks (bite-sized)
dressing
Romaine lettuce

2 tablespoons capers

Combine first eight ingredients and toss with dressing. Arrange on a bed of lettuce and sprinkle with the capers. Serves 4.

*Note:* "Great on a hot day."

## Dressing

½ cup mayonnaise
½ cup sour cream
¼ cup finely chopped watercress
2 tablespoons finely chopped parsley

½ teaspoon tarragon
1 teaspoon lemon juice
4 drops Tabasco sauce
shake of red pepper

salt and pepper to taste

Mix all ingredients together and refrigerate for a couple of hours before using on the salad.

## SALMON LOAF

1 cup cooked, flaked salmon
1 tablespoon melted butter
2 eggs, well beaten

1 cup hot milk
salt and pepper to taste
1 cup soft bread crumbs

½ teaspoon steak sauce

Mix all ingredients together well. Pour into a well-greased loaf pan and place in a preheated 350° oven. Bake for 30 minutes, until the custard is set. Serves 4.

# Shad

Shad, the "poor man's salmon," was a food fish long before it was known to have sporting value. Early colonists learned to enjoy shad flesh as the Indians had done before them, and the fish became a staple food. Smoked, it was carted to inland residents and used as a barter item.

About 100 years ago, rod-and-reel fishing for shad got underway. Surprisingly, a lot of early sportfishing for the white shad was done with dry flies. Present-day casters usually don't consider the shad a surface feeder, and when they do use fly tackle, weighted flies and sinking lines are preferred. Trolling seems to be the most popular way to catch shad in recent years. Small silver wobbling spoons and colorful jigs fished with spinning tackle are the favorite lures.

The American shad is found from Florida to the Gulf of St. Lawrence on the East Coast and from San Diego to southern Alaska in the West. Shad do not have the powerful homing instinct of the salmon and they don't always return to their parent stream. This is probably the reason they spread so quickly after being planted on the West Coast in the Sacramento River in the mid-1800s.

After spawning, the adult shad generally return to the ocean. Spawning starts during the winter months in the southern part of the United States where the shad wait until the water becomes cool enough to suit them. The spawning pattern continues northward along the coast during the spring until the fish reach the St. Lawrence in June. Newly hatched young stay in the freshwater streams until fall, when they make the trek to the sea for several years of eating and growing before they, in turn, return for the spring ritual.

American, or white, shad will average 4 pounds (they run from 1½ to 8) and are a hard-fighting game fish. Most fish that spend much of their lives in salt water seem to have more energy pound for pound than their freshwater cousins.

Shad, like salmon, do not eat (in fact, are not capable of eating) once they enter fresh water for spawning purposes. They strike lures, it is supposed, to "kill" that odd-looking creature lurking near them. A protective instinct or a remembrance of food in the past is the logical explanation. Even if they try to swallow the lure, it won't go down and is eventually released. They undoubtedly do the same thing with small minnows and other real food.

Shad, once caught, should be put on ice as soon as possible. If you wish to bake the fish whole or leave the skin on it, it is necessary to scale it. Otherwise, slit the female shad up the belly and remove the roe. Then fillet it as you would any large game fish. Once you have removed the back and rib bones, you still have to contend with two rows of "floating" Y bones. These are nearly impossible for an amateur fish cleaner to remove without much loss of fish flesh.

If you can find a professional shad deboner when you dock your boat, by all means hire him. His price is worth it. Otherwise, learn to cope with those bones. That is what my family has done. In my household, we eat shad with two hands, the right one guiding the fork to tender morsels of fish, the left hand deftly removing the bones from the flaking meat. It is really quite easy once you get the hang of it.

Some recipes advocate the "cook it to death" method of coping with bones. The bones become soft and are eaten with the meat. I tried that with the first shad I ever caught in the Susquehanna River. I hated it. The American shad is too delicate to overcook (most recipes suggest 6 hours).

# CHARCOALED SHAD

1 4-pound shad, cleaned and scaled
1 garlic clove, slivered
3 tablespoons butter

1 lemon, thinly sliced
lemon wedges
parsley sprigs

Wipe the fish well with paper toweling and place on a piece of buttered, heavy-duty aluminum foil. Put the garlic, butter and lemon slices in the fish cavity. Wrap the fish in the foil, leaving the ends open so the charcoal flavor can reach the fish. Place the fish on the grill about 3 inches from the coals for 15 to 20 minutes on each side. When you turn the fish, make sure the butcher-fold seal is tight so you don't lose any of the juices. Turn the ends up the other way. When the shad is done, discard skin, cooked lemon and garlic. Serve with fresh lemon wedges and sprigs of parsley. Serves 4.

*Note:* Penciled on recipe, "Excellent."

# ALMOND-STUFFED SHAD

1 3- to 4-pound dressed and scaled shad
juice of 1 lemon

salt
almond stuffing

Wash and dry the fish. Sprinkle inside and out with lemon juice and salt. Fill with stuffing and close opening with skewers. Bake in shallow pan at 350° in a preheated oven, 15 minutes per pound, until the flesh at the thickest part flakes when tested with a toothpick. Serves 4.

## Almond Stuffing

½ cup chopped onion
2 cups chopped celery
¼ cup butter
⅓ cup orange juice

1 teaspoon salt
⅛ teaspoon pepper
1 cup dry bread crumbs
¾ cup toasted, slivered almonds

Sauté the onion and celery in butter until tender. Add the rest of the ingredients and mix well.

# BLACK EDDY SHAD

2 pounds shad fillets, skinless
1 tablespoon minced onion
2 tablespoons lemon juice
parsley sprigs

3 tablespoons melted butter
salt and pepper to taste
½ teaspoon chervil

Place fish on a greased oven-proof shallow pan. Combine the other ingredients (except parsley) and spread over fillets. Place under a heated broiler, 4 inches from the heat, for about 10 minutes, until the meat flakes when probed with a fork. Garnish with parsley. Serves 4.

*Note:* "Simple but excellent."

## SHAD WITH SOUFFLÉ OF ROE

| | |
|---|---|
| 2 large shad fillets (or 4 small ones) | salt and pepper |
| ½ pound shad roe | grated nutmeg |
| ½ cup butter | flour |
| 4 tablespoons flour | 1 ounce dry vermouth |
| ¾ cup milk | 2 tablespoons chopped green onions |
| 3 eggs, separated | lemon butter |
| parsley or watercress sprigs | |

Melt half the butter (4 tablespoons) in a saucepan and blend in flour. Add milk slowly and cook and stir until mixture thickens. Add small amount of sauce to beaten egg yolks, blend and mix into rest of sauce gradually. Season with salt and pepper and a pinch of nutmeg and set aside to cool. Dust roe with flour and sauté in rest of butter for 10 to 15 minutes. Add wine for the last 2 minutes of cooking. Cut the roe into ½-inch slices and allow to cool in the butter/wine sauce.

Cut shad fillets into halves lengthwise. Butter 4 individual baking dishes and shape the fillets in a circle around the inside of the dish, leaving a hole in the center for the soufflé mixture. Salt and pepper the fish. Beat egg whites until stiff but not dry and fold into cooled sauce and roe. Divide equally between the 4 dishes, spooning into the center. Bake at 350° for about 30 minutes until soufflé is firm and fish flakes. If necessary, brown the top under broiler for a minute. Dribble a little butter mixed with some lemon juice on each dish and garnish with greens. Serves 4.

*Note:* "Great recipe adapted from one served by the Riverfront Restaurant in Philadelphia."

## HERB-BAKED SHAD

| | |
|---|---|
| 2 large shad fillets, cut in half | ¼ cup chopped parsley |
| 1 large onion, sliced | ¼ teaspoon thyme |
| 5 tablespoons butter | ⅛ teaspoon dill weed |
| 1 cup soft bread crumbs | ⅛ teaspoon sage |
| ⅓ cup chopped celery with leaves | ½ teaspoon salt |

Butter an oven-proof baking dish and place the fillets on it. Sauté the onion slices in 4 tablespoons of the butter until they are soft. Add the rest of the ingredients (except remaining butter) and mix well. Cover the fillets with the stuffing. Put a little chunk of butter on top of each fillet. Place in a preheated 450° oven and bake for 15 to 20 minutes, until the fish flakes when probed with a fork. Serves 4.

*Note:* Penciled on recipe, "Very good."

## SHAD ROE

Shad roe is a gourmet treat; it is a heavy food and a little goes a long way. Here are a couple of my favorite recipes. The first goes well with either scrambled or poached eggs as a special brunch or can be served as a companion to broiled fillet of shad. The second recipe is a sort of show-off thing. Invite your friends over for a bottle of beer, a glass of white wine or a cocktail and let them taste a little bounty of the earth.

## BROILED SHAD ROE

1 pair shad roe (from 1 shad)
2 tablespoons dry vermouth
rosemary

butter
garlic salt
4 slices bacon
parsley sprigs

Place the roe in a saucepan with the dry vermouth and a pinch of rosemary. Cover with boiling water and simmer for 8 minutes. Drain and cut each roe into two pieces. Place on foil on a broiler pan, sprinkle with garlic salt, dot with butter and cover each piece with a bacon slice. Broil 4 inches from the heat for 10 minutes. Serve on hot buttered toast, garnished with parsley. Will serve 4.

## SHAD ROE TEMPTIES

1 pair shad roe
2 tablespoons prepared mustard
2 teaspoons parsley flakes

1 teaspoon onion flakes
⅛ teaspoon garlic powder
½ teaspoon salt
½ teaspoon celery salt

Place the roe in a saucepan, cover with boiling water and simmer for 10 minutes. Break the drained roe into very small pieces and mix well with remaining ingredients. Spread thinly on crackers or thin toast points as appetizers. Serves 8 to 10.

# *Panfish*

Panfish provide a lot of sportfishing to youngsters all over North America because they can be readily caught with simple tackle and natural bait, such as worms, crickets and grasshoppers. Once the young angler knows where to look for the quarry, they are relatively easy to catch. Most panfish are school fish and are usually deliberate about taking bait. A too-fast strike can take the hook out of the fish's mouth. But youngsters don't ordinarily react to a nibble quickly and therefore are often more successful panfishermen than their more alert mentors. Because these little fish are the main target of many icefishing trips, the angling season is longer for them than for most other species. Another big plus is that panfish in many ponds need to be regularly harvested or they can become stunted from overpopulation.

Yellow perch, crappie, bluegill, bullhead, pumpkinseed and rock bass are the most common panfish. Although they are generally too small to be considered game fish, they do show the angler a good time when taken on very light tackle. But it's in the kitchen where they really shine and that, I suppose, is how the panfish earned that name. I don't know of a single angler who doesn't appreciate a well-cooked panfish.

Preserving the fresh, sweet meat of a panfish is easy when you're angling for them through the ice in the winter months. They can be tossed right on the ice. One word of caution: Watch out for your four-legged companion. More than one ice fisherman has lost his day's catch to a hungry dog. During the rest of the year, the catch of a boat fisherman can be kept on a stringer as long as the fish are alive and the water isn't exceptionally warm. Whenever possible, store your catch on ice in a cooler. When fishing from the shore, carry an old-fashioned wicker creel, which allows air to circulate around the dead fish.

To clean panfish, either gut and scale or fillet them. The fish should be cooked within a few hours of catching or frozen for future use. The thin panfish can spoil easily in the freezer so wrap extra-well or freeze in a block of ice to exclude all air.

Because panfish are lean meat, one of the easiest methods to prepare them is pan-frying. Scale, gut and remove the head. Douse in seasoned (salt and pepper) flour. Then place in a hot skillet with a half-butter, half-cooking-oil mixture and cook over moderate heat until the fish is browned on both sides. Don't use a lid and don't crowd the fish in the skillet. The crust should be crisp and the flesh moist. Five minutes on a side should be about right.

Deep-frying is popular with panfish fillets. Many people are using electric woks for this purpose since it is vital that the temperature of the oil be held at a stable level. I use peanut oil. Panfish dipped in a batter must be fried fast—at 390° to 400°—or it won't seal the fish and form a crisp crust. The panfish and the batter should be ice-cold to deep-fry properly. An excellent batter can be made from one part beaten egg, two parts ice water and three parts self-rising flour. Dip the cold fillets in the batter, then pop into the hot oil. When the fish floats to the surface, drain it on paper toweling and serve immediately. Don't overcrowd the pan or the temperature will drop too much.

## BROILED PANFISH WITH CUCUMBER TOPPING

2 pounds panfish fillets
½ cup unpeeled cucumber, chopped
1 cup mayonnaise
1 tablespoon minced fresh dill weed (or 1 teaspoon dried)
3 green onions, sliced
½ teaspoon lemon juice
4 drops Tabasco sauce
¼ teaspoon salt
lemon slices

Butter an oven-proof platter. Arrange fillets in a single layer. Combine the rest of the ingredients and spread evenly over the fillets. Broil in a preheated oven, 4 inches from the heat, for 4 to 5 minutes, until top is browned and bubbly and the fish flakes. Serve with lemon slices. Serves 6.

*Note:* Penciled on recipe, "Excellent."

## BAKED PANFISH WITH SWISS CHEESE SAUCE

| | |
|---|---|
| 1½ to 2 pounds panfish fillets | ½ teaspoon salt |
| ½ teaspoon celery salt | dash of nutmeg |
| ¼ teaspoon pepper | 1 cup milk |
| 2 cups shredded Swiss cheese | 2 tablespoons dry sherry |
| 2 tablespoons butter | 1 tomato, cut into wedges |
| 2 tablespoons flour | 1 green pepper, cut into rings |

½ cup bread crumbs, buttered

Sprinkle celery salt and a dash of the pepper on the panfish fillets and distribute 1 cup of the cheese on the fillets. Roll them up so the cheese is in the center (jellyroll fashion) and place seam-side down in a shallow, greased baking dish. In a large skillet, melt butter, add flour, salt, remaining pepper and nutmeg and stir until smooth. Add milk and stir until thick. Add remaining cheese and stir. Don't boil. Add sherry and pour over fillets in baking dish. Arrange tomatoes and peppers around and over the fillets. Sprinkle with bread crumbs. Bake in a 400° preheated oven for 30 minutes. Serves 4.

*Note:* Penciled on recipe, "Great."

## STRUBLE PANFISH

| | |
|---|---|
| 2 pounds panfish fillets | salt and pepper |
| butter | dry vermouth |

minced parsley

Place fillets on buttered foil on a broiler pan. Brush liberally with melted butter. Salt and pepper. Place under broiler (4 inches from the heat) until the fish is hot. Add more butter and a teaspoon of vermouth to each fillet. Broil 3 to 5 minutes, until the fish flakes. Garnish with minced parsley. Serves 6.

## PERCH ITALIAN

| | |
|---|---|
| 2 pounds perch fillets | ½ teaspoon salt |
| 1 large can tomatoes | dash of Pepper |
| 1 medium onion, chopped | 1 garlic clove, minced |
| 1 tablespoon minced parsley | 1 green pepper, chopped |
| 1 teaspoon Italian seasoning | ½ cup chopped mushrooms |

In a large saucepan, combine tomatoes, onion, parsley, seasonings, garlic and green pepper and cook 45 minutes. Add mushrooms and cook another

15 minutes. Put fish in a greased, shallow baking dish and cover with sauce. Bake in preheated 400° oven for 15 to 20 minutes, until fish flakes. Serves 6.
*Note:* Penciled on recipe, "Very good."

## GINGER FRIED CRAPPIE

2 pounds fillets
3 eggs, beaten
1 teaspoon grated ginger (fresh or preserved)

2 tablespoons soy sauce
2 tablespoons green onion, chopped
3 tablespoons dry or medium sherry
3 tablespoons butter

3 tablespoons cornstarch

Mix the eggs, cornstarch, ginger, soy sauce, onion and sherry thoroughly. Dip the fillets in batter and then fry quickly in hot butter. Serves 6.

## FILLET OF ROCK BASS

2 pounds fillets
½ cup finely chopped onion
1 clove garlic, minced
2 tablespoons butter
salt and pepper

¼ teaspoon basil
½ cup dry white wine
2 ounces mild cheddar cheese, thinly sliced
1 ounce brandy

Sauté onion and garlic in butter until soft. Add fish and sauté for 2 minutes. Add seasonings and wine to the frying pan. Cover and simmer until fish is done—about 7 minutes. Remove fish to heated platter and keep warm. Cook pan liquids down to about half the original volume. Add cheese and stir until melted. Add brandy and pour over fish. Serves 6.

## PANFISH WITH WHITE WINE

2 pounds panfish fillets
1 cup chopped celery
¼ cup minced parsley
½ cup white wine

½ cup fine bread crumbs
salt, pepper and cayenne
1 cup sliced mushrooms
¼ teaspoon dill salt

5 tablespoons butter

Place the celery and parsley on the bottom of a greased baking pan. Lay the fillets on top of the vegetables. Pour the wine over the fillets. Sprinkle with bread crumbs, salt, pepper and cayenne. Arrange mushrooms on top, dot with butter and a few shakes of dill salt. Bake uncovered in a preheated 500° oven for about 10 minutes or until the fish flakes, basting once with pan juices. Serves 6.

# BLUEGILL NIBBLES

bluegill fillets
1 bottle beer

½ cup catsup
1 tablespoon horseradish

Cut fillets into thin, bite-sized pieces. Pour the beer into a saucepan and bring to a boil. Add a handful of bluegill chunks at a time. Bring to a boil and cook for 3 minutes. Lift the fish out with a slotted spoon. Serve immediately with a sauce made of catsup and horseradish. A great cocktail or late-evening snack.

# *Other*
# *Freshwater*
# *Species*

So far in this part of the book I've devoted chapters to the eight freshwater species that I believe are the most commonly cooked in the United States. Practices, of course, can differ regionally. However, many of the recipes listed under northern pike can be used for muskies or pickerel. Grayling is delicate and should be treated like a walleye with lots of bones. Catfish are relatively lean and can be cooked like bass. Carp is often smoked in this country (check the smoking chapter). It can also be ground and used in fish cakes, fish loaf, and the like.

When in doubt, treat any species of fish with the simplest cooking method. *Any* whole fish or skinless fillet can be steamed or poached and the result will be enjoyable. Use the steaming recipe in the lake trout chapter (Trout With Cucumber Sauce) or the poaching recipe from the salmon section (Poached Salmon). Couple either of these with one of the interesting sauce recipes scattered through the freshwater and saltwater sections. You can't go wrong if you remember the 10-minutes-per-inch thickness cooking rule which I constantly refer to.

Although I touched on this in the introduction, the best method of freezing fish fillets is in a solid ice block. Stuff them in a half-gallon milk carton or lay them in a bread pan, cover with water and freeze. After the block is frozen, wrap in freezer paper and label. For whole fish, or fillets if freezer space is limited, use the double- and even triple-wrapping method. First, wrap the fish in Saran wrap, excluding all air. Ideally, the second wrap will be aluminum foil, again wrapping the fish tightly. Wrap the third time with freezer paper and label with a marking pen as to species, servings and date. When you place this package in the freezer, make a note on the master list—which should be taped to the door.

Here are a few of my favorite recipes for some of these species.

Grayling is a high-jumping gamefish with a delicate flavor and lots of bones. We release most of these sporting fish, but recently we enjoyed a shore lunch of delicious grayling. I filled a large frying pan with water, added salt and pepper and placed it on the fire to heat. The fish were cleaned and scaled and the heads removed, so they would fit in the pan. Ten minutes of simmering in the boiling water is about right. When done, the meat will easily flake away from the bones. Add a squirt of lemon juice and dig in.

To small children (and some bigger ones too), the sucker means unlimited fun and spells the difference between a fishless day and a full stringer. I used to think that suckers were good to eat only during the early spring months when the flesh was "firm." It's true that coldwater suckers do taste a bit better, but that firm flesh story is a tall tale. The reason summer-caught suckers become soft is that the air temperature is high. Suckers don't always get tended to as carefully as gamefish. Put them on ice as soon as they're caught and they'll be just fine.

Suckers can be deep-fried, smoked or steamed. Once steamed, the boneless fish meat can be used in chowder, fish cakes, a fish loaf or in the following sandwich spread.

## SAUCY SANDWICH SPREAD

| | |
|---|---|
| flaked, cooked sucker | minced onion |
| salt and pepper | minced parsley |
| garlic salt | prepared mustard |
| | mayonnaise |

Mix the fish with salt and pepper and garlic to taste. Add a little minced onion and parsley, a dab of mustard and enough mayonnaise to make the mixture spreadable. Taste while you are adding ingredients to get it just right for the family.

# CATFISH STEW BOURGUIGNON

2 pounds catfish fillets
court bouillon
4 slices bacon, chopped
3 tablespoons butter
10 small white onions

1 large carrot, cut in 2-inch strips
salt and pepper
3 tablespoons flour
⅓ cup heavy cream
pinch of garlic salt

2 tablespoons brandy

Place the catfish fillets in the court bouillon and simmer for 10 to 15 minutes, until the fish flakes. Drain the fish, break into boneless chunks, cover and place in a 200° oven to keep warm. Strain the court bouillon. In a small frying pan, brown the bacon in 1 tablespoon of the butter. Drain and add to the strained bouillon in the large pan. Brown the onions and carrot strips in the bacon pan. Place them in the bouillon and cook until just tender. Remove the vegetables with a slotted spoon and reduce the bouillon by boiling until it measures 1½ cups. Salt and pepper to taste. Mix the flour and remaining butter with your fingers until it forms small balls. Add these balls slowly to the simmering court bouillon, stirring until they dissolve and thicken the stew. Add the vegetables, cream, garlic and brandy. Stir and heat to the boiling point. Place hot buttered toast points on a warm plate, cover the toast with small chunks of fish and spoon the sauce over the fish. Serves 6.

*Note:* Can be prepared with any number of other fish, and even with a combination—half lake trout and half walleye, or bluefish/weakfish. "It's great."

## Court Bouillon

1 onion, quartered
1 carrot, scraped
1 stalk celery

1 bay leaf
3 tablespoons dry *red* Burgundy
salt and pepper

Add all ingredients to enough water to cover fillets. Boil, covered, for 15 minutes.

## BROILED MUSKIE FILLETS

1½ pounds muskie fillets
salt and pepper
1 teaspoon onion flakes

2 tomatoes
1 teaspoon chervil
½ cup grated Swiss cheese

2 tablespoons butter

Dry fillets thoroughly and put in buttered baking dish. Sprinkle with salt and pepper and onion. Chop tomatoes into small pieces and place on top of fish. Sprinkle with chervil and dot with butter. Place under broiler, 4 inches from the heat. Cook until the fish flakes, about 15 minutes. Sprinkle with cheese and return to broiler until the cheese is melted. Serves 4.

*Note:* Penciled on recipe, "Excellent."

## BAKED PICKEREL

1½ pounds of pickerel fillets
salt and pepper
1 10½-ounce can cream of mushroom
   soup

4 ounces sliced fresh mushrooms
¼ cup grated sharp Cheddar cheese
¼ cup dry sherry wine
1 tablespoon chopped parsley
paprika

Cut fish into serving-size pieces and arrange in a buttered, shallow baking dish. Add salt and pepper. Mix soup, mushrooms, cheese, wine and parsley and spread over the fish. Bake in a preheated 375° oven for 25 minutes. Just before serving, baste the fillets with the sauce, sprinkle with a little paprika and stick under the broiler for a couple minutes. Will serve 4.

*Note:* Penciled on recipe, "Great."

## CATFISH PATTIES

2 cups flaked, cooked catfish
1 cup crushed cracker crumbs
2 eggs, beaten
salt and pepper

1 tablespoon minced onion
1 tablespoon minced parsley
1 cup tomato juice (more or less)
cooking oil
tartar sauce

Mix all ingredients thoroughly, adding enough tomato juice to form patties. Fry in hot oil until well brown on both sides and hot in the center. Serve with tartar sauce. Serves 4.

# Bluefish

Breathtaking, exciting action best describes fishing for blues when they are on a feeding rampage. Bluefish are democratic about tackle and can be taken on anything from a hand line to a fly rod. The frantic feeding of a school of hungry blues is unique among fish. Not even sharks attack in such a seemingly blind dash through the water.

Periodically through our history, bluefish have virtually disappeared for long time spans, to reappear again. The wide fluctuation in bluefish population has been noted since the colonial period. We seem to be on an upswing now but the highs and lows come in an unpredictable pattern.

Bluefish occur all along the Atlantic coast from Florida to Cape Cod and even up to Nova Scotia during warm years. They are the most popular gamefish among trollers along the Middle Atlantic Seaboard because of the furious action when a school is located. Anglers have learned to be careful of the slashing teeth of the blue which are as dangerous in the water as on the deck. I would no more dangle my fingers in the ocean while a school of bluefish were nearby than try to remove a lure from a blue's mouth without hook-outs. Blues are the only fish I know that appear to kill for the sheer action. Birds are often seen scooping up the remains of the torn baitfish. Sometimes they dip into the water a bit too far when near a bluefish school—and no more bird!

As might be guessed from their appetites, the digestive enzymes of the bluefish are powerful. The flesh will spoil quickly if they are not gutted as fast as possible. Icing them while on a boat slows the deterioration and a chest should be used. The high oil content of the fish also contributes to a powerful flavor if it is not properly chilled while traveling.

Bluefish, like all fish and game, are what they eat. In the northern Atlantic, the bigger bluefish often feed on oily menhaden. They will be stronger-tasting than the little "snapper" blues that feast on crustaceans, mollusks and various inshore fishes.

Bluefish, at its very best in the smaller sizes, is soft-textured and mild-tasting. The larger the fish, the more difficult it is to prepare in the kitchen. The *very small* snappers can be gutted, scaled and pan-fried. Bluefish fillets up to about 8 pounds can be broiled or baked. Anything over 10 pounds should be broiled over a charcoal grill, poached, steamed or smoked—always in fillet form and, except for the charcoal method, minus the skin.

Smoking is one of my favorite ways to cook bluefish. Smoked bluefish is almost as good as smoked salmon (see smoking chapter). Many people insist that the dark strip of meat that runs lengthwise along the fillet should be removed from the bluefish before it is cooked. It can be a little "fishy," but I usually leave it alone. It is especially good in the fishcake recipe or when smoked. Much of the prejudice against this strip may occur because the blue has not been promptly chilled and this piece of flesh is the first to indicate spoilage.

The only exception to filleting everything over 10 pounds would be a whole large bluefish cooked on a covered charcoal grill. Scale and gut the fish, oil the skin and place over moderately hot coals. Cover and bake until the fish flakes at the thickest point on the back. It will probably take at least 30 minutes and possibly an hour, depending on the heat of the coals and the size of the fish. When it's done, strip the skin off the top side immediately if it is to be served hot. Serve with any of the sauce recipes in this chapter. The whole blue can also be served cold with the sauce recipe from Poached Salmon in the freshwater section. If serving cold, chill overnight, remove skin and decorate with lemon slices, parsley sprigs and the like.

# MARGATE BLUES

4 bluefish fillets, serving-size pieces
2 cups clam-vegetable juice
1 cup light cream

10 drops Tabasco sauce
salt and pepper
1 cup sliced mushrooms

In a heavy frying pan, mix juice, cream, Tabasco and salt and pepper to taste. Simmer for 5 minutes. Add fillets, cover and simmer for 8 to 10 minutes, depending on how thick the fish is. Check with a fork for flakiness. Transfer the fillets to a heated platter and place in a warm oven. Add the mushrooms to the frying pan and turn the heat up. Cook the liquid down until it is reduced to 1 cup. Ladle over the fillets and serve immediately. Will serve 4.

*Note:* "A favorite in our household."

# GRILLED BLUEFISH

large whole bluefish fillets, with skin
lemon slices
onion slices

1 cup tomato juice
6 drops Tabasco sauce
salt and pepper

Lay the fillets on a charcoal grill. Cover the flesh with slices of lemon and onion. Brush with the tomato juice laced with Tabasco. Broil, basting with more tomato juice, until the flesh flakes. Salt and pepper to taste. The fillets will take from 15 to 25 minutes to cook, depending on the thickness and the heat of the coals. A cover will help cook them faster. Figure ½ pound of fish to serve 1 person.

# STUFFED BLUEFISH

4 large bluefish fillets (1½ pounds)
salt and pepper to taste
1 cup finely chopped cucumber
1 large stalk celery, finely chopped
½ cup finely chopped green pepper
2 tablespoons chopped onion

2 tablespoons chopped parsley
½ cup chopped mushrooms
1 teaspoon sage
2 slices firm white bread, cubed
bread crumbs
6 tablespoons melted butter

Lay 2 fillets on an amply buttered shallow baking dish. Dust with salt and pepper. Mix cucumber, celery, green pepper, onion, parsley, mushrooms, sage, more salt and pepper and bread cubes together and spread over the 2 fillets. Top with the other 2 fillets. Add salt and pepper, sprinkle with some fine bread crumbs and pour the melted butter over it all. Place in a preheated 350° oven for about 30 minutes, until the fish flakes when probed with a fork. Serves 4.

*Note:* "Great recipe for those who say they don't like blues. Vegetables absorb the strong fish taste."

## VEGETABLE BAKED BLUEFISH

4 bluefish fillets, serving-size pieces
1 large onion, sliced
1 clove garlic, minced
4 teaspoons minced parsley
⅛ teaspoon dried basil

⅛ teaspoon thyme
1 tablespoon sugar
salt and pepper
1 large tomato, sliced thin
½ cup tomato juice

1½ tablespoons butter

Butter a shallow baking dish and lay fillets on it. Cover with onion slices. Mix garlic, parsley, basil, thyme, sugar and salt and pepper together and sprinkle on the onion-covered fillets. Top with tomato slices and pour the tomato juice over them. Dot with little chunks of butter. Place in a preheated 350° oven to bake for 25 to 30 minutes, depending on how large the fillets are. 4 servings.

*Note:* "Tomato brings out bluefish flavor."

## BUBBLY BLUEFISH

4 bluefish fillets
1 cup mayonnaise

½ cup horseradish
¼ cup green pepper, chopped
paprika

Place fillets on a buttered sheet of aluminum foil on a broiler pan. Mix mayonnaise, horseradish and green pepper and spread over fillets. Sprinkle with paprika. Broil, 4 inches from the heat, for about 10 minutes. The fillets will turn a bubbly light brown and flake to the touch when done. Serves 4.

*Note:* Penciled on recipe, "Excellent."

## VEGETABLE STEAMED BLUES

4 bluefish fillets
1 large onion, sliced
2 large tomatoes, sliced
½ green pepper, cut in rounds
1 medium zucchini, sliced

1 garlic clove, minced
¼ cup chopped parsley
¾ cup chicken broth
¼ cup dry vermouth
salt and pepper

chow mein noodles

Place onion, tomatoes, green pepper and zucchini in a large enough pan so the fillets will fit in a single layer on top. Add garlic and parsley and pour the broth and wine over the vegetables. Add salt and pepper, cover and simmer the vegetables for 10 minutes. Lay the fillets over the vegetables, salt and pepper them, cover and steam for 7 to 10 minutes, until the flesh flakes when probed with a fork. Serve vegetables and broth ladled over crisp noodles to go with the fish. Serves 4.

*Note:* "Good—delicate fish flavor."

## BLUEFISH WITH YOGURT

4 bluefish fillets, serving-size
1 cup plain yogurt
1 tablespoon brown sugar

1 teaspoon powdered ginger
½ teaspoon garlic powder
2 teaspoons grated orange peel

salt and pepper

Butter a piece of foil and lay the fillets on it. Place on a broiler pan. Mix the yogurt, sugar, ginger, garlic and orange peel together. Sprinkle the fillets with salt and pepper and cover with the yogurt mixture. Broil, 4 inches from the heat, for 8 to 10 minutes, until the flesh flakes. 4 servings.

*Note:* "Great—Oriental flavor."

## LUCKY'S BLUEFISH

4 bluefish fillets
3 tablespoons butter
2 tablespoons flour
1 cup light cream
½ teaspoon salt
1 teaspoon dry sherry

⅛ teaspoon pepper
⅛ teaspoon red pepper
¼ teaspoon celery salt
shake of paprika
½ cup chopped mushrooms

Steam the bluefish fillets by placing a little water in a large frying pan. Add a buttered cake rack. Bring the water to a boil, place the fillets on the rack, cover and steam until the fish flakes, about 10 minutes. Remove to a heated platter and keep in a warm oven until the sauce is ready. In a small saucepan, melt butter. Blend in flour. Add cream slowly, blending well. Add rest of ingredients except sherry and bring to the boiling point. Add sherry and serve over bluefish fillets. Serves 4.

*Note:* Penciled on recipe, "Great."

## BLUEFISH CAKES

3 cups flaked, cooked fish
5 tablespoons butter
5 tablespoons flour
½ teaspoon salt
dash of pepper
1½ cups milk

1½ tablespoons minced onion
1½ tablespoons minced parsley
1 teaspoon lemon juice
1 cup fine dry bread crumbs
1 egg
butter

chili butter sauce

Cook bluefish by using the steaming recipe from Lucky's Bluefish, or use leftover fish. Melt butter in saucepan, blend in flour, salt and pepper and slowly add milk. Cook until very thick, stirring constantly. Add onion, parsley, lemon juice and fish. Mix well and chill for several hours. Shape into 12 cakes, roll in crumbs, dip into egg mixed with 2 tablespoons cold water and roll in crumbs again. Chill 1 hour. Fry in butter in a heavy skillet until golden brown and heated thoroughly. Serve with chili butter sauce. Serves 6.

*Note:* "Great recipe—tastes like crab cakes."

### Chili Butter Sauce

1 cup chili sauce

3 tablespoons butter
1 tablespoon lemon juice

Combine ingredients, heat and ladle over cakes.

## BLUEFISH SALAD

2 pounds bluefish fillets, steamed
Romaine lettuce
½ pound small shrimp, boiled and
    cleaned
1 avocado, sliced
paprika

2 tomatoes, cut in thin wedges
1 stalk celery, cut in bite-sized pieces
1 cucumber, cut in thin slices
2 hard-boiled eggs, cut in wedges
mustard sauce

Steam fillets according to Lucky's Bluefish recipe. On a large platter, arrange a bed of lettuce. In the center, heap bite-sized chunks of the bluefish and the shrimp. Surround the meat with the vegetables arranged artfully like spokes of a wheel. Pour mustard sauce over the fish and vegetables and sprinkle with paprika. Serves 4.

*Note:* "Lovely summer meal with hot French bread."

## Mustard Sauce

1 8-ounce package cream cheese,
    softened
½ cup mayonnaise
2 tablespoons prepared mustard

¼ cup light cream
¼ teaspoon celery salt
⅛ teaspoon curry powder
2 shakes Tabasco sauce

Put all the sauce ingredients in a blender and blend until smooth. Check for salt and correct. Pour over the fish and vegetables on the platter.

# *Weakfish*

Squeateague was the original Indian name for this handsome gamefish. A freshly caught weakfish is beautiful, with its sides resplendant in tones of blue, green and purple with a golden tinge. It's a shame it has such a common name. But "weakfish" obviously refers to the delicate mouth. The angler has to be careful for it is easy to tear a lure right out of this fish's jaw. It can cause problems when you are catching both blues and weakfish in the same water. A blue must be horsed a bit or it could easily shake the hook. A bluefisherman soon learns to "put the rod" to the fish when it jumps and shakes its head at the same time. The weakfish, during its surging runs and dashes, must be fed line carefully with a little tension at all times. A sensitive but strong rod is a definite plus when weakfishing. Pound for pound, the weakfish will come in faster than the blue, but it will have to be handled with more care while it is still on the hook.

Sportfishing for weakfish usually runs from April into November along the northern Atlantic states. The southern form of the fish is the spotted sea trout (both are members of the drum family, as are the Pacific white sea bass and the various corvinas). Its range extends to the Gulf of Mexico. There are small differences between the weakfish and sea trout, but both can be cooked similarly.

As with the bluefish, weakfish populations and size fluctuate widely over the years. Just a few years ago, large weakies had seemingly disappeared. Now they are back again, with 10 to 12 pounders not uncommon. Some conservationists think that the ban on DDT has had a beneficial effect on the weakfish's food—shrimps, squid, crabs, mollusks and small fishes—hence, bigger and more fish.

The flesh of the weakfish is sweet, lean and finely textured. Again as with the blues, it is delicate and must be chilled upon catching to preserve the flavor. Weakfish roe is excellent. I like it better than the much-acclaimed shad roe. It isn't quite as "fishy." Use one of the shad roe recipes for its preparation or the one I devised for weakfish. It's at the end of this chapter. Hundreds of pounds of weakfish roe are wasted each year. What a shame!

If at all possible, store your frozen fish in an old-fashioned freezer that doesn't have the frost-free feature. It draws the moisture out of the freezer *and* the contents of the freezer, no matter how well you wrap the packages. We were lucky and managed to buy two small, thick-sided, chest-type freezers at a very reasonable price. They would have been a bargain at any price. Food stored in them will keep up to a year with no freezer burn. Once a year, I do have to defrost them. In my side-by-side freezer/refrigerator, I can only keep fish a month before it starts to go downhill in quality.

A special thanks must go to Ralph Stork of Capt. Andy's Marina, Margate, New Jersey. He shared three of his special weakfish recipes with me—all hits in my opinion.

## RALPH'S WEAKFISH FINGERS

| | |
|---|---|
| **1½ pounds weakfish fillets** | **yellow cornmeal** |
| **salt and pepper** | **cooking oil** |

Cut fillets into fingers, about 1 inch thick. Dry on paper toweling. Add plenty of salt and pepper to the cornmeal. Coat the fingers with the mixture. Heat cooking oil in an electric frying pan set at 375°. Fry the fingers, a few at a time, for 6 to 8 minutes, until golden brown and flaky. Serves 4.

*Note:* Penciled on recipe, "Great."

# CREAMED WEAKFISH

4 fillets, serving-size
4 tablespoons Madeira
1 cup light cream
1 cup mayonnaise

⅓ cup finely chopped onion
½ cup chopped mushrooms
1 tablespoon lemon juice
salt and pepper

parsley sprigs

Place the fillets in a buttered baking dish. Pour the Madeira over the fish and allow it to marinate for 30 minutes. Mix cream, mayonnaise, onion, mushrooms, lemon juice and salt and pepper to taste. Pour over the marinated fillets, cover and bake for 25 to 30 minutes in a preheated 350° oven. Baste once during the cooking if the fillets are not covered by the cream. Check for flakiness by probing with a fork. Garnish with parsley. Serves 4.

*Note:* Penciled on recipe, "A favorite—rich and creamy."

# STORK'S WEAKFISH

1½ pounds weakfish fillets
flour

milk
butter

salt and pepper

Coat weakfish fillets with flour. Put milk in a shallow dish and quickly dip the flour-coated fish in the milk. Place the fillets immediately in hot butter in a heavy skillet. Fry 5 minutes on each side until golden brown. (Ralph uses clarified butter so it doesn't burn. Unsalted butter or cooking oil would also work.) Serves 4.

*Note:* Penciled on recipe, "Great."

# DELAWARE BAY WEAKFISH

4 serving-size fillets
½ cup + 4 tablespoons dry white wine
4 tablespoons clam juice
6 tablespoons butter, 4 melted
1 6½-ounce can clams, drained

salt and pepper
1½ cups sour cream
3 tablespoons minced parsley
1 large tomato, sliced thin
bread crumbs

Place fillets in a buttered baking dish. Mix ½ cup wine, 4 tablespoons melted butter and juice drained from can of clams and pour over the fillets. Place the clams on top of the fillets, salt and pepper to taste. Blend sour cream, rest of wine and parsley and spread over fillets. Top with tomato slices. Put a chunk of butter on each fillet and sprinkle with bread crumbs.

Cover dish and bake in 400° oven for 15 to 20 minutes, depending on how thick the fillets are. When they flake when probed with a fork, uncover and run under the broiler until the bread crumbs are browned. Serves 4.

*Note:* Penciled on recipe, "Good."

## CARL'S WEAKFISH

4 serving-size fillets
1 cup dry white wine
1 cup chopped onion
1 cup chopped green pepper
½ cup chopped celery

¼ cup chopped parsley
3 tablespoons butter
1 15-ounce can tomato sauce
¾ cup sliced mushrooms
5 drops Tabasco sauce

⅓ cup grated sharp cheese

Place the fillets in a frying pan with the wine, cover and simmer for about 10 minutes, until the fish flakes when probed. While the fish is poaching, sauté the onion, pepper, celery and parsley in the butter in a small skillet for 7 minutes. Add tomato sauce, mushrooms and Tabasco and heat thoroughly. Place the cooked fillets on an oven-proof platter, top with sauce and sprinkle with grated cheese. Slip under the broiler for a minute to melt the cheese. Serves 4.

*Note:* "Delicious—spicy with a bit of crunch."

## STORK'S STUFFED WEAKFISH

1½ pounds weakfish fillets
salt and pepper
1 package frozen creamed spinach

butter
bread crumbs
lemon wedges

Butter a baking dish and lay half the fillets on the bottom of it. Add salt and pepper. Cover with thawed spinach mixture. Cover the spinach with the rest of the fillets. Add more salt and pepper. Dot with butter and sprinkle with bread crumbs. Place in a preheated 375° oven for 25 to 30 minutes, basting twice with melted butter. Remove when the flesh flakes when probed with a fork. Cut into slices to serve. Garnish with lemon wedges. Will serve 4.

*Note:* Penciled on recipe, "Great."

## WEAKFISH ITALIAN STYLE

4 weakfish fillets, serving size
2 tablespoons lemon juice
1 cup fish stock (or chicken broth)
salt and pepper
1 cup crushed cornflakes

4 tablespoons Parmesan cheese
1 cup chopped mushrooms
1 teaspoon basil
1 teaspoon oregano
½ cup melted butter

Place fish on a buttered baking dish. Pour lemon juice and fish stock over the fillets. Salt and pepper the fish. Mix the cornflakes, cheese, mushrooms, basil, oregano and butter together. Cover the fillets with the stuffing. Bake in preheated 350° oven for 20 to 30 minutes. The time depends on the thickness of the fillets—the ones I tested were from very large weakfish and required 30 minutes. Baste with pan juices once during the baking. Serves 4.

*Note:* Penciled on recipe, "Very good."

## WEAKFISH WITH CHEESE SAUCE

4 serving-size weakfish fillets
2 tablespoons butter
2 tablespoons flour
1 cup milk
½ teaspoon seafood seasoning

⅛ teaspoon garlic
½ teaspoon dry mustard
salt and pepper
½ cup shredded sharp Cheddar cheese
parsley sprigs

Place fillets on a buttered rack in saucepan. Put enough boiling water in pan to cover bottom but not touch fish. Bring water to a boil again, cover and simmer. Steam the fillets for 10 minutes, until they flake when probed with a fork. While the fish is steaming, make white sauce by melting butter in saucepan, add flour and blend in the milk slowly. When the sauce is thick, add seafood seasoning, garlic, mustard, salt and pepper and cheese. Stir until thoroughly mixed. Remove the fish fillets to an oven-proof dish, sprinkle with salt and pepper and ladle a little cheese sauce over each fillet. Slip under broiler until the sauce bubbles and browns. Serve with a sprig of parsley. Serves 4.

*Note:* Penciled on recipe, "Excellent."

# LUCKY'S WEAKFISH

4 serving-size weakfish fillets
1 small onion, chopped
2 tablespoons chopped sweet red pepper
2 tablespoons butter

½ cup chopped mushrooms
2 tablespoons minced parsley
½ cup Madeira
⅓ cup heavy cream

parsley sprigs

Steam fish according to instructions in Weakfish with Cheese Sauce recipe. Meanwhile, sauté onion and pepper in butter until the onion is transparent. Add mushrooms and parsley and simmer for 4 minutes. Add Madeira and simmer 1 minute. Add cream and bring just to the boiling point. Serve the sauce ladled over the steamed fish and garnish with parsley. Serves 4.

*Note:* Penciled on recipe, "A favorite with us."

# WEAKFISH ROE

weakfish roe
lemon juice
salt
freshly ground pepper

seafood seasoning
garlic powder
butter
parsley

Pour boiling water over roe in a skillet and simmer for 20 minutes. Drain, cool and then cut into small pieces. Squeeze a bit of lemon juice over pieces and sprinkle with salt, pepper, seafood seasoning and garlic powder. Dot each piece with butter and a bit of parsley. Place under broiler until brown and warm. Serve on crackers or rye bread.

*Note:* Penciled on recipe, "Super."

# *Striped Bass*

Striped bass have a history as long and as exciting as that of our country. The Plymouth colonists depended on them to help survive the rigors of the New World. The bass were captured in nets or on hand lines baited with pieces of lobster. (Imagine, lobster for bait!) Unlike the lobster, the striper's commercial value was recognized early, and an act was passed in colonial Massachusetts declaring that striped bass (and cod) could not be used as a fertilizer. As the pioneers moved west, striped bass also left their native shores. When biologists learned that the anadromous (saltwater fish that spawn in fresh water) stripers could survive inland without returning to the sea, the march was on. From South Carolina they spread through much of the big-lake country of the south (where they are usually called rockfish), and in some lakes they are beginning to compete with the black bass as the most popular sport fish, perhaps because of their great growth potential, calculated to be about a pound a year.

In the Atlantic, stripers are found from northern Florida to the Gulf of St. Lawrence. They inhabit the Gulf of Mexico from Florida to Louisiana. On the Pacific Coast, where they were introduced 90 years ago, they range from Los Angeles to Washington. As a landlocked sport fish they must be regularly stocked, except in South Carolina's Santee-Cooper Reservoir, since it takes about 60 miles of free-flowing water for the semibuoyant striper eggs to hatch into fry.

As with many other fish, the smaller striped bass are considered the best tasting. When the fish goes over 10 pounds, the flesh passes its prime and becomes a bit coarse. These fish should be scaled and cut into steaks or the skinless fillets can be poached or steamed. The cooked fish can then be served with a sauce or used in fish cakes, salad or a loaf. The recipes are endless. Smoking is another fine treatment for a large striper.

Another factor besides size can affect the quality of the striper's flesh. Because the fish is tolerant of polluted water, it survives in some pretty unsavory environs. This is great for the future of the species but can give grief to the chef. Striped bass taken from water such as the lower Hudson can be tainted with fuel oil and other pollutants. There is nothing much the cook can do—except work to clean up metropolitan wastes in the water.

Striped bass is lean meat, suitable for many cooking methods. Anything under 10 pounds can be baked whole, or filleted and broiled, poached or baked. It can also be pickled as well as smoked.

## STRIPER FILLETS, ORIENTAL STYLE

1½ pounds striper fillets (or steaks)  
¼ cup orange juice  
¼ cup soy sauce  
1 small tomato, chopped  
2 tablespoons peanut or cooking oil  

1 teaspoon lemon juice  
½ teaspoon oregano  
¼ teaspoon pepper  
1 clove garlic, finely chopped  
½ cup chopped fresh parsley  
parsley sprig

Put fish in a baking dish. Combine the other ingredients and ladle over the fish. Let stand for 1 hour, turning once. Remove the fish. Place it on a buttered piece of foil on a broiler pan. Broil, 4 inches from the heat, for 5 minutes on a side (10 minutes total cooking time) until the fish flakes. Baste once during the cooking time with the marinade. Serve with a sprig of parsley. Serves 4.

*Note:* Before chopping the tomato, remove as many of the seeds and excess moisture as possible. "Super!"

## BAKED STRIPED BASS WITH SHRIMP STUFFING

1 whole striper (5 to 8 pounds)
1 onion, chopped
2 tablespoons butter
1 teaspoon chopped parsley
½ teaspoon paprika

1½ cups chopped mushrooms
1 cup white wine
1 4½-ounce can small shrimp
1½ cups bread crumbs
melted butter

Sauté the onion in butter until it is soft (about 5 minutes). Add parsley, paprika, mushrooms and ¼ cup wine and simmer for 2 minutes. Just before removing from the heat, fold in the drained shrimp. Next, add crumbs and enough white wine to moisten the stuffing. Fill the fish with the stuffing and secure with skewers or toothpicks. Place the striper in a buttered roasting pan and brush with melted butter. Add ½ cup white wine to the pan. Preheat oven to 350° and bake about 55 minutes, until the fish flakes. Add more wine if necessary. Serve with lemon slices and parsley sprigs. Will serve 5 to 8.

*Note:* Penciled on recipe, "Very good."

## STRIPER/BROCCOLI OVEN DISH

1½ pounds striper fillets
fresh broccoli, cut into bite-sized pieces
    (about 3 cups)
salt and pepper
2 tablespoons butter

1 11-ounce can cheddar cheese soup
3 ounces light cream
1 tablespoon steak sauce
5 drops Tabasco sauce
paprika

Butter a baking dish and cover bottom with enough broccoli to serve 4 people. Salt and pepper broccoli and dot with butter. Place the striper fillets on top of the broccoli. Heat the soup, cream, steak sauce and Tabasco to the boiling point. Pour over the fillets. Sprinkle with paprika. Cover the dish and place in a preheated 375° oven for 35 minutes or until fish flakes when probed with a fork. Serve with biscuits and fresh garden salad. Serves 4.

*Note:* Penciled on recipe, "Very good dish."

## GRILLED STRIPED BASS

1 striped bass, scaled, filleted but not
    skinned

1 bottle Italian salad dressing

Pour bottle of salad dressing in a large shallow pan. Place the striped bass fillets in the dressing skin side up. Marinate for 30 to 40 minutes. In the meantime, let a charcoal fire burn down so the coals are white and hot.

Place marinated fish, skin side down, on the grill. Cover grill with either the top or a sheet of aluminum foil and bake fish for 15 to 30 minutes, until the flesh flakes when probed with a fork. The cooking time depends on the heat of the coals, thickness of the fillets and distance from the heat. Serve immediately. Count on about ¾ pound per person.

*Note:* This recipe can be prepared in the oven. Skin fillets, marinate, then place in a shallow baking dish. Cover and bake in preheated 400° oven for 15 to 20 minutes. "Pure striper flavor."

*Good*

## POACHED STRIPER PATRICE

1½ pounds striper fillets
¼ cup vermouth
2 bay leaves
10 peppercorns
salt
2 tablespoons butter

½ cup finely chopped cucumber
¼ cup finely chopped celery
¼ cup finely chopped onion
2 tablespoons flour
1 tablespoon orange juice
2 tablespoons minced parsley

pimiento bits

Bring vermouth, bay leaves, peppercorns, ½ teaspoon salt and water enough to cover the fillets to the boiling point and boil for 5 minutes. Add fillets, cut into 4 serving pieces. Cover and simmer for 10 minutes, until fillets flake. Drain and keep warm on a serving platter. Melt butter in a frying pan and sauté cucumber, celery, and onion for 7 minutes, until vegetables are soft but not brown. Blend in flour, then 1 cup of the poaching liquid. Just before serving, add orange juice and correct seasonings to taste. Pour over the fillets and sprinkle with the parsley and a little pimiento for color. Serves 4.

*Note:* Penciled on recipe, "Excellent."

## STRIPER COCKTAIL

2 pounds skinless, boneless striper fillets
2 bay leaves
¼ cup + 1 teaspoon lemon juice
1 sliced onion

1 teaspoon salt
freshly ground pepper
½ cup chili sauce
1 teaspoon steak sauce

Cube the striper fillets into chunks about 1 inch square. Boil a pot of water with the bay leaves, ¼ cup lemon juice, onion, salt and pepper added. Boil for 10 minutes. Add fish chunks, cover and boil for another 10 minutes. Drain the fish and cool. Serve as appetizers with a sauce made of the chili sauce, 1 teaspoon lemon juice and steak sauce.

*Note:* Penciled on recipe, "Excellent."

## STRIPED BASS SALAD

2 cups cooked, flaked striper meat
1 cup finely chopped celery
½ cup mayonnaise
2 tablespoons prepared mustard

½ teaspoon steak sauce
lettuce
ripe olives
1 large tomato, sliced
2 hard-boiled eggs, quartered

Toss fish, celery, mayonnaise (enough to moisten to your taste), mustard and steak sauce together until blended. Place on a bed of lettuce. Garnish with olives, tomato and eggs. Serve with hot, buttered French rolls. Will serve 4.

*Note:* Use leftover cooked fish for this recipe or prepare it by poaching, as in Poached Striper Patrice.

## STRIPER CROQUETTES

2 cups cooked, flaked striper meat
½ cup chopped mushrooms
3 tablespoons butter
1 small onion, minced
1 teaspoon lemon juice
1 teaspoon steak sauce

¼ cup minced parsley
¼ cup minced celery
½ teaspoon chervil
½ teaspoon dill weed
½ can cream of celery soup
1 egg, beaten
1 cup dried fine bread crumbs

Sauté the mushrooms in 1 tablespoon butter for 5 minutes. Combine fish, mushrooms, onion, lemon juice, steak sauce, parsley, celery, chervil and dill weed. Moisten to taste with celery soup. Press mixture into a pie dish and chill thoroughly (about 2 hours). Divide into 12 parts and shape into croquettes. Dip in beaten egg and roll in bread crumbs. Brown on all sides in 2 tablespoons butter and serve with mushroom sauce (see Wild Mushrooms chapter). Serves 4.

*Note:* To dry bread for crumbs, place in 250° oven until brittle. Crush with rolling pin until fine.

# *Flounder*

Flounder may well be the most popular saltwater fish on the dining table. There are over 200 species under the common name of flounder, which may be one of the reasons for this popularity. The flounders belong to any of three families of saltwater flatfishes ranging from the small dab to the giant halibut, and are found in both the Atlantic and Pacific oceans. The best-tasting of the Pacific flounders are the rex and petrale soles. On the Atlantic side, the lemon sole is considered to have the sweetest meat. But many of the other flounders are delicious. On light tackle, a flounder (or fluke) angler can have some lively action and come home with top eating fish.

One of the reasons given for a fondness for the flesh of the flounder is that "it doesn't taste like fish." It's accurate that, like walleyes, perch and panfish, well-cared-for flounder is delicately flavored. Because of this, I often favor simple recipes. But oddly enough, its flesh also has enough character to hold up to strong sauces, stuffings, spices and herbs. And this is the key, I think, to its great popularity. The only way flounder can be ruined is to overcook it. Unfortunately, I have found that many restaurants, especially inland, do just that and I've stopped ordering it except where I am sure the restaurant knows how to cook seafood. The usual flounder fillets are so thin that a few minutes of heat per side is enough. Dried-out flounder tastes like cardboard—ugh!

The old adage "You can't tell a book by its cover" certainly applies to the flounder. Lean and sweetly flavored flesh lurks beneath the skin of this ugly fish, which at first glance appears to be misformed, especially around the eyes. Most flounder caught range from 1 to 4 pounds. Fresh fillets are highly perishable and must be protected until they are cooked or frozen. When we are flounder fishing, I always carry heavy-duty plastic bags. Immediately after filleting, I seal the meat in these bags and place them on ice in a cooler.

Flounder should be cooked within 24 hours. If the fillets are to be frozen, double-wrap and mark the date on the package. They are best used in 3 months unless you freeze them in a block of ice (such as a milk carton of water). If this block of ice is then wrapped in freezer paper or heavy-duty foil, the fillets can be kept in the freezer for a year.

Filleting a flounder calls for a different technique than with other, more conventionally shaped fish. This is the way I do it. Lay the flounder, eyes up, on its side and make an incision from just behind the gill cover to the tail. Follow the spinal column, which in a flounder is almost in the center of the body. Push the tip of the knife blade tightly against the backbone and carefully follow the rib cage to the center of the back. Regulate the force to avoid cutting into the fillet. What you will remove is a half-moon shape of fish flesh. Do exactly the same thing on the other side of the backbone. Flop the fish over and repeat the maneuver. A flounder has four fillets instead of two, one on each side of the backbone, on both sides. The intestinal cavity is very small, so you run little danger of piercing the innards. The skin is easily peeled off by sliding the blade between the fillet and coarse outer hide. Using a flexible knife is especially important when filleting a flounder. Small flounder, those less than a foot long, can be scaled and broiled whole. But any fish larger than that ought to be filleted for better taste.

# CREEK ROAD FLOUNDER

1½ pounds flounder fillets
1 small onion, diced
¼ cup diced mushrooms
2 tablespoons butter
2 tablespoons cooking oil

¼ cup flour
salt and pepper
⅓ cup dry vermouth
parsley sprigs
lemon wedges

Sauté onions and mushrooms in butter and oil. Dust fillets with flour, seasoned with salt and pepper. When onions and mushrooms are lightly browned, add fillets to the frying pan. Simmer until done. If the fillets are thin, it will take about 3 minutes on a side, 6 minutes total cooking time. Just before serving, add vermouth and bring to the boiling point. Serve on a heated platter with parsley and lemon. Serves 4.

*Note:* Penciled on recipe, "Super."

## FLOUNDER WITH CHEESE SAUCE

1½ pounds skinned flounder fillets
16 ounces bottled clam juice
½ cup chopped green onion
3 tablespoons butter
2 tablespoons flour

3 tablespoons sour cream
2 tablespoons white wine
dash of salt
dash of Tabasco sauce
¼ pound grated mozzarella cheese

Bring clam juice to a boil in a large skillet. Add fillets, cover and poach for 6 to 8 minutes, until they flake. Drain the cooked fillets on paper toweling and keep warm. Reduce the clam juice a little by boiling. Sauté onion lightly in the butter until soft. Make a medium-thick cream sauce by stirring the flour into the butter and onion and then adding the clam juice. Add sour cream and wine and season to taste with salt and Tabasco. Arrange the fillets on a buttered, shallow oven-proof dish. Coat fillets with sauce and top with grated cheese. Broil until heated through and flecked with brown. Serves 4.

*Note:* Penciled on recipe, "Excellent."

## STEAMED FLOUNDER LISA

1½ pounds flounder fillets
1 carrot, thinly sliced
1 onion, thinly sliced
1 stalk celery, thinly sliced
3½ tablespoons butter

salt and pepper
2 teaspoons minced parsley
¾ cup chicken stock
¼ cup dry white wine
1½ tablespoons flour

Cook vegetables in 2 tablespoons of the butter in a large frying pan until soft but not brown. Lay fillets on top of the vegetables. Add salt and pepper, parsley, stock and wine. Cover and simmer until the fish flakes, about 6 to 8 minutes. Remove the fish to a heated serving dish. Turn heat up to reduce the liquid a little. Mix 1½ tablespoons cold butter and flour with your fingers. Drop by little chunks in the liquid. Stir constantly to thicken the sauce. Ladle sauce and vegetables over the cooked fillets and serve immediately. Serves 4.

*Note:* Penciled on recipe, "A winner."

## FLOUNDER FLORENTINE

| | |
|---|---|
| 1½ pounds flounder fillets | 1 tablespoon chopped parsley |
| 1 pound fresh spinach | 2 tablespoons flour |
| 4 tablespoons butter | 1 cup light cream |
| salt and pepper | 1 tablespoon Madeira |
| 1 teaspoon seasoned salt | paprika |

Wash spinach, remove stems and drain. Cook in a saucepan for a few minutes (without adding water) until wilted. Drain again and chop. Heat 2 tablespoons of butter in a small pan until it is brown. Mix with spinach. Add salt and pepper to taste. Put spinach in the bottom of a shallow baking dish. Sprinkle fish with seasoned salt. Roll each fillet up and place the rolls on the spinach. Sprinkle with parsley. Melt the rest of the butter in a saucepan and blend in flour. Slowly add cream and cook until thick. Correct salt and pepper. Add Madeira and blend. Pour sauce over fillets. Sprinkle with paprika. Cover and bake in preheated 350° oven for 25 to 30 minutes, until fish flakes when probed with fork. Serves 4.

*Note:* "Absolutely great."

## FLOUNDER AND OYSTERS

| | |
|---|---|
| 1½ pounds flounder fillets | dash of red pepper |
| 1 pint oysters with broth | 3½ tablespoons butter |
| 1 tablespoon lemon juice | 1½ tablespoons flour |
| ½ teaspoon seafood seasoning | parsley |

Place fillets in a buttered baking dish. Put drained oysters on top of them. Pour 1 cup of oyster broth (add water if necessary to make the cup) over the fillets and oysters. Sprinkle with lemon juice, seafood seasoning and red pepper. Dot with 2 tablespoons of the butter. Cover and bake in a preheated

400° oven for 15 to 20 minutes, until the fish flakes. Drain liquid into a saucepan and place on low flame. Keep the fillets and oysters warm. Mix the flour and 1½ tablespoons of cold butter with fingers. Drop little chunks of the mixture into the liquid and simmer until the broth is thickened, stirring constantly. Ladle sauce over flounder and oysters. Garnish with parsley. Serves 4.

*Note:* "A hit."

## BEACH HAVEN FLOUNDER

1½ pounds flounder fillets
4 tablespoons butter
½ cup mayonnaise
2 tablespoons dry vermouth

¼ teaspoon onion powder
salt
⅛ teaspoon pepper
½ cup crushed cornflakes

Put fillets on a buttered piece of foil on a broiler pan. Melt butter and mix with mayonnaise, vermouth, onion powder and salt and pepper. Pour over the fillets. Let the fillets marinate for 10 minutes. Sprinkle with the cornflakes and broil, 4 inches from the heat, for 6 to 8 minutes, until fish flakes when probed with a fork. Serves 4.

*Note:* Penciled on recipe, "Excellent."

## FLOUNDER STUFFED TOMATOES

1½ pounds flounder fillets
4 large tomatoes
¼ cup finely chopped green pepper
¼ cup finely chopped celery
¼ cup finely chopped onion
salt and pepper to taste

pinch of chili powder
¼ teaspoon minced parsley
2 tablespoons butter
3 slices white bread, 1 cut in squares and
    2 dried in the oven and crumbled
paprika

Cook flounder in court bouillon, cool and break into bite-sized pieces. Cut tops out of the tomatoes. Scoop out the insides and discard half of them. Mix the other half with the pepper, celery, onion, salt and pepper, chili powder, parsley, 1 tablespoon melted butter, hard bread crumbs and chunks of flounder. Stuff the mixture in the tomatoes. Put a few soft bread squares on top of each tomato with a dab of butter and a sprinkling of paprika. Place tomatoes in a baking dish with a little water in the bottom of the dish. Bake in a 375° oven for 25 minutes. Serves 4.

*Note:* "It's great with fresh corn on the cob and new boiled potatoes."

## Court Bouillon

salt and pepper          dill weed
1 bay leaf             celery salt

In a frying pan, put enough water to cover fillets, salt and pepper, bay leaf and a sprinkling of dill weed and celery salt. When boiling, add fillets, cover and simmer for about 6 minutes, until the meat flakes when probed with a fork.

## SNUGGERY DOCK FLOUNDER

1½ pounds flounder fillets    salt and pepper
2 tablespoons butter         white sauce
⅓ cup dry white wine        paprika
¼ cup lemon juice          parsley sprigs

Put butter, wine, lemon juice and salt and pepper in a large frying pan and bring to a boil. Place the fillets in the liquid, cover and gently poach for 6 or 7 minutes, until the fish flakes easily with a fork. Place fish on a hot platter, spoon sauce over it. Sprinkle with paprika and garnish with parsley sprigs. Serves 4.

*Note:* Penciled on recipe, "Very good."

## White Sauce

1 tablespoon butter                salt and pepper
3 tablespoons chopped green pepper  ¾ cup milk
1 tablespoon flour                  ¼ cup shredded sharp cheese

In a small saucepan, melt butter. Add green pepper and cook for five minutes, until pepper is tender but not brown. Add flour, salt and pepper. Add milk, blend and cook until the mixture thickens, stirring constantly. Add cheese and stir until completely melted. Spoon on cooked fillets.

# CATHY'S FLOUNDER CASSEROLE

1½ pound flounder fillets
salt and pepper
4 hard-boiled eggs, chopped
2 tablespoons chopped parsley
3 tablespoons mayonnaise
2 teaspoons Dijon-type mustard
2 cups cooked long-grain rice

2 cups broccoli, steamed for 5 minutes
  and chopped
1 cup light cream
½ cup chicken stock
¼ cup dry sherry
dash of red pepper
salt and pepper

Sprinkle flounder fillets with salt and pepper. Mix eggs, parsley, mayonnaise and mustard and spread on the fillets. Roll the fillets and secure with toothpicks. Combine broccoli and rice. Add salt and pepper to taste. Put the fish rolls in a buttered casserole dish. Spoon the vegetable/rice mixture around the rolls. Mix the cream, stock, sherry and red pepper. Pour it over the fish and rice mixture. Cover and bake in a preheated 350° oven for 25 to 30 minutes. If the dish seems a bit dry, add a little more stock. Serve when the fish flakes when probed. Serves 4.

*Note:* "Good, complete meal."


# LEE'S FLOUNDER

1½ pounds flounder fillets
freshly ground pepper
mayonnaise

crushed cracker crumbs
lemon wedges
parsley

Butter a sheet of aluminum foil and spread fillets on the sheet. Pepper them. Spread the mayonnaise in a thin, even layer over the fillets, covering completely. Sprinkle the cracker crumbs over the fillets. Broil for 5 to 7 minutes, until the fish flakes easily but isn't dry. Serve with lemon and garnish with parsley. Serves 4.

# *Other Saltwater Species*

This section will be a potpourri of the salty ones I've worked with. I have some favorite recipes for several saltwater fish, but not enough for a complete chapter on each species.

If you bring home a fish I haven't mentioned, be experimental with it. If the fish is oily, try a bluefish or mackerel recipe. A firm-fleshed fish can be prepared as I did the black drum. Lean, large fish can be cooked like weakfish or striped bass. The small, lean saltwater fish will benefit from a flounder treatment.

Most fish can be poached or steamed and then made into chowder, cakes, loaf or salad. You'll find plenty of these recipes spread through the saltwater and freshwater sections. Any fish can be successfully smoked and this should be considered as an alternate cooking method. Be innovative with the fish you catch. To waste this bounty is a shame.

There are times when no matter how hard you try, it will be impossible to use all the fish before it begins to deteriorate in the freezer. This is especially true with oily fish. They have a freezer life of about 2 months. A large tuna, for instance, will yield more meat than the average family will want to eat in a couple of months. Part of the fish may be canned. Preserved this way, it will have a storage life of a year. An additional benefit is that canning frees the freezer for other perishables.

## BOXFISH

The ugly exterior of the boxfish from the Florida and Caribbean flats hides a succulent meat. The fillets (three in each fish) are sweet and lean. I experimented with them once by poaching for 10 minutes in boiling water that had been laced with a little salt, pepper and celery seed. When the firm fillets were done, they were cut into small, bite-sized pieces and dipped into a cocktail sauce made from catsup spruced up with a dash of lemon juice and a bit of horseradish. What an appetizer the boxfish provided after a hard day of bonefishing! It was like eating lobster.

## SEA ROBIN

Another example of a jewel being covered by a strange-looking case is the sea robin. While fishing for flounder, I saved several large sea robins to experiment with. After they were filleted, I cooked them as follows.

## BROILED SEA ROBIN

| | |
|---|---|
| skinless, boneless sea robin fillets | salt and pepper |
| butter | lemon wedges |

Butter fillets. Broil, 4 inches from the heat, for 5 to 6 minutes. Salt and pepper lightly. Serve with lemon wedges. Serve 4 fillets per person.

*Note:* If poached, the pieces could be eaten as an appetizer (use boxfish recipe). "Very firm fish. Tasted much like northern pike."

## SEA BASS

A friend, Eji Suyama, a surgeon from Ellsworth, Maine, is a gourmet cook. He shared a special sea bass recipe with me.

# STEAMED SEA BASS

1 3-pound sea bass (or other firm fish)
1 teaspoon salt
1½ to 2 tablespoons fermented black
   beans
1 clove garlic, crushed
2 thin slices ginger root, shredded

2 scallions, minced
3 tablespoons soy sauce
1 tablespoon sherry
½ teaspoon sugar
1 tablespoon cooking oil
onion brushes

Clean and scale fish but leave it whole with head and tail on. Score crosswise on both sides and sprinkle with salt. Soak fermented black beans in water for about 20 minutes, drain and mash together with garlic. Mix other ingredients (except onion brushes) until blended and spread over the fish. Place fish in a steamer and steam for 30 to 35 minutes, until it flakes at the thickest place on the backbone. Remove from steamer and place on a heated platter. Decorate or garnish with onion brushes. To make the brushes, take a whole 2- to 2½-inch scallion, split in half lengthwise about ⅓ of the way up. Split again so that you have a crosswise cut, spread cut end out a little and place scallions in a bowl of ice water until they have curled fringes. Drain and use as garnish. Serves 4.

# BLACK DRUM

I've never found a good black drum recipe in a cookbook, especially for the large size we are now catching off the New Jersey coast. The flesh is firm, the firmest meat I've found yet in a fish. Here are two recipes that were hits at my table.

# CHICKEN FRIED DRUM

1½ pounds black drum, cut in thin serving
   pieces
flour
salt and pepper
1 egg, beaten

1 tablespoon milk
dry bread crumbs, finely crushed
2 tablespoons butter
2 tablespoons cooking oil
lemon wedges

tartar sauce

Dust fish pieces with flour seasoned with salt and pepper. Dip them in egg mixed with milk. Roll in bread crumbs and fry in butter and oil combined. Cooking time is a little longer than most fish because the flesh is firmer—12 to 15 minutes should be about right. Serve with lemon wedges and tartar sauce.

*Note:* Penciled on recipe, "Great."

# BAKED DRUM IN TOMATO SAUCE

1½ pounds black drum, cut in serving
    pieces
1 large onion, chopped
1 clove garlic, minced
2 tablespoons olive oil
2 tablespoons butter
3 cups canned tomatoes

1 bay leaf
2 cloves
½ teaspoon thyme
salt and pepper
2 teaspoons sugar
1 teaspoon lemon juice
parsley sprigs

Sauté onion and garlic in the oil and butter until they are tender but not brown. Add the tomatoes, bay leaf, cloves, thyme, salt and pepper, sugar and lemon juice and simmer for 30 minutes until the sauce is reduced and slightly thickened and the flavors well married. Place the pieces of drum in an oiled casserole and cover with the hot tomato sauce. Cover and bake in a 450° oven for 13 minutes per inch of thickness of the chunks. Garnish with parsley. Serves 4.

*Note:* "Very good."

# MACKEREL

So much mackerel is caught and then passed off to the family cat that anglers ought to be punished for bringing home more than they can use. Smoking is the most popular treatment for this oily fish and they are delicious this way. But they are also good broiled, baked or used as an appetizer.

# BROILED MACKEREL

4 large mackerel fillets (or 8 small ones)
butter

salt and pepper
lemon juice

Place the mackerel fillets on a buttered piece of foil. Spread soft butter on the fillets and sprinkle with salt and pepper. Broil, 4 inches from the heat, for 6 to 10 minutes, depending on their thickness. Sprinkle with lemon juice and serve immediately. Serves 4.

*Note:* "Delicious."

# BAKED MACKEREL GLENNA

1½ pounds fresh mackerel fillets (skinless)  
several sprigs parsley  
1½ teaspoons lemon juice  
⅛ teaspoon garlic powder  

1½ tablespoons butter  
2 tomatoes, sliced  
1 cup white wine  
1 green onion, chopped  
salt and pepper  

Lay the parsley in a well-greased baking dish. Put the fillets on top of the parsley. Sprinkle with lemon juice and garlic powder and dot with butter. Place tomato slices over the fish. Pour wine over the tomato and add chopped onion and salt and pepper. Cover and bake in a preheated 425° oven for 15 to 20 minutes, until the fish flakes when probed with a toothpick. Serves 4.

# CURRIED MACK

½ cup cooked, flaked mackerel (pressed firmly into measuring cup)  
3 ounces cream cheese, softened  
½ cup grated Parmesan cheese  
½ cup mayonnaise  

2 tablespoons grated onion  
1 teaspoon curry powder  
pinch garlic powder  
⅓ cup chopped ripe olives  
chopped parsley  
pimiento bits  

Mix cream cheese, Parmesan, mayonnaise, fish, onion, curry and garlic thoroughly. Add olives and blend. Toast small rounds of thinly cut French bread under the broiler on one side. Cut them in two if they are too large for canapés. Turn the bread over and spread the untoasted side with an ample amount of the mackerel mixture. Broil until it is hot and bubbly. Sprinkle each round with a bit of parsley and a small piece of pimiento for decoration. Serve while piping hot. Will serve 8 to 10 as appetizers.

*Note:* Cook fish by using Poached Striper Patrice recipe. "Absolutely great—would also be super with bluefish or salmon."

## TILEFISH

Tilefish is lean and delicious. I'll take all I can get.

# TILEFISH AMANDINE

1½ pounds tilefish fillets
¼ cup flour
½ teaspoon salt
⅛ teaspoon pepper
¼ teaspoon onion powder

4 tablespoons butter
½ cup sliced almonds
2 tablespoons lemon juice
½ teaspoon chili powder
parsley sprigs

Cut the fillets into serving pieces and douse in the flour. Place the fillets on a piece of amply buttered foil on a broiler pan. Sprinkle the fish with salt, pepper and onion powder. Melt 2 tablespoons of the butter and pour over the fillets. Broil, 4 inches from the heat, for 10 minutes per inch thickness of the fillets. Check for flakiness by probing with a fork. Fish will be opaque when fully cooked. Sauté the almonds in remaining 2 tablespoons of butter. Add lemon juice and chili powder. Place fillets on a heated serving dish and pour almond sauce over the servings. Will serve 4. Garnish with parsley.

*Note:* "Excellent."

# TILEFISH SALAD

2 to 3 cups cooked, chunked tilefish
lettuce leaves
1 cup shredded iceberg lettuce
6 large mushrooms, quartered
1 avocado, sliced
½ cucumber, sliced

½ cup celery, bite-sized chunks
slices of sweet green and red pepper
1 hard-boiled egg, sliced (optional)
fish sauce
paprika
parsley sprigs

Arrange lettuce leaves on a platter (garden lettuce is nice). Place shredded lettuce, fish, mushrooms, avocado, cucumber, celery and pepper and egg slices artfully on the platter. Pour fish sauce over the salad. Sprinkle with paprika and garnish with parsley. Serves 3 or 4.

*Note:* Cook fish by using Poached Striper Patrice recipe. "Very good."

## Fish Sauce

½ cup mayonnaise
2 tablespoons heavy cream
2 tablespoons chili sauce
½ teaspoon steak sauce

6 drops Tabasco sauce
1½ tablespoons minced green onion
1 tablespoon fresh lemon juice
1 teaspoon minced parsley
salt and pepper to taste

Mix all ingredients and refrigerate for 1 hour before using.

# TUNA

This simple recipe for fresh tuna is a favorite.

## CAPTAIN STARK'S TUNA

1½-pound chunk of tuna
⅓ cup + 2 tablespoons dry white wine
1 cup mayonnaise
2 tablespoons bland prepared mustard

1 teaspoon steak sauce
3 tablespoons catsup
dash of cayenne pepper
¼ teaspoon celery salt

Place the tuna in an oiled baking dish. Add ⅓ cup white wine, cover and bake in 375° oven for 40 to 50 minutes, until done. Make a sauce from the mayonnaise, mustard, steak sauce, catsup, pepper, 2 tablespoons wine and celery salt. Serve the tuna with the sauce. Will serve 4.

*Note:* "Delicious."

# SHARK

## SHARK TETRAZZINI

2 cups flaked, cooked fish
½ pound sliced mushrooms
¼ cup chopped onion
¼ cup butter
3 tablespoons flour
1 cup light cream
1 cup chicken broth

3 tablespoons dry sherry
½ teaspoon seafood seasoning
½ teaspoon salt
pepper
dash of Tabasco sauce
5 ounces spaghetti, cooked and drained
½ cup shredded Parmesan cheese

2 tablespoons chopped parsley

Sauté mushrooms and onion in butter for a few minutes. Blend in flour. Slowly add cream and broth and stir until thickened. Add sherry, seasonings and Tabasco. Toss the sauce with the flaked shark meat and spaghetti. If it seems a bit dry, add more broth. Put the mixture in a well greased 2-quart casserole, sprinkle with cheese and cover. Place in a preheated 350° oven for 30 minutes, or until the cheese is melted and the casserole hot. Sprinkle with parsley. Serves 4.

*Note:* Cook fish by using Poached Striper Patrice recipe. This would be good with tuna also.

# *Wines to Serve with Fish*

The wine most often associated with fish dishes is Chablis. By this time almost everyone who has read anything about wine knows that *real* Chablis comes from a small portion of the Burgundy region in France. This tiny area (you could lose it in Rhode Island) obviously can't produce all of the wine consumed by fish eaters so we've got to look elsewhere. But just once, everyone ought to buy a *premier cru* Chablis and enjoy it.

The California Chablis, for the most part, is made from the same grape, the Pinot Chardonnay, that is grown in France. It produces very good wine on these shores and the prices won't put a dent in the budget. Almadén's Mountain White Chablis is an excellent buy at under $4 for 1.75 liters. So is Louis Martini's Mountain White, Los Hermanos Chardonnay and Gallo's Chablis Blanc. But these are only a few of the good California jug wines. There is so much happening on the West Coast these days that the search for good American wine has never been more exciting. They are blending most of their white wines for American taste and are doing an excellent job of it.

Another wine to look for when fish are considered is Green Hungarian. This is a grape name and Sebastiani Vineyards does a great job with it. I love it with pan-fried or mildly sautéed flounder.

The rich-tasting (but still light) wines of Italy are fine with mildly spiced fish dishes, whereas the really robust stews and chowders will be better served by one of the inexpensive Portuguese Vinho Verdes (green wine).

From New York, Ohio and even Pennsylvania, look for wines made from the Seyval Blanc grape. It doesn't taste "foxy" like so many Eastern wines do and goes well with almost any fish.

The advertisements telling us that German wine goes with anything aren't far wrong, but the pleasantly sweet Moselles are at their best with a cold fish salad. The Rhines are equally good but less fruity.

As a rule I don't care much for rosé wines with fish but there are exceptions. I can't explain it exactly, but a pan full of crisply fried trout seems to be ideally complemented by a cold bottle of pink wine—if it's not too sweet.

The joy of wine drinking (and it's the same with cooking) is that life is not long enough to sample all of the fine white wines that go well with fish. But what a marvelous time we can have trying! Yet I must take this opportunity to make a confession. For many years, the wine I served most often with fish dishes to guests was an under-three-dollar (for a half gallon) California Chablis that was always served in a decanter. During my early fish-cooking days some of the experiments were flops—but the wine never was.

# Smoking

The Indians of the Northwest were smoking salmon long before the white settlers found their way to North America. In those early days, it was feast or famine. When food was plentiful, the colonists could gorge themselves. When it was scarce, they did without. Then slowly, despite frequent failures, they succeeded in preserving some of the local bounty for the lean weeks and months. Milk became cheese, apples became cider and pork became ham.

Just a short time ago, smoking was one of the favorite means of preserving meat for the long winter. Along with salting, pickling and drying, the smoking of fish, meat and game was a fall ritual in rural America. When I was a youngster, we had a smokehouse that was used once a year—when Dad butchered the pig or two that he had fattened up all summer on skim milk from the one cow we kept. Smokehouses were still common in the late thirties and early forties, but as more people moved to cities and away from the land, the art of preserving food by smoking was almost lost.

But American ingenuity came to the rescue. Today, every outdoor catalog and most sporting goods stores feature small home smokers of various designs. Most of them work well and are easy to operate. With today's trend back to natural ways, smoked foods are prominently featured in gourmet shops and catalogs. I've tried some of these and they are delicious, but the prices are astronomical. Why pay them when you can buy a smoker for nearly the price of a brace of smoked pheasants or ducks? Home-built ones are even cheaper.

I have used both a Little Chief and an Outers electric smoker for several years. These models are similar. One opens in the front for easy access to the racks; the other opens at the top and has a rack that lifts out. Both use a small electric hot plate to make smoke out of sawdust and dry the food. Each one is so simple to operate that you will find yourself including it in day-to-day menu planning.

We love to shock our friends by serving things like smoked carp as before-dinner appetizers. They are always surprised at how good a "trash" fish is when smoked. Smoke-cooking is an excellent way to use some of the meat from edible sharks, too. The list of saltwater and freshwater fish that can be smoked is extensive. Bluefish, bass, trout, mackerel, pickerel, salmon, grouper and marlin are just a few of our smokehouse treats.

A couple years ago, Jim and I were on Hilton Head Island in Georgia for a few days of cobia fishing. Although we had a successful trip, we were unable to transport any fresh fish home with us. As we left, our guide handed us a large package of smoked cobia that he had prepared in his home smoker. It's extra touches like that which make a trip memorable.

Once you start smoking fish and game, you'll want to experiment with using different quantities of salt, sugar, spices and herbs. Keep exact records on each batch so you can duplicate the ones that are superhits. Also, record the length of time you smoke the fish or meat and note the outside air temperature. The brochures that come with the smokers have suggested recipes and times. However, those times may be too long for your taste, or the outside temperature may be so cool that you'll have to run the smoker longer. If possible, set an alarm clock to remind you to add another pan of sawdust or to check for doneness. It's easy to forget the smoker and find the fish or meat overdone and on the leathery side.

Over the years I have been smoke-cooking I've found that most people don't appreciate heavily salted fish and game. Go easy on the salt at first. We always refrigerate (and on rare occasions have frozen) the finished produce, so preservation is no problem. Most of the time it disappears too fast for you to worry about storage. However, if the smoked food will not be consumed within two weeks, it should be frozen immediately after smoking.

Here is a favorite fish-smoking recipe. You can use it with fillets, whole small fish or chunks of about one inch in thickness.

# SMOKED FISH

| | |
|---|---|
| 4 pounds fish | 2 bay leaves, broken into pieces |
| ½ cup brown sugar | ¼ teaspoon freshly ground black pepper |
| ½ cup salt | sprinkling of chili powder |

Mix sugar and seasonings thoroughly with 4 quarts water in an earthenware crock or enameled pan (do not use metal). Add fish. Brine for 12 to 24 hours in the refrigerator. The pieces of fish must be covered with the brine. Remove the fish from the pan and blot with paper toweling. Air-dry for 1 to 2 hours on a cookie sheet until a glaze forms on the surface of the fish. Place on the oiled racks in electric smoker (don't let pieces touch). Smoke for about 6 hours, using 4 pans of smoke. Check earlier for doneness. Refrigerate pieces in a heavy plastic bag.

# BLACK FOREST SMOKED SQUIRREL

| | |
|---|---|
| squirrels, cut into pieces | 1 teaspoon minced garlic |
| 1 cup red wine | 1 tablespoon minced onion |
| ¼ cup salt | 1 tablespoon MSG |
| 4 tablespoons sugar | butter |
| ¼ teaspoon pepper | brandy |

Marinate squirrel pieces in a mixture of wine, seasonings and 1 cup water for 12 to 16 hours in a nonmetal container. If meat is not covered, mix up more of the brine. After marinating, drain squirrel on paper toweling and place on a cookie sheet to air-dry for 1 to 2 hours. Place in an oiled electric smoker for 2 hours (2 pans of smoke). Finish the squirrel in a 225° oven, basting twice with butter, for 2 hours.

We often make a pâté out of the smoked squirrel by grinding the boneless meat, mixing with an equal amount of softened butter and moistening with 1 or 2 tablespoons of brandy. Serve with crackers.

# SMOKED PHEASANT

| | |
|---|---|
| 1 cleaned, plucked pheasant | seasoned salt |
| | butter |

Sprinkle an ample amount of seasoned salt on a pheasant that has been dampened with a little water. Place in the refrigerator overnight. Using 3 pans of sawdust, smoke in an electric smoker for about 6 hours, until legbone turns easily in the socket. Baste once during the smoking with melted butter.

# SMOKED VENISON

4-pound boneless venison roast  
1 cup white sugar  
1 cup salt  
3 bay leaves  

½ teaspoon marjoram  
½ teaspoon chili powder  
2 teaspoons coarsely ground black pepper  
1 tablespoon soy sauce

Roll the roast and tie with a cord. Mix all the rest of ingredients in a deep bowl or pan (nonmetal) with enough water to cover roast. Add the roast and refrigerate for 48 hours. Remove roast from brine, drain on paper toweling and air-dry on a cookie sheet for 1 to 2 hours.

Smoke the roast in an electric smoker for 25 hours, 5 pans of sawdust. If the weather is cold, you may have to finish cooking the roast in the oven—300° for 2 hours. Cut thin and serve.

# SMOKED DUCK AND/OR CHUKAR

cleaned ducks or chukars (with skin)  
½ cup sugar  
½ cup salt

Brine the whole birds in water to cover mixed with sugar and salt for 24 hours. Drain on paper toweling. Let air-dry for 1 hour. Smoke in electric smoker, using 2 pans of sawdust. The chukar took 4 hours; the duck, 5 hours. The outside temperature was about 70° during this test.

# SMOKED DUCK SPREAD

1 cup ground meat from a smoked duck  
1 tablespoon minced onion  
1 teaspoon + 1 cup softened butter  
salt and pepper  
1 to 2 tablespoons brandy

Cut all the meat from legs, wings and back of smoked duck and put through meat grinder. Sauté the onion in the 1 teaspoon butter until tender. Cool and blend the softened butter and onion into the ground meat. Moisten with brandy. Serve spread on thin rye bread or bland crackers.

## *MOIST SMOKING*

I've experimented with a cooker called the Sportsman Smoker (Brinkmann Company). The main difference between this smoker and the others I've used is that it cooks with moist smoke. My Sportsman model uses charcoal as its heat source. Chunks of hardwood and a water pan between the heat and the meat add moisture and a woody flavor. I've tried pheasant and geese in the Sportsman Smoker and they were excellent. It's a roomy smoker and will take a wild turkey or a large venison roast.

The recipe used for the pheasant (and later the goose) was a snap. I simply marinated the bird for 12 hours in beer to cover. Just before smoking, I removed the bird from the liquid. It was drained on paper toweling and sprinkled with seasoned salt.

Liquid (spray-on) shortening is used to coat the entire inside of the new smoker and rack to make cleanup chores easier and to prevent food from sticking. Both the charcoal and water pans are covered with heavy-duty aluminum foil. I cut some green maple wood chunks (hickory or apple is great too) and soaked them in water for a half hour before starting the charcoal fire. Once the charcoal was burning, I added the wood chunks to the top of the pan, then dropped the water pan into place. This was filled with the beer that had been used to marinate the bird. (Add extra water if necessary to bring it near the top of the pan.) The grill was quickly inserted, the bird placed on it and the lid set in place.

In about a ½ hour, smoke started to seep out from around the lid. The urge to lift the lid was strong but I resisted. No peeking is allowed unless you think it may need more liquid. It would take at least a ½ hour to regain the heat lost in one peek.

I smoked my first pheasant for 6 hours. By that time, the charcoal was losing its heat and the leg joint of the bird moved easily. When I cooked a goose, it too was done in the same time but it was a warmer day and the fire seemed a bit hotter. Each smoking will be different and records should be kept with your smokers.

I now use my electric smokers for fish and small game and the charcoal smoker for large birds and roasts. There are entire books devoted to smoke cooking if you have the inclination to go into it in a big way and perhaps build your own smoker. Check the bookstores.

# Clay Pot
# Cooking

Cooking with clay pots has become more popular in recent years. One reason is the easy availability of reasonably priced pots in kitchen equipment stores and mail-order catalogs. Another is the worry about excessive fat in the diet. Clay-pot cooking doesn't utilize much fat, yet the food remains juicy.

For years I'd read about cooking with wet clay in camping magazines and books. But it always sounded so messy. To reach the cooked food, the improvised pot had to be smashed. Undoubtedly, cavemen originally invented clay-pot cookery when they discovered that game smeared with wet clay and placed in hot coals was juicier and easier to prepare than the usual over-the-fire roasting method.

With wild game to prepare, a cook will be especially pleased with clay-pot cookery. The meat is constantly bathed in steam. The pots come in glazed and unglazed models. The chief difference seems to be that the glazed ones are easier to clean. I have used only an unglazed pot, suspecting that the glaze might interrupt the steaming process to some extent—and game needs all the moisture it can get.

Basically, clay-pot cookery is simple. The pot is soaked in water before being filled with food. It is then placed in a *cold* oven. The heat is turned high and the meal forgotten until time to check for doneness. The porous clay allows some moisture to escape while constantly basting the food with steam. The game comes out beautifully tenderized and miraculously brown. All the good vitamins stay in the pot, too.

The first recipe I tried in the pot was Pheasant au Vin. The bird was tender and juicy, yet the carrots and celery placed in the pot at the same time retained their crunch. I can't explain it, but I was sold on the cooking method. And for those of us who have a tendency toward laziness, it's easy *and* fun.

There are several rules for clay-pot cooking but they are easy to follow as you work with the method. For instance, you must always soak the pot (top and bottom) in water for 15 minutes before filling and cooking. The pot is not tolerant of sudden heat changes so it must be placed in a cold oven and brought up to full steam. The same thing applies when it is removed from the oven. The hot container should rest on a heavy towel or cork trivet and never on a cold surface. It is said that you can mend a broken clay pot with epoxy glue, but I'm not going to test this until I have to. Because a clay pot never becomes as hot as a metal one, the heat used is higher than with most baking and roasting recipes.

The container should be cleaned with warm water and a stiff brush. Detergents are not used since they will clog the pores and impart a soapy taste. The unglazed pot will retain cooking spots and become mottled as it seasons. When it needs to be "freshened," it can be soaked in warm water with a couple of tablespoons of baking soda.

There are several books on the market devoted to clay pot cookery. I have a couple of them and found them interesting. One, however, calls for excessive salting of food. I think this is unnecessary. A tip suggests removing the lid for the last few minutes of cooking to brown a bird. I found this unnecessary for the pheasant, but the duck needed it. This could be because I buttered the breast of the pheasant or it may have something to do with the longer cooking time. Another tip concerned precooking firing of a new pot—a soaking and baking with nothing in it—a good idea. A weird odor comes from the clay that I was happy to be rid of. After that, it was pleasant smells all the way.

Both cookbooks praise arrowroot as a thickening agent. It is said to impart no taste of its own, leaving you with the pure flavor of the recipe. Arrowroot works fine but I'm not sure it's that much better than cornstarch or flour. I found arrowroot for sale with the spices at a cheese and specialty meat store in a nearby shopping center.

My clay pot is the chicken brick size (holds 1¾ quarts liquid). All the recipes in this chapter will fit in this clay pot. There are, however, larger clay pots which would work fine if you wish to double the recipes.

## PHEASANT AU VIN

1 whole pheasant (with skin)
1 cup dry red wine
⅓ cup wild rice
1 tablespoon butter
1 stalk celery, cut in 2 to fit pot
1 large onion, cut in 2

1 large carrot, sliced lengthwise, then cut
   in 2 to fit pot
2 parsley sprigs
salt and pepper
arrowroot (or cornstarch)
chicken bouillon

Marinate the pheasant in the red wine for 4 hours, turning often. Cook the wild rice. Place the clay pot in water for the 15-minute soaking time. Dry pheasant and stuff with wild rice. Tie legs together with string and rub the skin with butter. Place the bird in the wet clay pot. Add vegetables around the pheasant. Pour in the wine. Cover and place in the middle of a cold oven. Turn the heat to 480° and cook for 1 hour and 20 minutes. Check to see if the leg moves easily. If the bird is done, pour the pot sauce into a pan and thicken with a little arrowroot (or cornstarch) and water. If there isn't enough liquid for sauce, add a little chicken bouillon. Heat to thicken and serve in a gravy boat to be generously ladled over the pheasant and vegetables. With a sharp knife or poultry shears, split the pheasant in 2. Will serve 2.

## POTTED RABBIT

1 rabbit, cut into pieces
1½ tablespoons flour
salt and pepper
1 tablespoon butter
1 tablespoon olive oil

1 teaspoon rosemary
¼ teaspoon oregano
2 tablespoons fresh parsley
4 tablespoons bourbon
½ cup beef bouillon

arrowroot (or cornstarch)

Soak pot in water for 15 minutes. Douse the rabbit pieces in the flour seasoned with salt and pepper and brown in a hot skillet with the butter and oil. Place the rabbit in the wet pot with more salt and pepper, other seasonings and liquids. Place the covered pot in the middle of a cold oven and turn the heat to 480°. Cook for 40 minutes. Check the meat. If it is tender, remove pot from oven to a heavy towel or cork trivet. If it needs more cooking, return for another 10 to 15 minutes. Age of the animal will determine cooking time. Thicken pan sauces with arrowroot or cornstarch. Will serve 2.

# CARIBOU STEW

1½ pounds caribou stew meat
2 tablespoons flour seasoned with salt
  and pepper
1 tablespoon butter
1 tablespoon olive oil
2 cloves garlic, chopped
1 teaspoon salt
¼ teaspoon pepper
1 bay leaf

¼ teaspoon oregano
1 tablespoon lemon juice
½ cup beef bouillon
4 carrots, sliced once lengthwise
4 whole turnips, peeled
1 14½-ounce can tomatoes, drained
1 teaspoon arrowroot
2 tablespoons brandy
dash of nutmeg

Soak top and bottom of clay pot for 15 minutes. Douse the stew meat in the seasoned flour and brown in the butter and olive oil in a heavy skillet. Put the meat in the clay pot. Place the remaining flour in the frying pan with garlic, salt, pepper, bay leaf, oregano, lemon juice and bouillon. Simmer until thickened, cool slightly and pour into pot. Add carrots, turnips and tomatoes. Place the cold container in a cold oven. Set temperature to 450° and cook for 90 minutes. Thicken the sauce with arrowroot, adding the brandy and nutmeg. Bring to a boil and serve with the stew. Serves 4.

Venison, moose or elk meat would work equally well in this recipe.

# STEAMED BLUEFISH

4 bluefish fillets, skinned and boned
¼ cup chopped fresh parsley
2 bay leaves
1 small onion, sliced + 4 tablespoons
  chopped onion

½ lemon, sliced
4 tablespoons butter
salt and pepper
6 mushrooms, sliced thin
1 teaspoon arrowroot

Presoak the pot for 15 minutes. Place the bluefish fillets in the clay pot and add the parsley, bay leaves, onion slices, lemon, 2 tablespoons butter, ¼ cup water and salt and pepper. Cover the pot and place in a cold oven. Set temperature for 480? Count on 15 minutes to heat the oven and pot and then 10 minutes per inch thickness of the fillets. Check for flakiness after 25 minutes. Sauté the mushrooms and chopped onions in the remaining butter and add to the pot juices in a saucepan. Add arrowroot dissolved in water and heat until thick. Pour over fish and serve. Will serve 4.

# MICKEY'S DUCK

1 large duck (mallard size)
1 carrot, sliced
3 green onions, chopped
½ teaspoon salt
¼ teaspoon thyme

1 bay leaf
¼ cup Madeira
½ cup beef broth
1 tablespoon plum jelly
cornstarch

Soak clay pot for 15 minutes in water. Place carrot and onions in the bottom of the wet pot. Add duck. Sprinkle duck with salt and thyme. Add bay leaf, Madeira and broth to the pot. Cover and place in the center of a cold oven. Turn heat to 500° and cook 1 hour. Remove the cover for the last 5 to 10 minutes to brown, if you wish. Remove from oven and place pot on a heavy towel. Remove duck to a heated platter. With poultry shears, cut the duck in 2. Remove carrot and onions from pot with a slotted spoon and arrange around the duck. Pour the juice from the clay pot into a saucepan. Add jelly and thicken with cornstarch. Serve the sauce with the duck. Will serve 2.

Wild rice with sautéed mushrooms is a fine companion dish for this recipe. Try a little of the duck sauce spooned over the rice.

# CLAY POT VENISON

3-pound boneless venison shoulder roast,
    rolled and tied with cord
⅓ cup wine vinegar
¼ cup soy sauce
salt
½ teaspoon lemon pepper seasoning

⅛ teaspoon chili powder
4 whole carrots
4 whole medium potatoes
2 small onions
pepper
1 cup beef bouillon
cornstarch

Combine vinegar, soy sauce, 1 teaspoon salt, lemon pepper and chili powder in a bowl and add the roast. Cover and refrigerate for 24 hours, turning occasionally. Soak clay pot in water for 15 minutes. Remove roast from marinade and place in wet pot. Add carrots, potatoes and onions around the roast. Dust the vegetables lightly with salt and pepper. Add the bouillon to the pot. Cover and place clay pot in the middle of a cold oven. Turn heat to 450° and roast for 1¾ hours. Place meat and vegetables on a heated platter and pour clay pot juices into a saucepan. Thicken the juices with the cornstarch mixed with a little cold water. Serve the gravy ladled over slices of meat and vegetables. Serves 4.

# CLAY POT FRENCH BREAD

¼ cup milk, scalded
1 tablespoon margarine
¼ ounce fresh yeast

1 tablespoon sugar
2¼ cups all-purpose flour
1 teaspoon salt
½ teaspoon poppy seeds

Combine the scalded milk with ½ cup boiling water. Cool to lukewarm and add margarine. Whisk until melted. Combine the yeast with 2 tablespoons lukewarm water. Add the lukewarm milk mixture to the yeast. Mix the sugar, flour, salt and poppy seeds together. Add the liquid mixture and stir in thoroughly, but don't knead. Place the dough in a greased bowl. Cover with a damp tea towel and place in a warm place until it doubles in bulk, about 1½ hours. Soak the clay pot for 15 minutes. When the bread dough has doubled, form into a long loaf to fit the bottom of the clay pot. Butter a small sheet of lightweight aluminum foil (shiny side) and fit into the bottom of the wet pot, buttered side up. Smooth out any bumps so bread dough doesn't get stuck in the cracks. Place the dough on the foil. Cover with the damp towel and again allow the dough to double. When ready to bake, cover with wet clay top, place in cold oven and turn heat to 500°. Bake for 45 minutes. Remove pot to a heavy towel. Lift the bread out with the help of the edges of foil. Remove the foil and brush entire bread surface with butter.

*Note:* "Best French bread I've ever tasted."

# Dutch Oven
# Cookery

If I were to be marooned on a desert island with one cooking utensil, the Dutch oven would be my choice because of its versatility. There is no limit to its cooking capabilities. In addition to deep and shallow frying, stewing, braising and boiling, the oven will roast and bake. It can be hung over an open fire, placed on the ground over hot coals or buried underground in coals.

The cast-iron Dutch oven was an efficient cooking device in pre-Revolutionary days when the frontier was in the eastern part of the United States. It's hard to believe that Dutch ovens were sold for about the same amount of money then as now. Even a used one cost a week's pay in the old days. But it was worth it—and still is.

The secret is in the design. The outdoor model has three legs to keep the bottom of the oven from making direct contact with the ground, allowing air circulation beneath the oven. This simplifies the regulation of heat. The depth of the pot and the tight-fitting flanged (turned-up edges) lid, as well as the thick cast-iron walls, keep the heat in. Since you can bank coals all around and on top of the Dutch oven, the heat is uniform.

The indoor cast-iron Dutch oven has no legs so it can sit on a range. Its top is round without the raised edges. In a pinch, this oven can be converted for outdoor cooking by placing stones or bricks under it. Then either turn the metal lid upside down or use heavy-duty aluminum foil to form a ring to fit on top of the lid to hold coals.

The ovens come in a wide range of sizes from 8 inches in diameter on up. The 10- or 12-inch size is about right for most families, while the 16-incher will be useful for a group or large family. Any oven bigger than that is too heavy to carry around. The 8-incher has a capacity of 2 quarts and weighs 7 pounds; the 10-inch, 4 quarts and weighs 12 pounds; 12-inch, 6 quarts and 17 pounds; 14-inch, 8 quarts and 23 pounds; 16-inch, 12 quarts and 30 pounds. Camping supply stores stock Dutch ovens and they are also available from Boy Scout outlets.

Cast-aluminum Dutch ovens are also sold by outfitters. They are lighter in weight than the cast-iron models, but they are poor substitutes for the real thing, especially in the outdoors where even heating is essential. The aluminum heats rapidly, cools faster and develops hot spots whereas the cast-iron models heat slowly and evenly and then hold the heat for a long time.

The care and feeding of a Dutch oven is crucial. Virgin cast-iron is porous and must be cured to prevent food tastes from lingering. A new oven must be washed in hot, soapy water and then seasoned so it won't rust. Heat it in a moderate oven until it is hot. Then coat generously (including the bottom of the lid) with lard, suet, or any *salt-free* shortening. Heat again, until the grease starts to smoke. Remove from the oven and wipe the Dutch oven with paper toweling to remove excessive grease, leaving a thin film. The oven is now ready to use.

Most food particles can be removed with the swipe of a dish cloth or plastic scraper. Mild soap and water can be used to clean the oven, but detergents and soap pads will remove the seasoning and you'll have to start all over again. Every time I use water in my Dutch oven, I dry it thoroughly, either on top of the stove or over a campfire, and swab a little grease on it while it's still hot. It's an added precaution to keep the rust away.

The Dutch oven is excellent for shallow frying because it holds heat well. Frying can be done in the pot itself or on the lid. To use the lid, invert it on bricks, stones or a grill over a bed of coals. Eggs, meat or pancakes can be added when the lid is sizzling hot. Test with a few drops of water. Deep frying of fish, potatoes or chicken is easily accomplished in the Dutch oven. Regulate the heat of the cooking oil by moving coals around under the oven.

When boiling in a Dutch oven, arrange the coals so the water is at a slow boil rather than a vigorous one. The water temperature is the same but the food cooks without breaking up. When a Dutch oven is hot, never add cold water to it since it could warp the oven. Use warm or hot water and add slowly.

Stewing is simple in a Dutch oven. A good recipe to try is Caribou Stew from the chapter on big game. Two of our camping favorites are Dutch Oven Chili and Spanish Rice, both made with venison burger, although in a pinch, lean hamburger can be substituted.

## DUTCH OVEN CHILI

1 pound venison burger
1 tablespoon cooking oil
1 onion, chopped
½ green pepper, chopped
½ teaspoon chili powder (more or less according to taste)

salt and pepper
1 tablespoon sugar
3 cups chopped tomatoes (or 1-pound, 12-ounce can)
½ cup sliced mushrooms (or a 4-ounce can)
1 1-pound can kidney beans

Set the Dutch oven over hot coals and heat for 10 minutes. Add oil when the oven is hot and sauté the onion and green pepper. Add burger and brown. Add salt and pepper and chili powder to taste. Mix in sugar and tomatoes. Cover the Dutch oven and regulate the heat so the mixture simmers. Cook slowly for 45 minutes. Add kidney beans and mushrooms, simmer another 15 minutes and serve. Serves 4.

## SPANISH RICE

1 pound venison burger
1 small onion, finely chopped
⅓ cup finely chopped green pepper
2 tablespoons cooking oil
Tabasco sauce

1½ teaspoons salt
pepper
1 15-ounce can tomato sauce
1 cup long-grain rice

Set the Dutch oven over hot coals for 10 minutes to heat thoroughly. Sauté onion and pepper in hot oil. Add venison and brown. Add salt and pepper. Slowly stir tomato sauce and 2 cups warm water into the burger mixture. Add rice and mix well. Cover the oven and adjust the coals so the Spanish rice cooks slowly. The coals may be a bit hot and more water needed, so check a couple of times during the cooking. Simmer 45 minutes. If the rice is cooked and the water absorbed, add a dash or two of Tabasco, blend and serve. Cook a few extra minutes, if necessary. Will serve 4 to 6.

## FIRE-PIT OVENRY

For fussless roasting at camp, dig a fire pit slightly larger than your Dutch oven. Build a hardwood fire. While it's burning down, breakfast can be cooked over the flames. When the coals are glowing, mix up Dutch Oven Venison. Scoop out half of the hot coals. Place the filled Dutch oven in the bed, cover with the rest of the coals, place a piece of damp burlap over the coals (don't let it touch the coals) and seal with a layer of soil. That's all there is to it. You can spend the day hunting, fishing, hiking or just plain loafing. At suppertime, dig up the oven. While it's still piping hot, grab a loaf of bread and you're all set to eat. If the cooked venison has cooled a bit, place it over a small fire to reheat for a few minutes. Potatoes fare well in a Dutch oven used this way. And the Pheasant and Kraut recipe sold me on the cast-iron wonder for life.

## DUTCH OVEN VENISON

| | |
|---|---|
| 4-pound venison roast (or elk, moose, antelope, caribou or beef) | 4 potatoes |
| | 6 carrots |
| 3 tablespoons butter | 1 large onion, sliced |
| 1 can cream of mushroom soup | ¼ teaspoon basil |
| salt and pepper | |

Preheat Dutch oven over coals. Add butter and sear the meat on all sides. Add soup, ½ can water and onion slowly to the pot, stirring to mix. Cut potatoes and carrots coarsely or, better still, add them whole so they don't overcook during the day. Sprinkle with basil and salt and pepper. Cover the Dutch oven and bury in coals for the day—6 to 8 hours. Will serve 4.

## PHEASANT AND KRAUT

| | |
|---|---|
| 2 pheasants, cut in pieces | flour |
| 4 tablespoons butter | 1 large can sauerkraut |
| 1 apple, cored and cut into quarters | |

Allow a hardwood fire to die to glowing coals (or use plenty of charcoal briquets). Preheat the oven, melt butter in it and brown the bird pieces that have been dusted with flour. Cover the bottom of the Dutch oven with half the sauerkraut. Add bird pieces and then the rest of the kraut. Place the apple pieces on top. If the sauerkraut is not juicy, add a little water to the pot. Cover the oven and put in the coals, distributing lots of hot coals on the lid. Let it roast for 1½ hours before checking to see if the meat is tender. Serves 4.

*Note:* This would be equally delectable with quail, chukar, dove or woodcock or with a combination of any of these birds. The tight seal and the slow, moist roasting combine to make it a hit.

## STEAK AND POTATOES

2 to 3 pounds venison steak
6 tablespoons butter
6 large potatoes

1 large onion
salt and pepper
flour
milk

Heat the Dutch oven over hot coals. Add 2 tablespoons of butter and brown the steak on both sides. Remove the meat from the pot. Slice a layer of potatoes into the oven. Add a couple of slices of onion and a sprinkling of salt and pepper and flour. Add another layer of potatoes, onions, seasonings and flour. When potatoes and onions are all in the oven, slowly add milk until it almost comes to the top of the potatoes. Add a final dusting of salt and pepper and flour. Top with the rest of the butter (4 tablespoons) and the steak. Cover the oven and bury the pot in a bed of coals for the day. If the oven has cooled too much by dinner, you may have to add a little more milk and reheat over a small fire. Serves 4.

*Note:* This recipe would be excellent with ham too.

## *DUTCH-OVEN BAKING*

I get a kick out of baking in my Dutch oven when we are at camp. Any homemade pie, bread or cake recipe will work, but the ready-made biscuit, bread and cake mixes are ideal for a busy outdoor person. I find the easy way to bake is with charcoal briquets. For my 10-inch Dutch oven, I light a pile of thirty briquets and wait until the gray ash forms on the edges. Spread half of the briquets on the ground under the oven. Place the rest of the charcoal on the lid, using a pair of tongs. While the oven is heating (10 minutes), mix up the pan of goodies. Place the pan on a cake rack in the oven. This keeps the bottom from baking too fast. Put the lid back on and wait the minimum time on the recipe box before checking for doneness. You may have to add more hot briquets, but if the recipe calls for an hour or less baking time, one dose of charcoal should do the job nicely.

It surprised me to find that the cooking time varies little from that in indoor recipes—unless there is a wind blowing. Baking requires that the oven be level. See to this before you light the charcoal by setting the oven where you want to bake and pouring some water on the lid. In this way it's easy to see if any legs need to be propped up a bit.

In a large Dutch oven, two things can be baked at the same time, for instance a meat loaf in one loaf pan and scalloped potatoes in another. Another tip: If you don't have a round cake rack to fit your Dutch oven, place aluminum foil (shiny side up) in the bottom of the oven and bake in the foil.

# Venison
# Sausage
# and Salami

### SAUSAGE

Sausage has been an important meat staple in this country since colonial days. Today, more than a hundred commercial varieties are sold. Venison sausage has enjoyed a resurgence in the United States since the early 1960s. It was a favorite food of President Lyndon Johnson and was often served at his ranch in Texas.

For cooking purposes, sausage can be made from elk or moose, using exactly the same recipes as for deer meat. Many old-fashioned butchers make excellent venison sausage, bologna and salami for their favorite customers. But it's a kick to make your own sausage. When you do mix up a batch, it can be seasoned the way your family enjoys it and not the way someone else thinks it should be.

A butcher will grind your meat, but many sausage fanciers enjoy doing it themselves. If you choose this way, be sure the blades on your machine are sharp so the meat is sliced and chopped, rather than mashed. A butcher supply house can usually do a good job of sharpening grinder blades.

Venison sausage can be made into patties or stuffed into casings for smoking or for use without being smoked. Your butcher may be able to loan you a hand-stuffing machine. But you can also make your own stuffer by cutting off the bottom of a 2-quart plastic bottle and slipping the casing over the neck of the bottle. Then simply shove the sausage mixture as best you can through the neck of the bottle into the casing. Some grinders also have a sausage stuffer as optional equipment.

To make a sausage ring, don't cut off the filling until the ring has formed. If, however, you wish to make sausage links, give the casings a couple of twists every 5 inches or so to form the links. Individual links can also be tied off with pieces of string.

Butchers in some areas will have hog casings for sale. In our neck of the woods, the natural casings are much cheaper than the edible synthetic ones. The natural casings (made from intestines) should be kept refrigerated in a saltwater solution. If you have any left over after the sausage making, they'll keep this way indefinitely.

Rings of sausage are easier to smoke than links and are also more manageable if sandwich meat is your goal. Links work better for breakfast meat and for chunks to add to spaghetti sauce.

Using a small, home electric smoker, smoke the rings (or links) of venison sausage for about 6 hours using three or four pans of hickory sawdust, rotating the rings on the racks from time to time.

Because the sausage has a considerable amount of pork in it, you must make sure it is thoroughly cooked. There are several ways to accomplish this. The sausage can be boiled in water shortly after it is stuffed or just before final preparation. It can also be baked at 350° for an hour in a casserole dish in the oven. The links can be sliced lengthwise before frying for breakfast if time is short.

Traditionally, only the less-choice venison cuts are made into sausage, bologna, salami or deer burger. However, a few sausage lovers convert their entire deer into the spicy delicacy—a waste of delicious chops and steaks, I think. But if you're a sausage lover, go to it!

Most venison sausage recipes use a ratio of three parts venison to one part pork. The recipe for Bucky's Venison Sausage is one we have enjoyed. Try it as is or experiment with the ingredients a bit—the choice is yours. But for heaven's sake, don't put your whole deer in *any* sausage recipe without trying a little of it fried. When you get a small batch mixed up (before it is stuffed), fry a patty in a heavy skillet. Let the cooked patty cool for about 10 minutes to marry all the seasonings. Then taste it. Correct your seasonings and continue on with the sausage making.

I once had a letter from a *Field & Stream* reader who had mistakenly thought that a recipe which called for garlic cloves meant whole garlic bulbs. He spoiled 60 pounds of meat by adding much too much garlic to the sausage. If he had tasted his first batch during the mixing, most of the venison would have been saved.

Venison sausage has many uses besides being served with eggs or pancakes for a traditional breakfast. If the hot pepper is omitted from the recipe, it can be used for a stuffing for quail or pheasant. A few links (with the hot stuff) add terrific flavor to spaghetti sauce. Homemade pizzas are a Sunday evening favorite in our household and some slices of venison sausage (with the hot pepper) make the pies extra special.

For a super appetizer, I pour barbecue sauce over some venison sausage links in a casserole. They are then baked at 350° for an hour. Slice thin while hot and serve with melba toast rounds. It's a hit with family and friends.

The Camper's Sausage Sandwich is a favorite stick-to-the-ribs breakfast.

## BUCKY'S VENISON SAUSAGE

| | |
|---|---|
| 5 pounds ground venison (all fat removed) | 1 tablespoon black pepper |
| | ½ teaspoon powdered allspice |
| 3 garlic cloves, crushed | 2 tablespoons fennel seeds |
| ½ cup dry red wine | ¼ teaspoon paprika |
| 5 pounds ground fatty pork | ½ teaspoon meat and poultry seasoning |
| 8 tablespoons salt | ¼ teaspoon ground hot pepper (optional) |

Soak the crushed garlic cloves in the wine for 4 hours, then toss the garlic away. Mix all the ingredients together well. Use your hands to mix so it is thoroughly blended. Check seasonings by frying a patty. Allow it to cool for a few minutes and then taste. When the seasonings are to your liking, stuff the mixture in casings or form into patties. If the sausage is too dry to stuff easily, add a little more red wine. Smoke, if you wish, and then freeze rings, links or patties by double-wrapping in Saran wrap and then in freezer paper. Makes 10 pounds.

## CAMPER'S SAUSAGE SANDWICH

| | |
|---|---|
| 4 pieces venison sausage, thinly sliced | ½ teaspoon parsley flakes |
| 1 tablespoon butter | salt and pepper |
| 1 egg, slightly beaten | 1 slice sharp cheese |
| 2 slices buttered rye toast | |

Melt butter in a small frying pan. Combine sausage, egg, 1 teaspoon water, parsley and salt and pepper and add to the hot frying pan. Turn the heat down and simmer until the egg is just set. Turn the mixture over and place the cheese on top of it. Cover for 1 minute to melt the cheese. Serve immediately between slices of rye toast. Makes 1 sandwich.

## *SALAMI*

I've made excellent salami from venison. This recipe is so easy that it's surprising how good the finished product is. The first time I made it, I cut everything by a fifth—using 1 pound of the venison/beef suet mixture and a corresponding amount of spices. It made one log. I didn't want to waste all that venison if it was going to be too hot for my family's taste. It was just right, but you may want to take the same precaution. The cooked salami can be used as you would its commercial counterpart—cut thin for sandwiches, on top of pizza, chunks in spaghetti sauce, as an appetizer or for snacks with beer.

## LARRY'S VENISON SALAMI

| | |
|---|---|
| 4½ pounds ground venison (fat removed) | 2 teaspoons garlic powder |
| ½ pound ground beef suet | 6 teaspoons salt |
| 2½ teaspoons whole mustard seeds | 2½ teaspoons liquid smoke |
| 2½ teaspoons fresh ground pepper | 1½ teaspoons red pepper |

Thoroughly mix all ingredients in a bowl (nonmetal), cover and refrigerate. Once a day, using your hands, thoroughly knead the mixture. Do this for 3 days. On the 4th day, divide the mixture into 5 parts, knead and form into long, thin logs—about 12 inches long. Place the logs on a cookie sheet and bake for 10 hours at about 155°. Use an oven thermometer to monitor the oven. (I find that when I set my oven control at 200°, the temperature will fluctuate between 140 and 170°. This gives me an average of 155°.) Halfway through the baking time (5 hours), turn the logs over. Remove the salami from the oven after baking and roll in paper toweling to remove excessive grease. Cool, wrap in foil and refrigerate. The salami will keep in the refrigerator for about 3 weeks. To freeze, double-wrap, first in Saran wrap and then in freezer paper. May be kept up to a year in a good freezer. Makes 5 12-inch salamis.

# Jerky
## and Pemmican

### JERKY

Throughout history as our country expanded, explorers, hunters, soldiers and other backcountry adventurers had to travel as lightly as possible. The only practical way of carrying meat without its spoiling was to dry it. This also reduced the weight of the meat by about five to one. Drying was the way the nomadic Indians solved their feast or famine problems when they downed a large game animal such as a buffalo. Dried, the meat was easier to carry on their migrations and it didn't spoil.

Today, backpackers, canoeists, cross-country skiers, hunters and anglers can make use of jerky and pemmican, a by-product. They are readily available in camping supply stores, sporting goods stores and even some supermarkets—but they are expensive. Jerky, however, is easy to make at home from venison, elk, moose or caribou as well as beef. Bear, wild boar and javelina are too fat to be successfully dried. Homemade pemmican is a bit more trouble, but it's fun to make besides being tasty on the trail.

Technically, jerky is raw meat with all the moisture removed. The Indians "jerked" their meat by cutting long strips of lean meat and allowing it to dry in the sun. Early pioneers did the same thing. Plenty of black or red pepper was often added to the dry meat to keep the flies at bay. This pepper was washed off before eating. Jerky was eaten "as is" or added to a dinner such as pan-fried potatoes and onions. A few pieces of jerky plus a can of tomatoes made this a modern one-dish meal.

Meat for jerky should be cut from lean slabs of meat. From a deer, the round steak makes excellent jerky. The meat must be cut in long, thin slices. The easiest way to do this is to partially freeze the slab of meat. When it is firm but not thoroughly frozen, use a sharp knife and cut with the grain. If pemmican is to be produced from the jerky, cut the strips against the grain. It will be easier to grind or crumble the dried meat. Next, remove all the natural animal fat on the strips for it could turn rancid and spoil quickly.

The simplest way to dry the meat is to lay it on racks and place them on a hotwater radiator or in the sun to dry until the meat is black, hard and moisture-free. To eat the jerky, a piece is gnawed off and thoroughly chewed in the mouth to reconstitute with saliva. It's high in protein and highly nourishing. Most jerky fanciers like to dry it with a few seasonings to make it more appetizing. Also, many people use conventional ovens to do their curing instead of the sun or old-fashioned radiators. If an oven is used, an oven thermometer is highly recommended. The meat must be dried, *not cooked*. To dry, set your oven temperature so the thermometer (laid near the meat) averages 150°. The door on the oven must be ajar for successful moisture escape. I've found a folded potholder works well for this. Count on committing your oven for 12 to 14 hours of drying time.

Once the meat is cut into thin slabs and treated, it can be laid directly on the oven racks. Or cheesecloth can be pinned securely to the racks and the strips laid on the cheesecloth. Another method of drying involves the use of toothpicks. Stick a toothpick through one end of a strip of meat and suspend it, dangling from the oven racks. Whatever method is used, the strips can touch each other but they should not overlap or they will not dry properly. Treated strips of meat can also be dried in the popular home electric smokers. Use two pans of sawdust, then simply leave the meat in the smoker until it loses all its moisture. The time will vary according to the outside temperature. If a smoky flavor is not desired, use no sawdust at all.

Jerky should be stored in moisture-proof containers such as glass jars or plastic jugs with tight-fitting lids. Although the jerky will last for many months, storage is usually no problem. The concentrated protein is gobbled up by family and friends before it has a chance to get old.

# EASY VENISON JERKY

1 pound venison round steak
salt

pepper
liquid smoke

    Remove all fat from the venison. Freeze meat until icy. Cut into very thin strips. Cut with the grain for jerky, against for pemmican. Place strips in bowl, sprinkling each layer of strips with salt, pepper and liquid smoke. Cover and refrigerate for 12 hours. Drain strips on paper toweling. Place strips on oven racks (or use alternate drying methods discussed previously) and set the oven so temperature remains at 150°. Open door slightly and dry the strips for about 12 to 14 hours, until all moisture is gone. Store in a covered container.

# SPICY JERKY

1½ pound venison round steak
1 teaspoon seasoned salt
¼ teaspoon black pepper

1 teaspoon onion powder
1 teaspoon celery seed
¼ cup soy sauce

3 tablespoons steak sauce

    Trim all fat from the meat. Semifreeze, then cut meat into very thin strips. Combine rest of ingredients and mix thoroughly. Put strips of meat in a shallow pan and brush a little of the marinade on each layer. Marinate the strips (covered) in the refrigerator overnight. Drain on paper toweling. Dry venison in 150° oven or in a smoker (2 pans of sawdust) until all the moisture is gone.

# *PEMMICAN*

    Indians and frontiersmen often needed a more balanced diet than jerky (which is all protein) afforded them. Crushed berries, which supply vitamins and a little fat, were sometimes mixed with the ground jerky to make pemmican. Woodsmen could survive for weeks on pemmican. All sorts of wild berries were (and are) used in pemmican, but I've found that raisins are easier to work with since they have already been dried to some extent.

    The Indians pounded their jerky to make pemmican. I use a hand-cranked home grinder. Pulverizing the meat is difficult if you're working with jerky that has been cut with the grain. Cut it against the grain when pemmican is going to be made. Place the powdered meat in small, flat containers (I use 5-inch, square Tupperware boxes).

Using a butcher knife or a chopper, dice raisins to add to the pemmican. Use your own judgment on how many raisins you want in your pemmican. A half cup per pound of jerky is a good place to start. Don't make the mistake I did the first time I made pemmican and try to run the raisins through the meat grinder. There is just enough moisture left in them to clog a small crank model. What a mess! Hand-chopping is by far preferable. Mix the raisins with the ground jerky and press into the containers. Next, melt some clean (beef) kidney fat over a low flame. Your butcher can supply this. Don't let the fat boil, just melt. Cool it a little and then pour slowly over the jerky/raisin mixture. Add enough fat to glue the combination into a cake but not enough to coat the top. When the cake cools, it can be sliced into candy bar-sized chunks to be carried in a plastic bag on the next hiking, hunting or fishing trip.

With a cup of water, it is surprising how filling a small piece of pemmican can be. Try it on your friends—and then tell them it is mostly raw meat with a few raisins and beef fat. They won't believe it.

# Turtle

Over 200 million years ago, before snakes, birds, mammals or dinosaurs had appeared on earth. the turtle had already stopped its crawl through evolution. The slow-moving reptile has undergone only minor changes since that distant time. Most are still without weapons of offense, the exception being the snapping turtle. This prehistoric survivor is found in streams and ponds throughout North America from Canada to Mexico. The ferocious snapper's meat is considered a gourmet's treat in many parts of the East, especially around Philadelphia, although some connoisseurs declare it inferior to other turtles, such as the diamond-back terrapin.

The old-timers were expert snapper hunters, probing in the mud near ponds or streams with a pitchfork until they encountered the hard shell. Since the snapping turtle spends most of its time in the water feeding on insects, crayfish, carrion or fish, some people actually fish for them with a stout rod, using a chicken neck on a large hook as bait. Few anglers today set out deliberately to capture a snapper. Most snapper soup results from chance encounters by campers, hikers, anglers or hunters.

Recently, a neighbor's son saw one crossing the road in front of his car. He jumped out, grabbed the reptile by the tail and suddenly was at a loss as to how to transport it to his home, several miles away. He ended up driving one-handed with a death grip on the snapper's tail while it dangled out the driver's window. Surprisingly, he made it home without being bitten or causing a traffic accident.

Knowing that I enjoy snapper soup, he turned the 13-pound turtle over to me. I'd made snapper soup many times in the past, but always with cleaned meat furnished by some kind friend.

The traditional way of killing a snapper is to allow it to snap onto a stick, then extend the head and chop it off with an axe. Thus dispatched, it can be hung by the tail for 1 to 8 hours to bleed thoroughly. Sounds easy, doesn't it? Our turtle would not cooperate. It had to be shot in the head. We then followed through with the other steps. After the turtle had been bled for 2 hours, I plunged it, held by the tail, into a bucket of boiling water. This treatment loosens the skin and relaxes the muscles. Some experts think that the whole turtle should be boiled for half an hour, since the reflex action of reptiles continues for some time after decapitation. I was afraid of cooking the meat, so I only scalded it.

I've heard that some turtle cleaners take a sledgehammer and break the shell with a mighty blow to get at the meat. This seems a bit crude. Instead, I turned the snapper over, exposing the small underplate that covers the bottom side. I tried to remove this underplate with a knife on the sides where cartilage connects it to the main shell. This maneuver was tougher than it looked. Tree pruners proved ideal for cutting through the hard bone. They were also useful later in removing small rib bones that protect two hidden fillets.

Once the bottom shell was removed, with the help of a trout fillet knife, it was easy to see the different cuts. The skin must still be removed from legs, neck and tail, for which the sharp little knife works beautifully. Remove all four legs, the long neck with its snowy white meat and the tail section. Next, dump the viscera from the shell and you'll find two slim, white fillets firmly attached to the back shell beneath what look like rib bones. Using the tree trimmers, snap the little bones in two places along the back. Slip a finger under each fillet and strip it out. I'll bet a lot of turtle cleaners miss those tender morsels. With the sledgehammer method, they would be smashed to bits.

We came out of the operation with a great deal of meat, far more than I would have believed. Including leg bones, the meat weighed almost 7 pounds. For soup, I cook the meat with the bones intact. They add flavor and make the cleaning job much easier. The meat can be stripped after cooking.

Turtle cleaners should be aware that the reflex action of the reptile's primitive nervous system can be a bit unnerving at first. The turtle reacts much as a fresh-caught trout does when placed in a frying pan—by curling and twitching. Even though the head has been removed and the snapper has been scalded in boiling water, you are given a start, to say the least, when it moves.

I hate to blow the whistle on Philadelphia snapper soup, but some of it is *not* made with snapper meat. Even when you do find the real stuff, it is often supplemented with veal and other dubious things. There are many ways of making snapper soup. The following recipe, conceived by my husband, is the best I've ever tasted anywhere. I think you'll agree. I also believe you'll enjoy the Snapper with Madeira and Fried Turtle. Because turtles can live longer than any other backboned animal (over 100 years), be patient with the cooking. Allow extra time with the recipes, just in case the turtle is an old-timer. It will become tender eventually.

## BRANDYWINE SNAPPER SOUP

| | |
|---|---|
| turtle meat (3 cups) | dash of ground cloves |
| 1 bay leaf | dash of garlic powder |
| 3 beef bouillon cubes | dash of allspice |
| salt and pepper | ½ cup medium-dry sherry |
| 2 carrots, chopped | parsley sprigs, chopped |
| 2 onions, chopped | juice of 1 lemon |
| 1 stalk celery, chopped | 1 teaspoon Worcestershire sauce |
| butter | 1 teaspoon sugar |
| 1 can tomato soup | milk |
| 1 can consommé | flour |

Cook turtle meat (on the bones) in water to cover, with the bay leaf, bouillon cubes and salt and pepper until the meat is tender. Remove from broth and cool. Brown the vegetables in butter with some salt and pepper. Put them in a heavy Dutch oven with 5 cups of turtle broth, tomato soup, consommé and the rest of the ingredients (except for milk and flour). Simmer until the vegetables are just done. Thicken with milk and flour and add turtle meat, removed from the bones and cut into small pieces. Serve with additional sherry. Serves 14.

# SNAPPER WITH MADEIRA

| | |
|---|---|
| 1¼ pounds turtle meat, filleted from the bones and cut into paper-thin pieces | ¾ cup Madeira |
| 3 tablespoons butter | ½ cup heavy cream |
| flour | 3 drops Tabasco sauce |
| salt and pepper | chopped parsley |
| | paprika |

Heat butter in a heavy skillet. Douse meat in flour and brown lightly in butter. Season with salt and pepper. Add ½ cup of wine, cover and simmer until the meat is tender, approximately 1 hour. Add a little water if necessary. Just before serving, add the rest of the wine and the cream. Heat to the boiling point. Blend in the Tabasco. Serve on buttered toast points, topped with a little parsley and a sprinkling of paprika. Will serve 4.

# FRIED TURTLE

| | |
|---|---|
| 2 pounds turtle meat | 5 tablespoons milk |
| 1 bay leaf | 2 eggs, beaten |
| 1 beef bouillon cube | ¼ cup + 2 teaspoons cooking oil |
| salt | catsup |
| pepper | horseradish |
| ½ cup flour | lemon juice |

Cook the turtle meat in water to cover with the bay leaf, bouillon cube and a little salt and pepper. When tender, cut the meat into 2- to 4-inch pieces. Make batter with the flour, ⅛ teaspoon salt, milk, eggs and 2 teaspoons cooking oil. Dip the turtle pieces in the batter and fry in ¼ cup hot oil until brown, about 5 minutes. Serve with hot chili sauce made of catsup, horseradish and lemon juice. Serves 4.

# Berries
## and Fruit

When I was a kid, August "dog days" meant the blackberries were ripe. There was an abandoned railroad bed not far from our house that gave up the sweetest berries I've ever tasted. On Sundays the whole family would pile in the car and drive to a secret berrying place out in the country. There we'd really load up. Those berry bushes were very tall and at least once during such an outing we would hear a rustling in the bushes and all picking would cease. Was it a bear? We never saw one, but enough of our friends did to make every outing a little scary and exciting to a youngster. Mother canned most of the berries, usually enough so that blackberry pie was on the menu once a week all winter. We loved it even more because it was made with "our" berries.

When life was simpler in this country, berries provided variety to the colonists' monotonous diet and furnished needed vitamins. Today, they supplement freeze-dried rations with a pleasing change of pace for the backpacker and for other campers who know what to look for.

A lot of people wonder why anyone would waste their time getting scratched, sunburned and purple-fingered from picking wild fruit, especially when the tame ones are readily available in markets. But picking wild berries is fun when you have companionship. Besides, once the wild ones are compared with the hyped-up domestic varieties, the picker becomes a believer. The flavor of wild fruit is so superior there isn't any comparison.

If you have traveled your home country for more than a few years, you already know where to look for various berries. If you're a beginner, the best place to start is the site of an old forest burn or a recent clearcut. Pipeline and power company rights-of-way are good berrying locations too, if they haven't been doused with weed killer. Most thorny-stemmed and low-growing berries need ample sunlight; dense forests are not good berry producers for this reason.

Be on the lookout for game of all kinds when you discover a new blackberry or raspberry patch. Just about every sort of small game as well as black bears love the ripe fruit. You may want to remember the spot when autumn arrives, if you're a hunter.

Try to remain alert to a berry bonanza when on strange turf. For instance, driving across New Brunswick several summers ago with our two young daughters, we stumbled on a hot spot. The girls spotted what they thought were pretty purple flowers along the road. To keep them happy and to stretch our legs, we stopped—and were glad we did. The "little flowers" turned out to be wild blueberries. The ground was covered with them. In seconds we were all out picking and filling every available container with the sweet little fruit. For the next 4 days, while attempting to catch a salmon on the Miramichi River, we feasted on wild blueberries and milk. They were great, but some experimenting came up with a delicious blueberry pancake made with the ingredients at hand in our tent trailer.

## WILD BLUEBERRY PANCAKES

1 cup pancake or biscuit mix         1½ cups powdered milk, reconstituted
1 egg (or 1 powdered egg)            1 cup blueberries
butter

Beat the egg, then stir in the mix and powdered milk until well blended. The batter should be quite thin, so add more water if it is too thick. Fold in the berries. Drop by spoonfuls in a hot, buttered frying pan. Tip the pan to let the batter completely cover the bottom. Flip when the first side is brown. Leftovers can be cooled, rolled up and carried with you for a lunch snack. Serves 4.

# JAMS AND SAUCES

Most game is beautifully enhanced by wild berry jam or sauce. Much of the commercial jams and jellies are too sweet to accompany wild meat with style. A strong hint of tartness is much preferred.

Last summer, with some extra berries, I started out to make some jam. But I found when I attempted to cut the sugar from the usual jam directions, the mixture wouldn't thicken properly. To add more body, I cooked it twice as long as normal and then added pectin. The resulting Blackberry Game Sauce has been a hit with venison chops, roast goose and rare grouse breast. Almost any kind of wild berry will blend nicely with game.

Black raspberries grow plentifully along the lane to our present home. Most of these are quickly converted to fresh pie but a few are cooked for jam or jelly.

## BLACKBERRY GAME SAUCE

4 cups washed blackberries
½ lemon
½ lime

dash of salt
1 cup sugar
1 cup liquid pectin
paraffin

Slice the lemon and lime thin and remove the seeds. Place in a blender and chop until the rind is in small chunks. Place with berries and salt in a large pot and bring to a boil. Cook over moderate heat for 30 minutes. Add sugar and cook another 30 minutes. Remove from heat, add 1 cup of liquid pectin and pour into hot, sterilized jars. Seal with paraffin.

## BLACK RASPBERRY JAM

4 cups washed and drained black
   raspberries
¼ cup port wine
pinch of salt

1 teaspoon lemon juice
2 apples, pared, cored and cut in tiny
   pieces
2 cups sugar
paraffin

Place berries, port, salt, lemon juice and apples in a heavy saucepan. Simmer the fruit uncovered until soft before adding sugar. Stir in sugar until dissolved and bring to a boil. Reduce heat and simmer, uncovered, until the mixture thickens. Stir frequently to keep the jam from sticking to the pan. Cook until a small amount dropped on a plate will stay in one place.

Sterilize jam glasses by filling ¾ full of water and place in a pan of water (lids resting on the jars) and simmer for 20 minutes. Keep hot until ready to fill. Seal with hot paraffin and store in a cool, dark, dry place.

## WILD GRAPE OR PLUM OR BLACKBERRY JELLY

Mash fruit without crushing seeds. Barely cover fruit with water and boil until fruit is disintegrated. Strain fruit through cheesecloth, pressing it through. Strain again through flannel, without pressing. Bring juice to a boil, adding 1 cup sugar for each cup of juice. Slowly stir until dissolved. Broil until jelly point is reached on a thermometer. Seal in sterilized jars with hot paraffin.

## *STRAWBERRIES*

Wild strawberry picking during the month of June is another family pastime. A backbreaking chore for the lone picker becomes fun when competition is strong to see who fills their pail first. Wild strawberries are so good that they need nothing more than a touch of sugar and a little milk most of the time.

A special treat is Strawberry Fool. To make this easy dessert, whip half a pint of cream with a little sugar and a dash of vanilla. When the cream is whipped, fold in a cup or two of fresh, wild strawberries that have been washed, hulled and thoroughly drained. A great dessert!

Old-fashioned strawberry shortcake (the biscuit kind) has almost gone out of style, but when I was a kid, my mother made a big deal out of our first wild strawberry picking of the year. Our Sunday supper consisted of a huge shortcake with all the berries and whipped cream we could pile on. What a feast! Here's the recipe she used.

## WILD STRAWBERRY SHORTCAKE

| | |
|---|---|
| 4 cups wild strawberries | ½ teaspoon salt |
| 2 cups flour | ⅓ cup butter or margarine |
| 4½ teaspoons baking powder | ½ cup milk |
| 1½ tablespoons sugar | 1 well-beaten egg |
| 1 cup whipping cream | |

Sift flour, baking powder, sugar and salt. Cut in the butter until mixture is like coarse bread crumbs. Beat milk into egg and add to the flour mixture. Stir only until the mixture is moistened. Butter a pie pan. Divide dough in half and press half of it in the bottom of the pie pan. Brush the top with some softened butter. Press the other half on top. Bake in a preheated 450° oven for 15 minutes, until a toothpick inserted in the center comes out clean. Cut pie in wedge-shaped pieces. Break pieces in 2. Pile on the strawberries and whipped cream. Will serve 8 to 10.

## DRYING

Our freezer space is limited and is mainly saved for preserving fish and game. The horn-of-plenty situation that I often encounter when picking berries or apples taxes my ability to cram everything into the freezer. I've never been much of a canner, probably because I *had* to help can when a youngster. Then we moved to the Pennsylvania Dutch country and I learned that they "schnitz" their apples, which means dry them. The old-fashioned way was to peel, core and slice them. They were then spread out on brown paper on top of the furnace or in some other warm place for 2 to 3 days. It is really just as easy today with the added plus of being fun. It's economical too and requires little storage space. Basically, when drying food the idea is to remove enough moisture from the fruits and vegetables to prevent spoilage and bacteria growth. In a hot, dry climate this can be accomplished by sun-drying. Most of us live in a humid area where it's better to use your oven set at 150° to accomplish this.

A few manufacturers have gotten into the drying business and several small home dehydrators are now being marketed. You can also build your own dryers. But they are for those who want to get into the drying in a big way. Most of us only do it occasionally and our ovens work fine.

Drying is not complicated, but it will keep you in the kitchen during the entire day because the food has to be stirred, trays have to be switched and the temperature must be watched. Once you have started, the process should be continued without interruption, or mold could grow on the semi–dry food. It would then have to be thrown out.

Preparation of food to be dried is similar to that for canning or freezing. Choose fresh fruit (or vegetables), picked the same day if possible. Wash and discard any moldy or bruised parts. Fruit should be treated to protect flavor, color and vitamins.

Since strawberries were in season, strawberry leather was my first attempt at drying fruits, and I couldn't have chosen anything easier to prepare or more delicious a treat to taste.

# STRAWBERRY LEATHER

5 cups strawberries                    ¼ cup sugar or honey

Wash and hull strawberries. Cut away any bad parts. Place the berries, a cup at a time, in a blender. Purée until smooth, then mix in the sugar. Line two 15½ × 10½ × 1-inch pans with plastic wrap. Try to eliminate any folds. Secure edges with tape. Spread the strawberry mixture in the pans. Put them in a 150° oven to dry.

Place a candy thermometer in the back of the oven on an upper rack to check the temperature. (With my oven I have to set the temperature control at 180° to maintain an even 150° on the thermometer. All ovens will vary, so you may have to check to get yours just right.) It is necessary to prop the oven door open during the drying process to let the moist air escape. (I used a folded pot holder to keep my electric oven open, but gas ovens may need a gap of up to 8 inches to maintain the desired heat.) Check temperature periodically and rotate pans every 2 hours. The leather is dry when the surface is no longer sticky to the touch. Check the sides to be sure the plastic wrap is smooth. Any puree caught in a fold will not dry properly.

The total drying time will be from 6 to 12 hours, depending on the humidity the day you try it, how well you've watched the temperature and other variables. Start early in the day if you are using the oven to cook the evening meal. (Better still, plan a cookout or top-of-the-stove meal for dinner.)

When the leather is dry, remove from the oven. Turn it out on a counter and pull away the plastic wrap. Check again to be sure it is completely dry. Let it cool. Then rewrap in plastic wrap, rolling like a jelly roll. Leathers can be stored at room temperature up to 1 month, in the refrigerator for 3 months and in the freezer for 1 year. (I had a hard time saving a little from eager eaters, but a piece I placed in the refrigerator was just as tasty after 6 months. It was a bit brittle compared with the fresh product.) There is no need to worry about storage, though, since your family will be crazy about it. It is superb in school lunch pails, on backpacking or fishing trips.

## APPLES

Apples were next on my drying experiments. The fruit selected should be fresh, sound and just right for eating. Most enthusiasts use drying trays made from scrap lumber (free from pitch) and stainless-steel hardware cloth. The idea is to circulate the warm air to all parts of the fruit (or vegetable) equally. For my experiment I used one layer of cheesecloth stretched tightly over my oven racks and pinned securely at the four corners and several places along the sides. It worked beautifully.

The apples were washed, cored, pared (with a stainless-steel knife to avoid discoloring) and cut into thin slices of uniform thickness so they would finish drying at about the same time. The next step is to pretreat to retard enzyme activity and therefore help halt loss of color, flavor and vitamins. I decided on an easy 10-minute dip into a half-gallon of water into which was mixed 2 tablespoons of salt and 1 tablespoon of lemon juice.

After the 10-minute dip, drain the slices thoroughly on paper towels before transferring to the drying trays. Use the same method to dry as with the strawberry leather, except start with 130°, gradually increase to 165° and finish at 145°. The slices will take about 6 hours and will be leathery and suedelike when done. Cut the thickest slice and check for moisture to be sure it is completely dry.

To condition dried food, place the pieces in a heavy-duty plastic bag (such as Ziploc), seal tightly and refrigerate for 2 days. Any moisture left in the food will be distributed evenly. Check again for moisture. If you find any, the fruit can be returned to the oven. The dried food should be stored in heavy-duty plastic bags and then doubly protected by placing it in coffee cans or glass jars. Keep them in a cool, dry, dark place. You can even freeze the containers; just be sure to protect them from light, heat and moisture. They have a storage life of between 6 and 12 months.

There are many books on drying fruits and vegetables but one of the best comes to us from the food editors of the Farm Journal. It is titled *How to Dry Fruits and Vegetables at Home* (see Bibliography).

Try dried apples with your first pheasant of the fall season.


## PHEASANT IN CREAMY APPLE SAUCE

1 pheasant, cut in serving pieces
1 cup cranapple juice
¼ cup butter
1 tablespoon brandy

1½ cups dried apples
1 teaspoon steak sauce
sprinkling of cinnamon, mace, salt, pepper

½ cup light cream

Heat the juice, melt the butter in it, and add brandy and apples. Soak for 1 hour. Place half the apple mixture in the bottom of a Dutch oven. Put the pheasant pieces (reserving the breast pieces) on top of the apples. Add rest of apples. Mix steak sauce with cream and pour over meat and apples. Add spices and cover. Heat on top of the stove for a few minutes to warm all ingredients. Pop into a preheated 350° oven for 45 minutes. Add breast pieces and bury in the apples. Bake another 45 minutes. Serves 2 to 3.

*Note:* I use skinned pheasant in this recipe. If your bird has its skin, you may wish to brown it in butter before proceeding with the recipe.

# Wild Greens

### WATERCRESS

Would anyone be foolish enough to buy a house because the property had watercress? We did! After three visits we were still trying to make up our minds. The property was private and quiet, the house was comfortable and well built but it lacked the one extra room that was needed for an office. The owner, who had also built the house, offered to put an office in the basement for a reasonable price. While we were contemplating his offer, he said, "Say, you know a lot about outdoor things. Maybe you can tell us what it is that people keep picking at the end of our drive. It's where the spring overflow runs down to the creek." Jim and I looked at each other incredulously. Could it be watercress? It was—and that was the end of the bargaining. Three months later, the house was ours and so was a supply of almost year-round watercress.

According to some historians, early immigrants brought the first watercress to this country in sailing ships. It provided vitamins for crew and passengers on the long crossing. Like a lot of other plants, watercress has to be started in an area sometime. But it then does its own thing in the wild, naturally. It needs no care. It will freeze—but only that part of the plant which is above the running water. Low water conditions *and* an extremely cold winter will damage the supply but only for a few months. The roots are prolific and if only a remnant survives, it will eventually fill in the gaps. The biggest danger to watercress is a flock of wild turkeys. Turkeys are drawn to spring seeps in January and February for water and grit. Those tiny green sprigs are irresistible. Roots and all are consumed. I have seen turkeys completely wipe out a large bed of watercress in one winter.

We "help" our watercress by trimming it to encourage new growth and by periodic mass pulling when it threatens to choke the little run. It rewards us with an ample supply of fresh greens much of the year. It is probably appreciated more in February and March than any other time. At that time of the year in Pennsylvania, nothing else has its brilliant green color. The young plants are at their tender best in early spring—a special treat.

Watercress has long been used as an edible garnish. Sandwiches made of watercress have been treated as somewhat of a joke in the United States, but anyone who has really tried them comes back for more. They are delicious. Butter a couple of slices of homemade bread, pile on some well-washed and drained watercress tops, spread on a bit of mayonnaise and go to it. A glass of chilled Chablis and you have a lunch fit for any nature lover. Add a few crisp fried pieces of bacon and a thin slice of homegrown tomato and you have a BLT unlike any other.

Watercress sprigs are excellent in salads with other greens such as lettuce. A half-and-half ratio is about right. Our watercress supply is often so bountiful that I've come up with two excellent but simple dressings to complement a salad made totally of tender watercress sprigs.

Watercress is also excellent in fish sauces. Included here are some recipes I often use. I break the rule that says that cold sauce must only be used with cold fish and often serve the Sauce Verte with hot fish as well.

## THOUSAND ISLAND DRESSING

| 1 cup mayonnaise | ⅓ cup chili sauce |
|---|---|
| | 1 teaspoon steak sauce |

Mix all ingredients together, refrigerate for 1 hour and serve over well-washed and well-drained watercress sprigs. Makes 1⅓ cups.

# BLUE CHEESE DRESSING

¼ cup olive oil
2 tablespoons wine vinegar

2 ounces blue cheese, crumbled
salt, pepper and garlic powder to taste

Mix all ingredients well and let set for 15 minutes. Shake well and toss with well-washed and drained watercress sprigs. Makes ½ cup.

# SAUCE VERTE

1 cup mayonnaise
¼ cup chopped watercress leaves

1 teaspoon lemon juice
salt and pepper to taste

Mix all ingredients well. Refrigerate for 1 hour and serve with cold or hot fish as a sauce. Makes 1 cup.

# WATERCRESS SAUCE

2 tablespoons butter
2 tablespoons flour
1 cup milk

1 teaspoon steak sauce
salt and pepper
¼ cup chopped watercress leaves

In a small saucepan, melt butter and blend in flour. Slowly add milk and cook until thickened. If the sauce is too thick for your taste, add a bit more milk at this time. Add steak sauce and salt and pepper to taste. Blend in watercress and serve immediately with hot poached, steamed or broiled fish. Makes 1 cup.

# *DANDELION*

Our colonial ancestors considered dandelion greens a spring tonic and blood purifier. It was also said that heart problems and rheumatism were remedied by a good "mess" of greens in the spring. Vitamin deficiencies in late winter were a serious problem until recent times. The dandelion (a source of vitamins A, C and iron) was undoubtedly a boon to good health.

Once our supermarkets started selling greens year round, the dandelion fell from favor and soon became a despised weed. A couple of generations have now grown up fighting the dandelion, digging it out by the roots, applying selective poisons and hiring small children to pick the blossoms. Neighbors argue over seeds blowing from yard to yard. How far we've come from the real values of this earth when a few wild plant seeds can cause the loss of friendships. Even worse are the communities that enforce "weed laws" and fine those who don't conform to the mowing rules.

When I was a kid, dandelion-green salad was served with the first, pan-fried brook trout of the season. They seem to go together in my mind because of all the pleasant memories. Salad is best made with the very young leaves of the spring. If your lawn is organically grown and relatively dog-free, it is the easiest place to find greens. Pastures, fields and even vacant city lots are also sources for dandelion greens.

To pick the dandelions, I use a narrow trowel, lifting a portion of the root with the leaves. I find it is easier to do the first washing or two if the leaves are attached to the crown. For the last dunking, cut them off and wash the leaves singly in a giant pan of salted, cold water. Drain well and refrigerate until ready to toss with dressing.

There is more to the dandelion than just the greens. The roots can be used as a substitute coffee. Wash and peel the roots. Roast in a slow oven for four hours, until they are brittle. Then grind and use as you would coffee; except you will need slightly less to make a brew of equal strength as coffee. The root can also be peeled, sliced and cooked like carrots in a bit of water with salt and pepper. Served with butter, it is a nutritious vegetable.

The yellow blossoms are delicious when dipped in pancake batter and quick fried. Gather all the blossoms you'll need and wash well in cold, salted water (the salt in the water draws out any insects). Drain thoroughly on lots of paper toweling. Mix up your favorite pancake batter or use a mix. Dip the blossoms in the batter and quickly fry in hot vegetable oil in a 365° to 375° electric fry pan. It will only take a minute or two until they are crisp and brown. Drain on paper toweling, add salt and pepper and serve immediately. I have a friend who does the same thing with pumpkin and squash blossoms. They are equally good.

The dandelion blossoms are also made into wine. There has been a resurgence in wine making in this country in recent years and I have tasted some great dandelion wine. Unfortunately, I have never tried to make it myself. Many cookbooks have recipes for dandelion wine. Most call for a combination of a gallon of blossoms, 3 pounds of sugar, the juice of 3 oranges and 1 lemon plus their peel and a bit of ginger root. Someday, soon, I'll try it.

At least one town in the United States celebrates the coming of the dandelion each spring with a festival—queen, formal banquet and all the hoopla. Vineland, New Jersey, in the midst of the truck farms, grows dandelions for their annual dandelion festival. Besides the traditional salads and wine, the banquet menu includes dandelion soup, dandelion ravioli, veal tips with dandelion and a dandelion dessert. I'll bet Vineland cooks know all one would like to learn about dandelions—and perhaps more.

## MOTHER'S DANDELION DRESSING

| | |
|---|---|
| 3 slices of bacon | 2 tablespoons wine vinegar |
| 1 beaten egg | 2 teaspoons sugar |
| 2 tablespoons flour | salt and pepper to taste |

Cut the bacon into small slices and fry. When the bacon is done, add ½ cup water to the pan. Mix the beaten egg with flour, vinegar and sugar. Add that mixture to the pan, stirring constantly. Add salt and pepper. Heat and stir until the mixture thickens. Makes enough dressing for 4 servings.

The dressing must be poured over the greens just before serving, otherwise you will have a soggy salad. Toss quickly at the table. Then bring on the trout and some hot French bread—gourmet fare!

## *WILD LEEKS*

The wild leek grows in dense, shaded woods from North Carolina to the northern New England states and west to Minnesota and Iowa. While in grade and high school, I was certain there were far too many of them in northern Pennsylvania. Mondays were particularly trying during March and April each year. The country kids would have been gathering and eating wild leeks all weekend. A small number of raw leeks were fine but I'm sure the boys prided themselves on eating so many that the garliclike aroma poured out of their pores. The teachers would usually place them near an *open* window (in March) and, at last resort, would send them home—a drastic measure in those days. Even churches were not safe during early spring.

It was years before I realized that it was the number of raw, wild leeks eaten and not the leek itself that caused the awful odor. Cooking leeks eliminates the afterpresence. As far as I know, the Hebron Grange in Potter County held the first public leek supper, at least in Pennsylvania. It was back in March of 1934. They served cooked and raw leeks, baked ham, potatoes and gravy, cabbage salad, rolls and pie—all for 35¢ for adults and 20¢ per child. It was a money-making scheme, and went over well. Now the leek suppers are recognized as a harbinger of spring in upstate Pennsylvania.

The leek in Europe was the original "onion" in French onion soup. I think this dish is where the wild vegetable really shines. But my favorite is a version called Venison and Leek Soup.

# VENISON AND LEEK SOUP

2½ pound venison roast with bone
2 teaspoons salt
5 stalks celery (with leaves)
1 large carrot
2 large potatoes

5 dozen wild leeks
pepper
2 bay leaves, crumbled
4 tablespoons butter
chopped parsley

Remove all fat from the venison roast and place in a large pot with 4 quarts water. Add the salt and bring to a boil. Cut celery, carrot and potatoes into small pieces and add. Clean and wash 3 dozen of the leeks. Cut their bulbs into small pieces and add to the pot. Add pepper and bay leaves. Cover and simmer until the meat is tender. In a saucepan, melt the butter. Wash the last 2 dozen leeks and cut the bulbs into small pieces. Drain well and sauté in the butter. Cover and cook over low heat for 5 minutes. Dip a cup of the broth from the big pot and add it to the saucepan. Cover and simmer for a half hour. Remove the meat from the large pot, cool and cut into bite-sized pieces. Put the rest of the soup, a little at a time, in a blender and purée. Return to kettle. Add the sautéed leeks and the meat to the kettle. Salt and pepper to taste before serving. Garnish each served bowl of soup with a little chopped parsley. Makes 16 servings.

# Wild Mushrooms

To avoid all wild mushrooms because some are poisonous is to miss one of our finest wild treats. Of course, it is vital to acquire and use a good guide book with pictures and descriptions before you pick a single specimen. Anyone hunting mushrooms for the first time should go with someone who is over 50 and has been picking and eating wild mushrooms all their life. It's the same philosophy as the bush pilot story: "An old bush pilot is a good bush pilot—he's alive, isn't he?"

Forget all the old wives' tales about shortcuts on how to test for poisoned mushrooms. They are worthless. Mushrooms that look as if they'd been nibbled on by mice may well have been eaten by insects that are immune to the poison. A silver spoon held against the flesh of a mushroom indicates absolutely nothing. Varying degrees of unpleasantries can be suffered from mushrooms, all the way from a slight stomach upset to death. Some individuals are allergic even to certain of the edible species, so the first time you serve a new mushroom, eat with moderation. Just as some people are sensitive to milk or eggs, there are those who cannot tolerate mushrooms.

The puffball is one of the common mushrooms that my Pennsylvania expert, Ned Smith, places in the "foolproof four" category. Others are the morel, shaggy mane and sulphur mushroom. Most people can recognize puffballs without much trouble, especially the giant puffball (*Calvatia gigantea*). The first one I ever ate was presented to me with a flourish by a guest. He was obviously very proud to have discovered such a fine specimen (it was volleyball-sized). Frankly, I didn't know what to do with it, but he quickly took over the kitchen and produced delicious slices of sautéed puffball to awe the rest of the party guests. He thinly sliced the mushroom with a bread knife, removed the outer skin and gently cooked it with butter in a frying pan until brown on both sides—about 10 minutes. A splash of white wine and a sprinkling of salt were added a few minutes before it was done. Success!

Puffballs are excellent served raw in a salad. They should be white clear through and firm when cut into. If they have begun to turn yellow and a bit watery, they are past their prime. In most parts of their territory, they appear in August and September. A large puffball will go a long way. To avoid wasting any of it, you may preserve it by peeling, thinly dicing, sautéing in butter and then packing in jars and freezing.

Most mushrooms dry easily and take up little space on the kitchen shelf. For preserving (both drying and freezing), choose young, firm specimens, wash and dry thoroughly, dice and place in a 180° oven (with the door propped open) for 3 to 5 hours. They are done when dry and leathery. Put in a sterile glass jar and store.

Become familiar with a few common kinds of edible mushrooms in your locale. They are so far superior to the commercial varieties that you wouldn't believe it. The difference is like that between fresh peas straight from the garden and canned ones.

A few years ago we moved to an area in Pennsylvania where there are many Amish farms. Shaggymane mushrooms grow with abandon in their manure-covered fields. What a kick each fall to drive the back lanes with one eye watching the road and the other looking for the telltale lineup of "little soldiers." Shaggymanes look just like the guidebook pictures and are best picked in the button stage before the gills darken. They are solid when immature. You know as soon as you get a bagful in the car that you have a treat coming. The aroma is breathtaking.

Shaggymanes must be used within a day of picking or they will deteriorate into an inky mess. Hold upright under a faucet to wash off the dirt. Dry thoroughly and place in damp paper toweling in the refrigerator until ready to cook. They can be diced and sautéed in butter like any other mushroom, but our family has a special way of preparing them creamed.

Another favorite way of serving wild mushrooms is for breakfast. Cut them in small pieces and sauté in a little butter for a few minutes. Add some slightly beaten eggs. Scramble, add salt and pepper and serve with buttered toast.

I enjoy using wild mushrooms with fish and game dishes. Fish that have been broiled, poached or steamed are complemented by mushroom sauce. It is especially tasty with fish cakes. The following sauce recipe is great with wild mushrooms, but you can cheat a bit and use the commercial variety if that's all that is available. Fresh wild mushrooms are also an excellent first course when company comes to dinner. It's a show-off appetizer that is guaranteed to wow them.

## MUSHROOM SALAD

1 pound mushrooms, peeled and cut into
    bite-sized pieces
1 large celery heart, cut in pieces
4 hard-boiled eggs, cut in chunks
2 green onions, minced

salt and pepper
olive oil
vinegar
garlic powder
lettuce leaves

Place the first five ingredients in a salad bowl. Make a dressing of 4 parts olive oil and one part wine vinegar with a pinch of garlic powder. Toss the salad with the dressing for a couple of minutes. Place in the refrigerator for 1 hour. Serve on lettuce leaves. Will serve 6.

## CREAMY MUSHROOMS

½ to 1 pound shaggymanes, cut into
    pieces
3 tablespoons butter

salt and pepper
1 tablespoon flour
hot buttered toast

Place the mushrooms in the top of a double boiler with 2 tablespoons of butter and a little salt and pepper. Simmer over hot water for 15 minutes. Brown 1 tablespoon butter, blend in flour and add the liquid from the cooked mushrooms. Stir until thickened into a gravy. Add the mushrooms to the sauce and serve on hot buttered toast.

*Good*

# MUSHROOM SAUCE

2 cups chopped mushrooms
¼ cup sliced green onion
¼ teaspoon salt
dash of pepper
1 tablespoon flour

2 tablespoons butter
⅓ cup milk
1 tablespoon Dijon-type mustard
¼ cup sour cream
2 tablespoons dry vermouth

Combine mushrooms, onion, salt, pepper and flour. Sauté in butter. Blend in milk and mustard. Cook until thickened. Add sour cream and vermouth. Heat until almost boiling. Serve with hot fish or fish cakes. Makes 2 cups.

# JIM'S MUSHROOM APPETIZER

1 cup fresh mushrooms, cut in chunks
3 tablespoons butter
dash of onion salt

hint of chili powder
2 tablespoons chili sauce
2 tablespoons heavy cream

2 slices of toast, quartered

Sauté mushrooms in butter until tender, about 5 minutes. Place in center of plates with toast points surrounding them. Add rest of ingredients to pan, heat and top the mushrooms and toast. Serve immediately. Serves 2.

# MUSHROOM DIP

1 cup finely chopped mushrooms
2 tablespoons butter
1 teaspoon steak sauce
2 teaspoons Dijon-type mustard

salt and pepper
pinch of garlic powder
⅓ cup sour cream
¼ cup mayonnaise

Simmer mushrooms for 10 minutes in the butter. Remove from heat, blend in steak sauce, mustard and a bit of salt, pepper and garlic powder. Add sour cream and mayonnaise and mix well. Refrigerate for 1 hour and serve with potato chips or crackers. If the mixture is to be used as a cracker spread, refrigerate overnight before serving.

# MUSHROOM CROUTONS

1 pound mushrooms, sliced
1 medium onion, minced
3 tablespoons butter
¼ cup dry vermouth
salt and pepper

2 tablespoons minced parsley
¼ teaspoon thyme
¼ teaspoon chervil
toast
grated cheese

Cook onion in the butter. As it starts to become tender, add the mushrooms and vermouth. When cooked, season with salt and pepper. Place the mixture in a blender and reduce to a purée. Return to the pan and add the parsley, thyme and chervil. Cook down until it is fairly firm. Spread the mixture on toast and broil until hot—a little grated cheese can be added before the broiling. Cut the toast into quarters diagonally and serve around meat. Can also be served as an appetizer with before-dinner drinks.

# MUSHROOM AND VENISON BURGUNDY

1½ pounds venison round steak, cut in
   bite-sized pieces
2 tablespoons flour
2 tablespoons butter
½ cup chopped onion

1 small clove garlic, minced
1 bay leaf
salt and pepper to taste
1 cup mushrooms, large chunks
½ cup Burgundy

½ cup water

Coat meat with flour. Brown in butter in a heavy skillet. Add rest of ingredients. Blend in well and bring to a boil. Lower heat to simmer, cover and cook until meat is tender, about 1½ hours. Add more water if necessary. Serve over hot, buttered rice. Serves 4.

# *Wild Nuts*

Early North American colonists found a plentiful supply of wild food. The mature forest regularly produced a large annual crop of good-tasting and nutritious nuts. Chestnuts, hickory nuts, walnuts, pecans, chinquapins, beechnuts and acorns were the most abundant. Taking their cue from the Indians, the early settlers quickly learned to make the most of this earth bounty. The nuts were roasted, added to stews, eaten out of hand and ground to make breads and puddings. When stored in their natural covering, most nuts could be kept for a year or longer before drying. This was appreciated by the early Americans in those days of no refrigeration. Today, we can enjoy the same rich nut flavors. While the huge groves of nut-bearing trees no longer exist, the North American continent is still heavily laced with this excellent source of natural energy.

## HICKORY NUTS

Of all the nuts I've sampled, the American hickory nut offers the most unusual and delicious flavor, according to my taste buds. Like many of the good things in this world, the rich, pungent nutmeats of the flint-shelled hickory are not easy to get at. A common nutcracker will not even dent the shell of a hickory nut; at least mine won't. I've tried clamping them in a vise, beating them with rocks, running over them with a car and at one time considered training a pet squirrel to crack the shells for me.

I once mentioned in a magazine article how much trouble I was having cracking hickory nuts and that I finally resorted to using a hammer to strike the shell on a cement floor. Trouble was, even though I was able to crack the shells, the meat was squashed and hard to extract. Then, a kind reader, Benjamin James from Weedville, Pennsylvania, gave me the benefit of his 82 years of nut picking and cracking. He wrote that he managed to get hickory halves out intact, most of the time, by using an old, sturdy, well-dried apple stump. He made a small depression in the stump, just big enough to take the round end of the hickory nut. With the nut in the hole and holding it in his fingers, he taps the blossom end of the nut with the flat end of a small machinist's hammer. A couple of taps and both sides of the shell crack and the meat halves will be exposed. It takes a little practice to get the tapping right, but the resulting whole nuts are worth the trouble.

Once the meat is out of the shell, I usually air-dry the nuts for several days to draw out the moisture that could cause mold. The nuts are then put in glass containers (usually peanut butter jars) and stored in a cool basement. Another good way to keep nuts—all nuts—is to freeze them. Wrap well, excluding all air. The nuts will keep up to 7 months.

Hickory nuts added to sweet rolls lend a touch of elegance that even the most casual breakfast eater will notice. The flavor is best described as "intense." Not many nuts are needed to add the extra something. They make a great topping, too, for cookies and cakes. Green hickory nuts were used as a sort of butter by the early settlers on their corn bread, a trick they learned from the Indians.

The next three recipes really shine with hickory nuts but other wild nuts can be substituted successfully.

# HICKORY NUT CUSTARD PIE

¾ cup coarsely broken hickory nuts
1 cup sugar
2 tablespoons cornstarch
¼ teaspoon salt
1 cup water

½ cup molasses (light)
4 large eggs, slightly beaten
1¼ teaspoon vanilla
9-inch pie shell
ice cream or whipped cream

In a saucepan, combine the sugar, cornstarch and salt. Stir in 1 cup water and molasses. Cook and stir until thickened and bubbly. Slowly stir the hot mixture into the eggs. Add vanilla. Bake unpricked pie shell at 350° for 5 minutes. Remove it from the oven and pour in egg mixture. Top with nuts and return pie to oven. Bake at 350° until a knife inserted off-center comes out clean (about 35 minutes). Cool and serve with a dab of ice cream or whipped cream. Makes 6 to 8 servings.

# CRANBERRY-NUT BREAD

¾ cup chopped hickory nuts (or black walnuts)
¾ cup orange juice
2 teaspoons freshly grated orange rind
1 tablespoon Madeira (optional in place of 1 tablespoon of orange juice)
2 tablespoons butter

1 egg
1 cup sugar
1⅓ cups chopped cranberries
2 cups flour
1 teaspoon baking powder
½ teaspoon baking soda
½ teaspoon salt

Place orange juice and rind in a small pan with the butter. Heat enough to melt the butter. Add Madeira and cool. Beat egg and sugar. Add to the orange juice mixture and blend. Fold in the berries and nuts. Sift flour, baking powder, soda and salt together. Stir into the rest of the mixture. Pour into a greased 9 x 5 x 3-inch loaf pan. Bake in a preheated 350° oven for 65 to 75 minutes. Cool on rack and store overnight before slicing. Makes 1 loaf.

# FRANK CASE'S SHELLBARK CAKE

2 cups hickory nuts
¾ cup butter
2 cups sugar

2½ cups flour
1½ teaspoons baking powder
1 cup milk
5 egg whites, stiffly beaten

Cream butter and sugar. Sift the flour and baking powder together and add to the butter/sugar mixture alternately with the milk. Stir in the nuts. Fold in egg whites. Bake in 2 round cake tins in a preheated 350° oven for about 35 to 40 minutes. Frost with your favorite butter frosting.

# BLACK WALNUT

Black walnuts are found across much of the United States and while they are messy to handle when the outer shells have turned black and sticky, they are well worth the trouble. I've found that removing the outer hull while it is still green simplifies the task. The hammer-on-cement technique works well for shelling black walnuts. The taste improves when the shelled nutmeats are dried on a screen in a sunny, dry place for a couple of weeks.

Mr. James had an elaborate method for shelling black walnuts, as well as hickory nuts. But it involved using a Model T Ford and since there aren't very many of those around these days, I decided that not too many people could take advantage of his Wisdom on this chore.

However, another old friend, Hayes Englert of Harrisburg, advised me that black walnuts should be cracked in about 10 days from the time the outer hull is removed. Hayes said that if the shell dried too long the pieces would fly all over when cracked. He also suggested a 3- or 4-hour water soaking for shells that were too dry. It will "tame them down."

Black walnuts are most frequently used in cakes, but I love to substitute them for English walnuts in many recipes such as pinwheel cookies. Here are a couple of unusual black walnut desserts.

## BLACK WALNUT AND HONEY ICE CREAM

1 cup coarsely chopped black walnuts
2 cups milk
¾ cup honey
3 beaten eggs
2 cups heavy cream
1½ teaspoons vanilla

In a saucepan, blend milk into honey. Cook and stir until hot but don't boil. Remove from heat and stir the hot mixture slowly into the eggs. Return to saucepan. Cook 2 minutes longer, stirring constantly. Cool to room temperature. Blend in the cream and vanilla. Stir in walnuts. Freeze in ice-cream freezer according to maker's directions. Will make 2 quarts.

## APPLE-NUT BARS

1 cup chopped black walnuts
1 cup flour
¼ teaspoon baking powder
¼ teaspoon salt
1 cup granulated sugar
¼ cup melted butter
2 eggs, beaten
¼ cup raisins
¾ cup finely cut dried apples
powdered sugar

Sift flour, baking powder, salt and granulated sugar and then add rest of ingredients (except powdered sugar). Mix well. Pour into a buttered 13 x 9 x

2-inch pan. Bake in a 350° oven for about 25 minutes. While warm, cut into bars. Sprinkle with powdered sugar. Makes 39 bars.

## *BUTTERNUT*

Butternut tree leaves resemble those of the black walnut, but the outer hull of the fruit is smaller and is egg-shaped whereas the black walnut is round. Butternuts are delicious and sweet. They can be used in place of the hickory nuts in the cake or bread recipes in this chapter or in the following two concoctions.

## BUTTERNUT SAUCE

| | |
|---|---|
| 1¼ cups shelled butternuts | ½ cup imported olive oil |
| ¼ cup chopped fresh parsley | salt and pepper |
| pinch of tarragon | 2 tablespoons lime juice |

Place butternuts, parsley, tarragon and olive oil in a blender. Blend until mixed well. Add salt and pepper to taste and blend in lime juice. Use sauce with cold poached salmon or trout. Makes 1½ cups.

## NUT BUTTER

| | |
|---|---|
| 1 cup finely ground butternuts | ¼ teaspoon salt |
| ½ cup butter | 1 tablespoon steak sauce (optional) |

With the back of a wooden spoon, mix the softened butter with the rest of the ingredients. The nut butter can be used in many ways, such as for appetizers or on nut bread. Makes 1 cup.

## *CHESTNUTS*

The native American chestnut tree once flourished from New England to Alabama, but an Asian fungus destroyed most of our stock. The chestnut blight of the twenties and thirties brought chestnut gathering to an end until it was discovered that the Chinese variety was immune to the blight. These have been planted widely across the nation and a good supply, cultivated and semiwild, now exists.

As with all nuts, the chestnut is easily adapted to a variety of uses. Boiled or roasted and then eaten with a dash of salt or butter is one of the favorites. They can also be served mashed or whole as a vegetable or chopped as garnish for almost any green vegetable. They are especially good with peas or snap beans.

To boil, slash the flat side of the nuts with a knife and place them in a pan of cold water. Bring the water to a boil and simmer for 10 minutes. Remove one at a time from the water and peel immediately. The skin will slip off easily. To roast, slash the shell and spread the nuts on a cookie sheet. Roast in a 400° oven for twenty minutes. Serve them hot with a cup of melted butter.

While chestnuts are traditional at Thanksgiving, any wild nut can be added to turkey stuffing for an authentic old-time American flavor. The important thing is to use and enjoy our wild bounty of nuts.

# Dishes to Serve
## with Fish
## and Game

This chapter is an afterthought. Most of my favorite recipes for salads, sauces, appetizers and other "go withs" are scattered through the book, if not with different fish, bird or game chapters, then in the berry, greens, mushroom or nut chapters. But a few of my longtime specialties to serve with fish and game didn't fit in any category. They are a mixture, ranging all the way from soups to desserts. Some Jim and I have concocted, others were passed down in our families and a few have been given to me by friends. All are especially tasty with wild things. They don't fight with the flavor of the main dish but complement it. I couldn't leave them out of this book.

You'll notice that I'm heavy on carrots. It's because they are good, plentiful, cheap *and* provide a spot of color. It's important to color-coordinate dinners, even for the family. If it looks pretty, it tastes better. Zucchini and tomatoes are also favorites because I grow them, like them, and they too are colorful.

Simple desserts are best, in my opinion. And lemon-based ones win first place in my heart. They complement fish and game with style. Lemon meringue and key lime pies are often on my menu, but they are in every cookbook. The desserts included here are standouts—light, delicious and satisfying.

## JIM'S CREAMED CARROT SOUP

4 large carrots, sliced
1 onion, chopped
salt and pepper to taste
3 teaspoons sugar

dash of chervil
dash of marjoram
4 cups warm milk
dash of Tabasco
chopped parsley

Cook carrots, onion, salt and pepper, sugar, chervil and marjoram in water to cover until the vegetables are tender. Remove cover and allow stock to reduce. Place the carrot mixture in a blender and puree. Return to pan, add milk and slowly heat for 20 minutes, adding the Tabasco. Do not allow the soup to boil. Garnish with parsley. Makes 6 to 8 servings.

## LUCKY'S ONION SOUP

6 medium onions, chopped
½ cup butter
5 beef bouillon cubes
½ teaspoon chervil
dash celery salt

dash red pepper
2 tablespoons medium-dry sherry
salt and pepper
toast wedges
grated Parmesan cheese

Sauté onions in butter until they are golden and limp. Add 2 quarts water, bouillon cubes, chervil, celery salt, red pepper, sherry, and salt and pepper to taste to the pot. Simmer for 30 minutes with lid off. Ladle into bowls. Float toast wedges on top and dust with Parmesan cheese. Will serve 8.

## COTTAGE CHEESE/TOMATO SALAD

1 envelope unflavored gelatin
½ teaspoon salt
2 tablespoons wine vinegar
1 small onion, grated

½ pound cottage cheese
1 8-ounce can tomato sauce
coleslaw
green pepper rings

Soften gelatin in ¼ cup cold water. Add ½ cup boiling water and stir until dissolved. Add salt, vinegar and onion. Add 3 tablespoons of this mixture to the cottage cheese. To remaining gelatin, add the tomato sauce. Pour half of the tomato mixture into a lightly oiled 1-quart mold. Chill until set. Keep the cottage cheese and rest of tomato mixture at room temperature. Next, add cottage cheese mixture to mold. When this is set, add rest of tomato mixture and chill. To serve unmold on a bed of coleslaw and garnish with pepper rings. Serves 6.

## GARDEN CUCUMBERS

| | |
|---|---|
| 2 large cucumbers | ⅛ teaspoon tarragon |
| salt | pepper |
| 2 tablespoons wine vinegar | ¼ cup sour cream |

Grate the cucumber (or slice thinly), salt and cover with ice water. Place (covered) in the refrigerator for 3 hours. Drain well. Add the vinegar, tarragon, pepper and sour cream and toss. Serves 4.

*Note:* "Great with fish."

## CUCUMBER SALAD

| | |
|---|---|
| 3 cucumbers | ½ cup minced celery |
| salt | 1 teaspoon dill weed |
| wine vinegar | 3 tablespoons minced green onion |
| sugar | pepper |
| 4½ teaspoons unflavored gelatin | lettuce leaves |
| 2 drops green coloring | mayonnaise |

Peel cucumbers, halve them lengthwise and scrape out seeds. Grate into bowl and sprinkle with 1 teaspoon each of salt, wine vinegar and sugar. Let stand 1 hour. In a bowl, sprinkle gelatin over ⅓ cup cold water to soften for 10 minutes. Pour 2 cups boiling water over it and stir until dissolved. Add coloring and stir. Chill until the mixture is cool and syrupy. Drain cucumber and add celery, dill and onion. Stir into gelatin with ¼ cup vinegar, 1 tablespoon sugar and salt and pepper to taste. Place in a 1-quart ornamental mold or in a pan, to be cut into squares. Serve on lettuce leaves with a dab of mayonnaise. Serves 6 to 8.

*Note:* "Excellent with goose or venison."

# GARDEN SALAD

3 small zucchini, cut in bite-sized pieces
2 medium tomatoes, cut in bite-sized
 pieces and seeded

1 small head of cauliflower, broken in
 bite-sized pieces
salt and pepper

Italian salad dressing

In a large bowl, combine vegetables. Toss with some dressing, cover and refrigerate 1 hour. Drain and serve. Serves 6.

# MILDRED'S CARROT SALAD

6 to 8 grated carrots
1 small onion, diced fine
1 pecan (2 halves), cut fine

2 tablespoons mayonnaise
salt and pepper to taste
lettuce leaves

Mix all ingredients except lettuce together. Add a little more mayonnaise if necessary to properly dampen the carrot mixture. Serve on lettuce leaves. Serves 6.

*Note:* "My favorite salad with fish and game—it goes with everything."

# GARDEN LETTUCE DRESSING

¼ cup mayonnaise
¼ cup sour cream
¼ cup buttermilk
2 tablespoons tomato juice

1 tablespoon grated Parmesan cheese
¼ teaspoon dry mustard
⅛ teaspoon paprika
⅛ teaspoon celery seed

shake of salt, pepper and garlic powder

Blend all the ingredients well. Cover and chill. Serve on garden lettuce or spinach. Makes 1 cup.

# GOOSEBERRY SAUCE

2 cups gooseberries
¼ cup chopped spinach
1 tablespoon butter

⅛ teaspoon lemon juice
⅛ teaspoon grated nutmeg
pinch of salt

sugar to taste

Cook berries with 1 cup water until they are soft. Add spinach and cook another 3 minutes. Drain (keeping juice in a saucepan). Force the berries and spinach through a food mill. Add the puree to the juice. The mixture should be about the consistency of applesauce. If you wish a thicker sauce, simmer until enough liquid evaporates to suit you. Add butter, lemon juice, nutmeg, salt and enough sugar to suit your taste. Simmer for 2 minutes, stirring constantly.

*Note:* "Good side dish with pheasant, duck, goose or mackerel."

## COLLINS POTATOES

4 large potatoes
2 medium onions

2 tablespoons butter
salt and pepper
chervil

Peel potatoes and slice thin. Chop onions fine. Heat butter in an iron skillet. Layer potatoes and onions with potatoes first. Salt and pepper to taste and add a couple shakes of chervil. Brown the bottom layer of potatoes well over a hot fire. Cover the skillet and place in a preheated 350° oven for 30 to 40 minutes. Check to see if potatoes are done before removing from oven. Loosen potatoes with a spatula. Place a heated platter over the skillet and invert. The potatoes will come out on the plate all beautifully brown. Serves 4. Great with salmon or trout.

## CREAMY POTATOES

3 large baking potatoes
3 tablespoons butter
⅓ cup heavy cream

¼ cup crumbled blue cheese
¼ cup grated Parmesan cheese
2 tablespoons chopped parsley
parsley garnish

Cook the potatoes in salted water until tender. Cool, peel and cut into cubes. In oven-proof casserole, place melted butter and cream. Add the potatoes and blue cheese. Top with Parmesan cheese and parsley. Cover. Bake in 325° oven for 30 minutes. May be browned under broiler before serving. Add parsley garnish and serve. Serves 4.

## CARROTS VICHY

2 cups thin carrot sticks, about 3 inches
　　long
2 tablespoons butter
1 tablespoon sugar

¼ teaspoon salt
1 teaspoon lemon juice
paprika (optional)
chopped parsley (optional)

Place carrots, butter, sugar and salt in saucepan. Cover with boiling water (¼ cup) and simmer until done, about 10 minutes. Add lemon juice, sprinkle with paprika and parsley for color and serve. Serves 4.

# BROILED TOMATOES

4 ripe garden tomatoes
butter
salt
pepper

celery salt
sugar
bread crumbs
Parmesan cheese, grated

Peel firm, ripe tomatoes and cut in halves. Place on foil on a broiler pan. Spread each half with soft butter. Sprinkle each with a little salt, pepper, celery salt and sugar. Slash each half several times in the middle so the good flavors go into the tomato. Sprinkle the tomatoes with bread crumbs and cheese. Place under a preheated broiler (4 inches from the heat) until the top is brown. Then place in a 400° oven for 5 minutes or until the tomato is a bit soft. Transfer to a heated platter and serve. Serves 4.

# BROILED ZUCCHINI

2 zucchini (about 6 inches long)
2 garlic cloves, mashed
4 tablespoons butter

salt and pepper to taste
¼ teaspoon marjoram
dash of oregano

½ cup Parmesan cheese, grated

Steam the whole zucchinis for 10 minutes. Cut into lengthwise slices from ¼ to ½ inch thick. Mix the garlic, softened butter, salt and pepper, marjoram and oregano and spread over the slices of vegetable. Place slices on a greased broiler pan. Sprinkle with cheese and broil until lightly brown and hot throughout. Serves 4 to 6.
   *Note:* "A Jim favorite."

# SAUTÉED ZUCCHINI

1 large zucchini
butter
cooking oil

salt and pepper
garlic powder
Parmesan cheese, grated

Grate zucchini or slice thin. Place a little of the grated zucchini at a time in a dish towel and squeeze the excess moisture out. Sauté in a half-and-half mixture of butter and cooking oil in a heavy skillet. Turn with a spatula as the vegetable browns. Add salt and pepper and garlic powder to taste as the zucchini cooks. After 10 to 15 minutes, sprinkle with cheese and serve immediately. Serves 3 to 4.

## TERRY BELL'S ITALIAN-STYLE POTATOES

4 potatoes, sliced thin
2 tomatoes, chopped
salt and pepper

oregano
Parmesan cheese, grated
2 tablespoons butter

Butter a casserole dish. Place a layer of tomatoes in the dish, then add a layer of potatoes. Add salt and pepper. Add another layer of tomatoes and sprinkle with oregano and a generous amount of cheese. Repeat layers, ending with tomato. Dot the top with butter, cover and bake in a 375° oven for 1½ hours. Serves 4. This is a family dish so exact proportions are sketchy, but I'm sure you'll enjoy it as much as our family does.

*Note:* "Delicious with fish and game entrées."

## MOTHER'S LEMON FLUFF

1 3-ounce package lemon-flavored gelatin
1 13-ounce can evaporated milk, chilled
   until ice-cold

¼ cup lemon juice
1 cup sugar
2½ cups vanilla wafer crumbs, crushed
maraschino cherries

Dissolve gelatin in 1 cup very hot water and add ¾ cup cold water. Chill until partially set. Whip until light and fluffy. Add lemon juice and sugar and mix. Whip milk until it forms soft peaks and fold into gelatin. Line bottom of greased 9 x 13-inch pan with 2 cups of crumbs. Pour gelatin mixture over crumbs and top with remaining crumbs. Chill until firm—4 to 5 hours. Can be made the day before. Top with maraschino cherries for color (or large strawberries). Serves 15.

*Note:* "Perfect light dessert for game or fish."

## LEMONADE COOKIES

1 6-ounce can frozen lemonade
   concentrate, thawed
1 cup butter

1 cup sugar
2 eggs
3 cups sifted flour
1 teaspoon soda

Cream the butter and sugar together. Add eggs and beat until light and fluffy. Sift together flour and soda. Add alternately to the creamed mixture with ½ cup lemonade concentrate. Drop dough from teaspoon 2 inches apart onto ungreased cookie sheet. Bake in preheated 400° oven for about 8 minutes, until lightly brown. Brush hot cookies with remaining lemonade and sprinkle with more sugar. Makes about 4 dozen small cookies.

*Note:* "Penciled on recipe, Great."

## TABLE OF WEIGHTS AND MEASURES

| U.S. Customary | Metric |
| --- | --- |
| 1 teaspoon | 4.95 milliliters |
| 1 tablespoon (3 teaspoons) | 14.8 milliliters |
| 2 tablespoons (1 liquid ounce) | 29.6 milliliters |
| 1 jigger (1½ liquid ounces) | 44.4 milliliters |
| ¼ cup (4 tablespoons) | 59.2 milliliters |
| ½ cup (8 tablespoons) | 118.4 milliliters |
| 1 cup (16 tablespoons) | 236.8 milliliters |
| 1 pint (2 cups) | 473.6 milliliters |
| 1 quart (2 pints) | 947.2 milliliters |
| 1 gallon (4 quarts) | 3.788 liters |
| 1 ounce, dry (2 tablespoons) | 28.35 grams |
| ¼ pound (4 ounces) | 113.37 grams |
| ½ pound (8 ounces) | 226.74 grams |
| 1 pound (16 ounces) | 453.59 grams |
| 2.21 pounds (35.3 ounces) | 1 kilogram |

## OVEN TEMPERATURE CONVERSION

| Fahrenheit | Celsius |
|:---:|:---:|
| 200 | 93 |
| 225 | 107 |
| 250 | 121 |
| 275 | 135 |
| 300 | 149 |
| 325 | 163 |
| 350 | 177 |
| 375 | 191 |
| 400 | 204 |
| 425 | 218 |
| 450 | 232 |
| 475 | 246 |
| 500 | 260 |

Water boils at 212 degrees Fahrenheit at sea level. Water boils at 100 degrees Celsius at sea level.

# Bibliography

Boorman, Sylvia. *Wild Plums in Brandy*. New York: McGraw-Hill Book Company, 1962.

Dickey, Charley. *Bobwhite Quail Hunting*. Birmingham, Ala.: Oxmoor House, 1974.

Fegely, Thomas D. *Wonders of Geese and Swans*. New York: Dodd, Mead & Company, 1976.

Food Editors of Farm Journal. *How to Dry Fruits and Vegetables at Home*. Philadelphia: Countryside Press, 1975.

*The Great Cooks' Guide to Clay Cookery*. New York: Random House, 1977.

Grigson, Jane. *The Mushroom Feast*. New York: Alfred A. Knopf, 1975.

Holm, Don. *Old-Fashioned Dutch Oven Cookbook*. Caldwell, Idaho: The Caxton Printers, 1970.

Latham, Roger M. *Complete Book of the Wild Turkey*. Harrisburg, Pa.: Stackpole Books, 1976.

Luttringer, Leo A., Jr. *Pennsylvania Birdlife*. Harrisburg: Pennsylvania Game Commission, 1966.

Madson, John. *The Cottontail Rabbit*. East Alton, Ill.: Olin Mathieson Chemical Corp., 1960.

————. *Gray and Fox Squirrels*. East Alton, Ill.: Olin Mathieson Chemical Corp., 1964.

————. *The Mourning Dove*. New York: Winchester Press, 1978.

————. *The Ring-Necked Pheasant*. New York: Winchester Press, 1962.

————. *Ruffed Grouse*. New York: Winchester Press, 1969.

McClane, A. J. *The Encyclopedia of Fish Cookery*. New York: Holt, Rinehart & Winston, 1977.

————. *McClane's New Standard Fishing Encyclopedia*. New York: Holt, Rinehart & Winston, 1974.

Pfeiffer, C. Boyd. *Shad Fishing*. New York: Crown Publishers, 1975.

Sales, Georgia MacLeod and Grover. *The Clay-Pot Cookbook*. New York: Atheneum Publishers, 1977.

Sleight, Jack and Hull, Raymond. *Home Book of Smoke-Cooking Meat, Fish and Game*. Harrisburg, Pa.: Stackpole Books, 1971.

Woolner, Frank. *Timberdoodle!* New York: Crown Publishers, 1974.

# Index